The Last Days Series

Volume 1

These chapters are messages that were preached during a live service broadcast.
There has been a minimal amount of editing for this publication. I am indebted to
many people for bringing this work into existence.

Please email us at info@1017media.com if this has
encouraged and strengthened your faith.

Write us at
1017Media, Inc.
3436 Magazine Street, #7155
New Orleans, LA 70115

Contents

Introduction

The Last Days is an in-depth eschatological teaching series utilizing the Old Testament, New Testament, secular history, plus many other resources for the purposes of restoring this fascinating subject matter to clarity while providing its reader with a sense of understanding from a scripturally verifiable point of view. Unless otherwise noted, all scriptural references will be in the King James version.

Just a few of the topics that will be covered in this series are:

- The history of current prophecy preaching: where it came from, how we got it, who were some of the principle contributors behind it, and why it is still being taught and preached today
- The 70 Weeks
- Hebrew idioms (e.g. time, times, and a half) and timelines
- The Two Witnesses
- The Two-horned Beast
- The Abomination of Desolation
- The Olive Trees and the Candlesticks, and how the current definition of those trees and candlesticks has missed the mark
- Anti-Christ and what it could be, or who it could be
- The False Prophet
- Where the United States, England, and Israel occur within prophecy and their interrelationship.
- The Great Tribulation
- The Rapture—a term which is never used in scripture
- The Mark of the Beast

But thou, O Daniel, shut up the words, and seal the book, even to the time of the end: many shall run to and fro, and knowledge shall be increased. –
Daniel 12:4

Only the last days ministries and the persons that were called to preach this would have the full knowledge of what to expect and how to accurately interpret the Scriptures. Daniel could not receive the interpretations because they were reserved for the "time of the end," and for preachers that exist in the last days. That is not only clearly expressed by Daniel, but also John. That means theories and doctrines developed two to five hundred years ago would be flawed in part, if not entirely. Those that are flawed need to be discarded and replaced with the verifiable Word of God. And because these are the last days, we can see the things that have already occurred, but even more exciting, the events that are occurring now. This series will be pointing those things out to you and begins with the topic of The Mark of the Beast.

The Mark of The Beast Part 1

Revelation 13:15-18, *"And he had power to give life* [or breath] *unto the image of the beast, that the image of the beast should both speak, and cause that as many as would not worship the image of the beast should be killed. And he causeth all, both small and great, rich and poor, free and bond, to receive* [or to give them] *a mark in their right hand, or in their foreheads: And that no man might buy or sell, save he that had the mark, or the name of the beast, or the number of his name. Here is wisdom. Let him that hath understanding count the number of the beast: for it is the number of a man; and his number is Six hundred threescore and six* [understood as 666]. *"*

Nothing divides Christians more than end-time prophesy, nothing. They get heated over this subject and they have question after question: What is this mark? What is this 666? People want to know because if they can identify what this mark is, obviously they want to try to avoid it; and secondly, they know the time until the end of time is right at the door. In fact, the door is open, so they are curious. They want to know. They want that sign. There is nothing more on Christians' minds concerning prophesy than to know what the mark of the beast is.

We will look at these verses using, as I always do, the whole Bible because unless you use the whole book you are going to have trouble. If you think you can use only the New Testament or the book of Revelation, then you won't figure it out and you will end up developing your own *Christian Science Fiction* theory. Believe me, there are plenty of those circulating. There have been countless numbers of theories and opinions concerning this mark and 666 but I am telling you up front that it is associated with Islam, the Beast, and the Koran. It is necessary to use both the Old and New Testament to show how we arrived at that and prove God's Word. That is the mistake people make, even for people that understand Islam, the Beast, and the Koran. And they are missing one important element that clearly identifies what this mark is and how it relates to Islam, that we have in history, and the 8th Beast, which we are dealing with now.

According to the scriptures above, we see that the mark is both in name and number and we will know the beast when we know the mark. Well, I could flip that. We will know the mark when we recognize the beast. The only problem with that last statement is everybody has been looking for the wrong mark because they have not seen what Scripture says. "You mean it is in Scripture?" Absolutely. Between the front cover and the back cover, the mark is clearly identified. You just have to be trained to look for it. You must be taught to look for it. Unfortunately, we have too many people more interested in *Christian Science Fiction* than thus saith the Word of the Lord. "Can you prove that?" We will see. Before I get to that, let's look at some of the cockamamie theories that are out there from the last 100 years about this mark and 666.

This one only goes back to 1990:

> *I personally believe that the mark will be either an invisible laser tattoo or a microchip which will be placed under the skin having the uniform product code* [the UPC code]. *This mark, a type of barcode in the skin or on the microchip, will be scanned at that point of trade.*

Sorry, wrong.

> *The UPC code* [or the barcode] *with leading information on each person will be placed. Concerning the name of the beast, this, I believe, will be a name with six letters in each name invisibly coded into a laser tattoo or microchip. A computer could pick up this as six digits in each name; for example, Ronald Wilson Reagan.*

I remember when Reagan was President. Some Christian authors even actually wrote some books pinpointing that they discovered who the 666 was using Gematria. They had figured out mathematically that Ronald Wilson Reagan added up to 666. Well last time I checked, that didn't happen unless they are planning on Reagan rising from the dead. I guess they could use that the beast's wound was healed and therefore he would come back to life again if they are still going to hang onto that theory. They could hope for that I guess. It is silly, folks.

Here is another one:

> Instead of social security cards and credit cards, the number will be printed on the forehead or hand so that all who receive it will carry it at all times. Using modern technology, it would be a method to eliminate loosing such cards or having them stolen or duplicated. Just how the number will be imprinted? Will it consist only of the number 666? We do not know for certain, but it is possible a small computer chip will be embedded under the flesh, or even in the bone of the forehead or hand. That kind of technology is already in place. Another method may be used but the results will be the same - instant identity and little or no likelihood of counterfeiting or reproducing. I suspect the number 666 will be a prefix followed by other numbers, but I do not know.

Here is another person:

> Yet the Apostle John describes the reality that has only recently come into focus, global banking, laser scanning and the universal barcode. It is a tiny step to go from using a Visa card or a bank card on the Plus System, and other ATM machines, in which the electronic strip is attached to the card, to print in that same strip of information on the human body so they can be laser scanned. This has already been done with laser tattoos and implanted microchips. Again, what better descriptive term could have John

found in the ancient world than the mark which would enable every citizen to buy or sell who had it.

First, do not assume from what John wrote down. All he was, was a scribe and he wrote it all down as Jesus dictated it to him. Do not assume this is referring to a worldwide mark that all peoples on a global scale are going to receive. I will have more to say about that later. Do not assume that. That is the first mistake. I will not leave you dangling in all this.

Let's read somebody else:

> *Europeans believe that the monetary system called ECU or the European Currency Unit* [or even the Euro now] *will be in place and will serve as the medium of commercial exchange and trade. However, the Bible reveals that a mark (or the symbolic number 666) on the right hand or forehead will replace the ECU and become the mandatory currency expression necessary to conduct trade and commerce in much of the world. Those refusing to accept this mark will be killed.*

Let's go to 1978:

> *What will be his mark? It appears that it will be some sort of credit card number and loyalty badge combined into one. Possibly it may be a tattoo invisible to the naked eye, but visible upon some type of light beam scan. It, however, in its numerical aspect has some liberal type connection with the number 666 or code based on these digits which will be related directly to the name of antichrist.*

This is 1996, another author:

> *It is my well-researched opinion that the mark of the beast...*

"My well-researched opinion" - now we better listen to this individual.

> *...as related in scripture, is absolutely literal.*

That is right. It is too bad you have no clue what the literal meaning is. And this is one you cannot look up in your Greek dictionary and try to figure it out. It takes more than that.

> Soon all people on earth will be coerced into accepting a mark on their right hand or forehead. I am convinced that it will be an injectable passive RFID transponder with a computer chip, a literal injection with a literal electronic biochip mark. I believe that such an implanted identification mark will literally become Satan's mark of the beast as we discuss further in this chapter.

A different era, 1962:

> All religions will be placed in the control of a counterfeit ruler or false Christ making a single world religion. He will have the power to enforce his mark 666, known as the mark of the beast. This mark or stamp of antichrist will be placed on the foreheads or right hands of all living persons where antichrist rules.

Not one single person yet has a clue what they are talking about. This is nothing more than science fiction. Does this technology exist? Sure. I can tell you right now if I had a medical chip put under my skin, because it is the thing that is happening, did I receive the mark? No, because that is not what the mark is.

Let's read someone else's, 1988:

> It appears that there will be three separate things or marks which will qualify a man to buy or sell.
>
> The first is called the mark of the beast. If indeed the antichrist is the leader of the Soviet Union...

Okay, now we have an antichrist and he is the leader of the Soviet Union.

> ...then the mark may well be the red star, the universal communist symbol. This may be a simple tattoo of the communist red star.

A second possibility concerns what is meant by the name of the beast. I do not think it will be the name of a specific man. This mark again might be a simple tattoo indicating that the bearer is a member of the communist party and loyal to the antichrist.

The third may be more complicated, the number of his name. I do not believe that this means simply the number 666. With the recent advancements in computer chip technology, especially in the miniaturization of them, it is now possible to make them microscopic enough to be injected beneath the skin. Although the microchip could possibly be the ultimate in the antichrist's control of people's lives, this would take considerable time to implement and the cost would be enormous. A much simpler form would be the use of a series of bars utilizing the universal products code already in place in most supermarkets. This code could be tattooed, possibly the dye only visible under ultraviolet light on either the hand or forehead.

Oh, this one is from "The Complete Book of Bible Prophesy":

This passage in Revelation 13 provides five key clues that is the interpretation of the mark of the beast: 1) the name of the beast; 2) the number representing his name; 3) the number of the beast; 4) the number of a man, and 5) the number of 666. When these five clues are followed through their logical progression, the number or mark of the beast is the number of man who is the antichrist or final world ruler. This number is the number of the antichrist's own name.

After reading that, do you now have any more of a clue what the mark is than you did before reading it? Think about it. More blah, blah, blah confusion.

Another author:

A timely computer chip painlessly and quickly implanted just under the skin in the hand or forehead will likely become the means of fulfilling this prophesy.

Everybody has heard of Grant Jeffrey:

What kind of mark will it be? It will be a physical mark, possibly visible, that the false prophet will force every man and woman to receive on his right hand or forehead. The mark will be related to both the name of the beast as well as the number of his name, 666. Possession of the mark will indicate that you willingly worship the beast. The number 666 indicates that the letters in Greek form the name of the antichrist would add up to 666.

Really!

There is a slim possibility that his name will equal 666 in the Hebrew language since antichrist will be Jewish...

Oh wow! Now we have an antichrist and he is going to be Jewish.

...yet the numeric system does not work in English or in languages other than Greek or Hebrew, so it is useless to calculate the value of his name in these modern languages.

The number 666 will be a finance number, perhaps invisibly tattooed on every person's right hand or forehead.

Here is someone in 1978:

One day in the tribulation period you will need proper identification to withdraw or deposit money in your bank. That identification will be an invisible mark either on the back of your hand or on your forehead. Your Social Security Number will become your identification number and will be prefixed by 666, and quite possibly followed by your own personal zip code. The government knows you by a number. Your most universal number is now your Social Security Number. Quite conceivably it could be the mark. Technology is already here whereby the Social Security Number could be painlessly imprinted on your forehead or right hand in invisible ink revealed only by a special light.

Next, everyone has heard of Tim LaHaye. He is the one who put together the *Christian Science Fiction* novel series "Left Behind":

One of the best known prophesies of the tribulation is the beast, or antichrist will have the ability to put his mark 666 on the forehead or hand of the world's people. Revelation 13:13-18 teaches that after the midpoint of the tribulation, all men and women will be ordered to bow down before the image of the beast and worship him. Those who do will receive a mark on the foreheads that is the name of the beast, or the number of his name, later identified as 666.

He goes on to say more *Christian Science Fiction*, folks. Let's just go right by that.

Here's another author:

The microchips currently used in smart cards could easily fulfill the definition of the mark which will be issued under the antichrist regime.

Let's go back a little further, almost 100 years to Clarence Larkin (1918). I have referred to him a couple of times before. All his stuff on the last days is *Christian Science Fiction* but, you know, he is popular:

The mark will be branded or burnt on. It will probably be the number of the beast or 666.

Hal Lindsay. Everybody has heard of "The Late Great Planet Earth":

Everyone will be given a tattoo or mark on either his forehead or forehand only if he swears allegiance to the dictator as being God. Symbolically this mark will be 666.

Here is a different twist from another author:

The prince... will exclude everyone who does not have an approved cashless account. Because of the importance of that account to daily existence and to protect it from theft, account information will be bio-implanted, leaving a small mark on the hand or temple.

Here is another author:

Could a microchip be programmed with the number of the beast and be inserted under a person's skin? And what of the barcode? Could the laser be used to 'brand' people with the mark? In light of the meaning of the biblical word mark, as used in Revelation 13, I do not see this as a viable possibility. For one thing, I believe the coming new age world leader will promote the mark as a spiritual status symbol that people will probably covet. It will be a mark of distinction. Like the commercial for a well-known credit card says, you wouldn't want to leave home without it. To hide or somehow mark it indistinguishable would defeat its purpose.

Here is another one:

Will the implantable microchip, link in with the L.U.C.I.D. worldwide control net, become the basis for the mysterious, but diabolical, Mark of the Beast? It seems possible, even likely that this will be proven to be the case.

It goes on and on. Pretty much everyone says the same thing over and over.

Let's look at Jack van Impe. Many have heard of him. What is his take on the mark of the beast?

This mark will consist of either the name of the beast, antichrist, or his number 666. It is likely that the image of the beast, a forthcoming master computer, will give antichrist all the information necessary for him to govern the world. Its memory banks will know the number, record and history of every living person. Perhaps this number will be composed of an international/national area computer plus individual numbers such as one's Social Security Number.

By the way, they have those kinds of computers and systems in place now, folks. There are very few places left you can hide if you want to live. You use a gas card. You use a credit card. You use a checking account. You have a job. Everything is recorded. You get on the internet, they can track you. Unless you are going to plant yourself on top of the Rocky Mountains and somehow be able to survive at that altitude with no one around, it is hard not to be identified any longer in these systems. Christ knew that. Do you really think that Christ wanted all Christians to go hide out on top of the Rocky Mountains, or in a cave, or in a hole somewhere? It goes against everything Christian discipleship is all about. We do not have to hide, crawl in a hole, or climb the tallest mountain that we think we could breathe on to hide ourselves. We are to be light bearers until the end. You cannot hide and be a light bearer. That is like putting the bushel over the lit candle. Who is going to see it? No one. So, what are we to do, I mean if it is not one of these things?

I have even more updated material on the RFID's, and the digital chip currency that is being entertained, which will produce a cashless society, but that is not the mark. It identifies that the EU is now trying to put something like that together.

The plan, to be unveiled in the coming days, is even more ambitious than the Commission's previous legislative attempt, as Brussels now wants to extend the electronic authentication to a number of services, beyond e-signatures. They plan to 'widen the scope of the current Directive by including also ancillary authentication services that compliment e-signatures like electronic seals, time date stamps, etc," and it reads as an internal paper prepared by her [Kroes] cabinet.

I mean, there are documents there that you can read, the actual papers and how they are pursuing this.

"It is proposed that all member states recognize and accept all formally notified e-IDs from other EU member states."

If that was not scary enough, they want to put a human barcode which could organize society in a more systemized way because big government knows what you need better than you do. You might forget something. You might forget to go in for your health checkup. Well, big government will, I don't know... buzz your chip, do what they have to do to notify you that it is time for you to go for your checkup. There are all kinds of microchip companies. I have list after list of those producing all this kind of technology.

Now, the latest fad surrounds Turkey's present leader, Recep Tayyip Erdogan. He hates Israel. Someone did a Gematria on his name and using the English Gematria, the number comes out to 666 when you mathematically add up all the numerical values of each letter of his name. I mean there is theory after theory out there by different people all guessing at what this mark is and who they consider antichrist to be. Everyone is looking.

I am not going to bore you with all the details. I am just generally covering this right now, but every single source we just looked at is wrong. It is not what God's Word has declared about what this mark of the beast has always been.

Listen, marking is nothing new. You can label it as marking or label it as sealing, but marking is nothing new. As Christian believers, as disciples of Jesus Christ, we want to be marked by Him, not by the Beast that exists today; or for the believers of times past, the beast that existed then. Marking or sealing has always existed. There has not been a single person that has ever existed on this planet that has not been marked with one type of mark or another. We will cover more on that and what that is in the following chapters. The evidence of what the mark of this beast is has always been in God's Word.

The Last Days Study Guide
The Mark of the Beast Part 1

1. List some of the theories given to explain the mark of the beast.
2. Is the mark of the beast a worldwide mark that will be placed on all peoples? And Why?
3. What does Christian discipleship call us to be?
4. What is Gematria?

The Mark of the Beast Part 2

I am going to present just a very general review of who we are talking about in this chapter, starting with Revelation 13:1-2.

"And I stood upon the sand of the sea, and saw a beast rise up out of the sea, having seven heads and ten horns, and upon his horns ten crowns, and upon his heads the name of blasphemy. And the beast which I saw was like unto a leopard, [circle leopard] *and his feet were as the feet of a bear,* [circle bear] *and his mouth as the mouth of a lion:* [circle lion] *and the dragon gave him his power, and his seat, and great authority."*

I want to establish the historical map of where these beasts existed that are described as a solitary beast in verse 2. So, let's geographically put borders in the areas of the Middle East and a little bit beyond the Middle East of what we find in Scripture for the Leopard, the Bear, and the Lion empirical empires not only here in the book of Revelation but also in Daniel and where they once existed.

The map above depicts the Babylonian Empire. That would be the Lion beast in verse 2. This is a beast that was, came and gone, and then was resurrected to become the 7th and 8th Beast.

<u>The 8th Beast is who the beast is today and that 8th Beast is Islam.</u>

Islam includes, as we will see on all the maps, not only the lion and bear but also the leopard empires of the past that have now been resurrected.

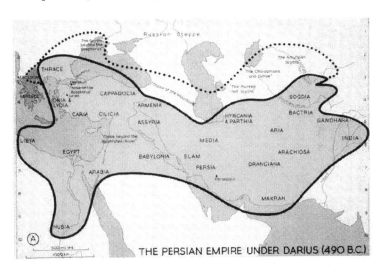

THE PERSIAN EMPIRE UNDER DARIUS (490 B.C.)

What I want you to get a feel for is the territory these empires covered.

The Babylonian Empire (depicted in pink on the map) covered about half of Saudi Arabia, goes into Iraq, the present western portions of Iran, Israel, Lebanon, Syria, along with a very small portion of present day Turkey, a section of Egypt including both the Sinai Peninsula and the areas around the Nile. That was the Babylonian Empire.

The next beastly kingdom's geographical territory is the Persian Empire under Darius. The Persian Empire in verse 2 is represented by the Bear. Some call it the Medo-Persian Empire, but this map shows what it covered as far as conquered territory. Now this map falls a bit short because their territory actually extended over Libya to its western border.

Looking north of Libya, we can see the empire covered the Grecian area, all of Turkey, all of Lebanon, Israel, Syria, the more northern parts of Saudi Arabia, Iraq, all of Iran, all of Afghanistan, followed by Pakistan and all the way to the borders of India. That was the Persian Empire's geographical territory.

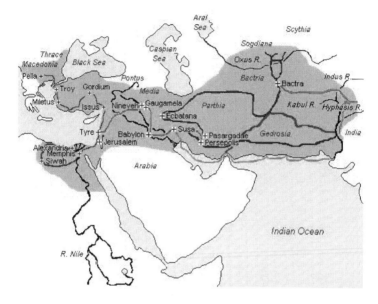

The final map depicts in gold the Grecian Empire under Alexander the Great. It is represented by the Leopard in Revelation 13:2.

Once again it is like the Persian Empire map. The Grecian Empire's territory covered Egypt, the Sinai Peninsula, the north-eastern part of Egypt, the Grecian area, all of Turkey, present day Armenia, Lebanon, Israel, obviously present day Jordan, Iraq, the most northern part of Saudi Arabia, Iran, Afghanistan and then Pakistan all the way to the borders of India, plus territories of some of the 'stans' that we now find on the map that were created following the breakup of the Soviet Union (e.g. Turkmenistan and all those other 'stans'), which by the way are also at present mostly Islamic countries. I think there are like two or three 'stans' that can be included in the old Grecian Empire's territory.

By superimposing all three maps each on top of the other, the Babylonian Empire over the Persian Empire over the Grecian Empire, that gives us some type of visual of the total geographic area of all three beasts combined, which forms the Lion+Bear+Leopard (LBL) Beast's territory of Revelation 13:1-2. Now this does not include and should not include the areas after Muhammad's death when the Muslims were conquering not only into the Baltic States but also westward on the northern part of the continent of Africa, crossing the Gibraltar into Spain, Portugal, and the southern tips of France and so forth. That is not included because that is not part of the 7th and 8th Beast. That was not a part of the Leopard beast, the Bear beast, or the Lion beast whether it was the Babylonian Empire, the Medo-Persia Empire, or Alexander the Great and the Grecian Empire. Make a mental picture of that because this chapter lays out for us who it is referring to.

Now the error in *Christian Science Fiction* doctrines is to make this a worldwide prophesy. I am sorry, this is not a worldwide prophesy. Verse 2 makes very clear who it is including. The prophesy is directed toward the Middle East in the geographical area where the 8th and final composite Beast resides. This is not even the 7th Beast because the 7th Beast was a beast that extended itself further out than the geographical areas on the maps. This LBL Beast is the final beast, and like I said, it consists of the Leopard, the Bear, and the Lion.

Now, even though I say this is not a worldwide prophesy, the whole world is affected by it. It is a prophesy directed towards these Middle Eastern and African areas, even some of the most eastern portions of the Baltic States of Eastern Europe and includes some of the 'stans' that used to be part of the Soviet Union or Russia. Still, it not a worldwide prophesy. It is only a prophesy directed towards this final 8th Beast and where it resides according to Scripture. To take it out of this geographical location is adding something to Scripture that just is not there. The only thing you can find in this chapter before we get to verse 16 is in verse 11 where it talks about the Two-horned Beast that is like a lamb but spoke as a dragon. Now that does take it and extends it out, but it is not part of the LBL Beast. We will cover that in the future and what the Two-horned Beast did when it came on the scene. That is the only area outside of the LBL geographical area mentioned in this chapter, but that is not the 8th Beast. It empowers the 8th Beast and I will give the explanation of how when we get to that segment.

This chapter in the book of Revelation is about that beast in the Middle East and its relation to Israel, how they will not only feel the repercussions of this 8th Beast, but eventually how the Lord will deal with it. This 8th Beast is Islam in the geographic areas we looked at. It is Islam and it is Jihad, period. Now, there is no question, after it is all said and done, that the effects of this 8th Beast will be felt worldwide, but it is still not a worldwide prophesy. That is important to make note of. Make no mistake, folks.

Now I gave a list of multiple possibilities for 666 that *Christian Science Fiction* theory people have put together from chips, to tattoos, to cards, to all kinds of things such as lasers, scanners, this and that, and how this Beast will require people worldwide (even though this is not a worldwide prophesy) to have placed either on or under the skin some device, or carry a card around (or whatever their theory is) or else they cannot buy and sell. I have told you that it is all a bunch of nonsense. It is all a bunch of *Christian Science Fiction*, even though a lot of it is not science fiction because you do see those things being developed to put into commerce, so you can buy and sell whatever.

I remember when the barcode scanners began to be used. I do not know, I think this was back in the early '80s, maybe '82 or '83. A supermarket that was near to where I was living in Glendale, California at the time installed one. There was one lane where the cashier could ring up your product by scanning its barcode. Of course, as a few more of those came out everybody was saying this is the 666, or this is the beginning of the 666. Everybody was going crazy. That was some thirty plus years ago now but then, everybody was convinced. There were pamphlets, materials, even books being printed that this was the beginning of the end. The mark is just around the corner. I mean the technology is there, so it is not a stretch to be creative if you twist Scripture and use that technological information to say it is a possibility. And since some of the book of Revelation is written in a figurative language, they did not see any problem in making it stretch, making it feasible. After all, like I said, the technology is there.

The problem with that theory is it does not line up with the verifiable Word of God and I use a system called the verifiable Word of God. I try not to base anything that I preach about on opinion, even though there might be some. There have been times when I have said that it is just an opinion. That means I do not have verifiable verses in God's Word to back up that opinion. It just seems like it is the logical choice. Then you must decide whether I am right or whether I am wrong. I don't do it much but when I do, I like to point that out to you. Well, I am saying to disregard all the *Christian Science Fiction* nonsense. It really does not add up. It is just interesting like sci-fi, especially for you sci-fi enthusiasts. I am sure it is intriguing, but it does not add up. See, God's Word can verify itself. In fact, I cannot find any of it that does not. I make it my effort to try to – not to disprove God, but to make sure what I am preaching is the correct and rightly divided Word of God. I need something other than intriguing *Christian Science Fiction* theories. I want facts, and can we find the facts.

Revelation 13:15, *"And he had power to give life unto the image of the beast, that the image of the beast should both speak, and cause that as many as would not worship the image of the beast should be killed. And he causeth..."* Well, causeth is not really the right word there. *"And he makes all, both small and great, rich and poor, free and bond, to <u>receive a mark</u>..."* Who? This beast. *"to receive a mark in their right hand, or in their foreheads: And that no man might buy or sell, save he that had the mark, or the name of the beast, or the number of his name. Here is wisdom. Let him that hath understanding count the number of the beast: for it is the number of a man; and his number is Six hundred threescore and six."* Or 666.

Now back to the question that I left you with the last time I spoke on this subject: What is this mark?

I can say from those that I've talked with and that have communicated to me, Satan is having a hay day convincing people to look for something that never arrives. They think the time is extended and the Lord is not just around the corner. They know He is near but certain things, they think, have not happened yet. So, their bottom line is He cannot be that near. I was reading a message from a person who just could not understand why it was not going to be just the number 666. Their dilemma is a result of being indoctrinated with that system of teaching which says it will be some form of 666 or another, whether it is the number 666, a barcode system of 666, or some kind of 666. Their thinking is that until that is really put in place and the plans are carried out worldwide (even though this is no worldwide prophesy) they still have some time. I am sure some people are still thinking they'll have enough time to get it together when the time comes because He is not at the door now. I am telling you, not only is He at the door, He has one-foot in. There is not that much time, and many are going to be unprepared in dealing with what is coming down because they are not prepared. This is not placed here in the Bible just to fill in pages, just to create a thick book. This is here for our instruction.

The Old Testament is full of instruction on the First Advent and the Second Advent. The same is true with the New Testament. The New Testament just covers some of the things in its historical aspect that happened in the Old, but it still has information of things yet to come in the New as we wait for the Second Advent, the return of Christ. It is there for a reason. Christ instructed His disciples for a reason. So, they could be ready. There are many parables that Christ uses to teach us that there are going to be many that are not ready. They squandered their time that they could have been helping the ones that are trying to prepare others for the Second Advent, because they just did not see the importance of it, or it was not necessary because for some reason they think they still have time. I am telling you right now, no you don't.

Now back to this mark. You circled the word *mark*. It just means a stamp in the Greek. If you look at the Greek word it means a mark, an imprint, etcetera. Can we, with that definition alone, identify with certainty what that mark could be? Do you have any clue? We could speculate like many others have, but do you really have a clue? Put another way: Could someone possibly have an idea of what it means if they do not have a clue based on everything that came before this chapter, from the beginning in the book of Genesis onward? I am telling you the answer is no. That is why there are so many *Christian Science Fiction* theories. Many have tried by just using this definition alone. Many have tried creating all types of theories to prove their viewpoints, and they think they are successful. Tens of thousands of messages have been preached. Hundreds upon hundreds, if not thousands, of books have been written. With all the mountains of information and speculation, the Christian world is no closer to identifying this mark than they were 100 years ago. Even the people that listen to me and follow this ministry and have listened to this Last Days series teaching and who have gone exploring in other places, they think they have it figured out. They think it is the Koran or something related to Islam. Well, even though it is associated with the Koran, that is not it. You may think, "Well, I have seen if you use a numerical value system that adds up the letters in a certain language, the Koran would add up to 666." Okay, but what about the mark? The name of the beast is simple to figure out, but what about the mark and what about the number? "Well, you just said the number could be added to the holy Koran." I did not want to call it "holy" but to play the devil's advocate I guess, let us just call it that. We know one thing, one will not be able to buy or sell. It is kind of humorous to see the world trying to figure this out. They do not even realize about 80-90 percent of the geographical area we looked at on the maps is already in place, and soon the system is going to be completely in place where you cannot buy unless you buy something they control, that they can identify with. Scripture has prophesied that, and I will get into that later. There is so much information and speculation, but we are no closer than we were 100 years ago. The reason why we are no closer is not so much because of the name of the beast, because like I said that is simple to figure out, but because of the mark and also the number, and more so the mark than even the number, but still both. That is where a lot of speculation has come in, those two features in Revelation 13.

So, then the question becomes, can we possibly find other marks in history that can help us identify what this mark might look like? The short answer to that question is yes, and that is what we are going to do. But to do so, we are going to have to put our biblical detective hats on and not just deal in speculation.

Men have been marked throughout history with the purpose of identifying whether they were one of God's chosen or if they belonged to the Devil. To see that, all we have to do is look at the Scripture for some clarity on this subject. If you go back to the very first book in the Bible, Genesis 4, you will see the first murder committed by Cain killing his brother Abel. Assuming you know the story, let's just pick it up with verse 9,

"And the LORD said unto Cain, Where is Abel thy brother? and he said, I know not: Am I my brother's keeper? And he said, What hast thou done? the voice of thy brother's blood crieth unto me from the ground. And now art thou cursed [cursed] *from the earth, which hath opened her mouth to receive thy brother's blood from thy hand. When thou tillest the ground, it shall not henceforth yield unto thee her strength."*

Now this is a matter of opinion, based on other scriptures but still opinion because I cannot say with 100% certainty that this is fact but, I believe the ground itself, what God created and what it could provide for physical growth, changed from this point on. I do not want to get off into that subject right now but there are other scriptures I could provide for that opinion. It is just a sidebar.

"When thou tillest the ground, it shall not henceforth yield unto thee her strength; a fugitive and a vagabond [a fugitive and a vagabond] *shalt thou be in the earth. And Cain said unto the LORD, My punishment is greater than I can bear."*

Do you know what Scripture is really saying Cain said? *"My iniquity is greater than that it may be forgiven."* Think about that statement for a minute. *My iniquity is greater than that it may be forgiven.* Cain nowhere asked the Lord for forgiveness. There is no remorse. If there is any remorse it was because of the punishment he was receiving was greater than he could bear. He was not remorseful or sorry for his crime.

Verse 14, *"Behold, thou hast driven me out this day from the face of the earth; and from thy face shall I be hid; and I shall be a fugitive and a vagabond in the earth; and it shall come to pass, that everyone that findeth me shall slay me."*

He was not worried or concerned about his eternal existence. He was not worried or concerned about the sin he committed – and not just against his brother but more so, unto God himself. No, he was just worried about if he was going to survive, if he himself would not also be killed, probably because of the story passing along from generation to generation. Who knows. The way he was possibly thinking was one of Abel's kin would come after him and try to kill him. Everyone thinks that these two men (that's right, I said men) were boys when this event occurred. They were not boys, they were men already.

Verse 15, *"And the LORD said unto him, Therefore whosoever slayeth Cain, vengeance shall be taken on him sevenfold."*

There is a lot of speculation about why God even did this. Why did God give a level of protection to Cain? I do not want to get sidetracked with this particular part of this message, so we will go right over this, but it is an interesting verse.

Verse 15, *"And the LORD said unto him, Therefore whosoever slayeth Cain, vengeance shall be taken on him sevenfold. And the LORD set <u>a mark</u> upon Cain, lest any finding him should kill him."*

So obviously, whatever this mark was had to be visible for others to see. The story had to be told, "Hey, do not touch Cain. God placed that mark on him. He is untouchable. He is God's problem. Even though you might want to seek your revenge... **Don't**." This was God's way of saying hands off to anybody that would entertain the thought of doing any harm to Cain.

"And Cain went out from the presence of the LORD...".

What a horrible way to exist from that point on. Up to this point, including even after the murder, he was still in the Lord's presence. Do you think the Lord would have forgiven him, even after the murder? Maybe we would not but the Lord sure would have. But Cain never even presented that option that he was going to be remorseful for what he did and ask for God's forgiveness. He did not care about the type of sacrifice. His was not an animal sacrifice because he brought the fruit of the ground as an offering to the Lord. But Abel brought the first fruit of the flock and the fat which was necessary for the offerings of sin and trespasses, period, even before the Mosaic Law was in place. Cain did not care about that. I guess he thought he was sin free and did not believe in all this sin nonsense. And God was pleased and respected Abel's offering but Cain and to his offering He had no respect, and Cain was very wroth. He became angry but still even with all that going on, even the murder, he still was in the presence of the Lord. He had an opportunity to repent.

I have people listening to me who think what they have done is so horrible that it cannot be forgiven. Well, in a sense you are right if you walk away out of the presence of the Lord forever. Yes, you are correct. But if you do not, I do not care what you have done in the past, forgiveness is there. Christ in our day already paid the ultimate price, and once and for all He gave man the opportunity, the gift of being able because of His grace to come at His feet and say, "Lord, forgive me. From this day forward, I want to walk in Your presence until I go home, or You come and get me. Either one is fine with me. This day I will no longer walk away from Your presence, but I will run towards Your presence." Now, that is not the message but any time I can preach true salvation I want to.

Moving on from that we see here that God knows, He marked: *"And the LORD set a mark upon Cain"*. God knows and identified him because of the type of offering that he did not present. Keep that in mind. There is a lot of gobbledygook that is preached about these offerings of Cain and Abel. They miss the point of the types of offerings that were presented and not presented by each individual. God knows when your desire is to walk away from His presence and not recognize the true offering for our sin, in our case, Jesus Christ. He knows just as He did here with Cain. God knows and identifies those who refuse salvation, including Cain, by what? By the blood. He marks them as lost. I am going to come back to Cain later.

Another example of marking is found in Ezekiel 9. At the beginning of the chapter, Ezekiel is in the middle of having a second vision. The vision is dealing with the city of Jerusalem and Israel that has forsaken God. So, let's backtrack a little to chapter 8 for the cause of the vision.

Ezekiel 8:4, *"And, behold, the glory of the God of Israel was there, according to the vision that I saw in the plain. Then said he unto me, Son of man, lift up thine eyes now the way toward the north. So I lifted up mine eyes the way toward the north, and behold northward at the gate of the altar this image of jealousy in the entry."* Verse 6 continues, *"He said furthermore unto me, Son of man, seest thou what they do? even the great abominations that the house of Israel committeth here, that I should go far off from my sanctuary? but turn thee yet again, and thou shalt see greater abominations."*

So, in short, get ready Ezekiel. In the vision you are having, you are going to see abominations above abominations, some worse than others. And of course, God brings him to the door of the court and he looks through a hole in the wall and he starts seeing one abomination after another. Ezekiel is looking through this hole in the wall that he had to dig because they are trying to keep all this secret. They think they are worshipping these false idols and false gods in secret. God sees it all, my friend. You cannot hide anything from God. Who are you fooling? So, Ezekiel in the vision is instructed again.

Ezekiel 8:13, *"He said also unto me, Turn thee yet again, and thou shalt see greater abominations that they do."*

He is going to see something that is worse than what he had seen so far. What is it?

Verse 14, *"Then he brought me to the door of the gate of the LORD'S house which was toward the north; and, behold there sat women weeping for Tammuz."*

Who was Tammuz? Cush, a son of Ham—who I believe started all the upheaval again shortly after the flood—had sons and one of his sons was Nimrod. Nimrod married Semiramis and she supposedly had a child miraculously after Nimrod died, Tammuz, who in a sense was a resurrected Nimrod, mimicking what was to come with the virgin birth several thousand years later. But here about 1500-1700 years later, they are still worshipping this Tammuz. But how? Was it a statue? Was it a relic? What was it? We will get to that.

And then we get to Ezekiel 9:1, *"He cried also in mine ears with a loud voice, saying, Cause them that have charge over the city to draw near, even every man with his destroying weapon in his hand. And, behold, six men came from the way of the higher gate, which lieth toward the north, and every man a slaughter weapon in his hand; and one man among them was clothed with linen, with a writer's inkhorn by his side: and they went in, and stood beside the brasen altar. And the glory of the God of Israel was gone up from the cherub, whereupon he was, to the threshold of the house. And he called to the man clothed with linen, which had the writer's inkhorn by his side;"* And here is the verse I want to get to: *"And the LORD said unto him, Go through the midst of the city, through the midst of Jerusalem, and set ... "* The Hebrew for 'set' says *mark a mark*. Write it in your Bibles there. *"...__and mark a mark upon the foreheads__ of the men that sigh and that cry for all the abominations that be done in the midst thereof."*

So here we read, go and mark a mark. Now, remember Ezekiel is still in the vision format. He is not seeing this in the physical world. He is seeing this in the vision. So, in a sense, he is seeing this in the spiritual world.

II Chronicles, written by Ezra, is another location where we see this same story being carried out, but there it is being carried out in the physical world. Zedekiah was ruling currently in Judah, the Southern Kingdom.

II Chronicles 36: 11-16, *"Zedekiah was one and twenty years old when he began to reign, and reigned eleven years in Jerusalem. And he did that which was evil in the sight of the LORD his God, and humbled not himself before Jeremiah the prophet speaking from the mouth of the LORD. And he also rebelled against king Nebuchadnezzar, who had made him swear by God: but he stiffened his neck, and hardened his heart from turning unto the LORD God of Israel. Moreover all the chief of the priests, and the people, transgressed very much after all the abominations of the heathen; and polluted the house of the LORD which he had hallowed in Jerusalem. And the LORD God of their fathers sent to them by his messengers, rising up betimes* [quickly]*, and sending; because he had compassion on his people, and on his dwelling place: But they mocked the messengers of God, and despised his words, and misused his prophets, until the wrath of the LORD arose against his people, till there was no remedy. "*Remembering what we just read in Ezekiel 9, we pick it up here in verse 17, *"Therefore he brought upon them the king of the Chaldees, "*now we have the identification of who is doing the slaying, *"who slew their young men with the sword in the house of their sanctuary, and had no compassion upon young man or maiden, old man, or him that stooped for age: he gave them all into his hand."*

Referring back to Ezekiel 9:4, *"And the LORD said unto him, Go through the midst of the city, through the midst of Jerusalem, and <u>mark a mark upon the foreheads</u> of the men that sigh and that cry for all the abominations that be done in the midst thereof. And to the others, "*corresponding to the II Chronicles account, *"he said in mine hearing, Go ye after him through the city, and smite: let not your eye spare, neither have ye pity: Slay utterly old and young, both maids, and little children, and women: but come not near any man upon whom is the MARK* [the mark that is on their foreheads] *and begin at my sanctuary. Then they began at the ancient men which were before the house."*

What Ezekiel saw being carried out in the spiritual world II Chronicles 36 shows being carried out in the physical world.

II Chronicles 36:17-18, *"Therefore he brought upon them the king of the Chaldees, who slew their young men with the sword in the house of their sanctuary, and had no compassion upon young man or maiden, old man, or him that stooped for age: he gave them all into his hand. And all the vessels of the house of God, great and small, and the treasures of the house of the LORD, and the treasures of the king, and of his princes; all these he brought to Babylon."*

The princes, the ones with the mark, were spared slaughter and carried into Babylon.

Now both in II Chronicles and in Ezekiel 9 we saw marks that were to be placed on their foreheads, in Ezekiel's case in a vision. Ezekiel is in the spiritual world seeing what is going to be played out. So, he can see things in a spiritual sense that in the physical world cannot be seen. Now we just touched on one mark that I believe others could see, the mark of Cain. That mark was in the material world and others could see it. Here in the Ezekiel 9 vision it is seen in the spiritual world only. As the Zedekiah story is being played out in the physical world, you will notice there is no reference in this story anywhere where anyone was able to see any type of literal mark of any kind on people's foreheads. Why? Because Ezra recorded what he saw in the material world, what people can see with their eyes. Those in the spiritual world saw the mark. Those in physical world did not. So, we have two classical cases: one in the physical world that could be physically seen and one in the unseen spiritual world that couldn't be seen, yet played out upon the players in the story. God sees the spiritual realm that is unseen to us. That is what He is looking upon. He knows.

Now that is not the only marks or stamp or even seals. We read in the New Testament that Christians are also marked. They are marked or sealed with the Holy Spirit.

II Corinthians 1:20, *"For all the promises of God in him are yea, and in him Amen, unto the glory of God by us. Now he which stablisheth us with you in Christ, and hath anointed us, is God. Who hath also* <u>*sealed us*</u>, *and given the earnest of the Spirit in our hearts."*

He has sealed us, and it is not a seal that we can physically see. Can you imagine if someone invented some type of camera that could capture this seal of the Holy Spirit by taking a picture? Can you imagine having one of those cameras? Boy, one could make a mint off Christians if they did. Maybe non-Christians too. Boy oh boy! imagine the snake oil salesmen that would be peddling this Christian Jesus junk. I bet you would have scores of Christians either going to a place and paying a hefty sum to get their picture taken or buying one of these expensive cameras to see if they had the Holy Spirit aura, or whatever you want to call it. Here we have the mention of a seal and also an earnest of the Spirit which is a down payment of the Spirit, a necessary amount the Holy Spirit in us that we need to get through this as a disciple of Jesus Christ.

Now go to Ephesians 1:13-15. I have preached on these many times in the past. *"In whom ye also trusted, after that ye heard the word of truth, the gospel of your salvation: in whom also, after that ye believed,* [in this case *pisteuo, had trust and confidence in*] <u>*ye were sealed*</u> *with that Holy Spirit of promise...."* Ye were sealed; there we go again, another marking by God that only He can see. *"Which is the earnest* [the down payment once again] *of our inheritance until the redemption of the purchased possession, unto the praise of his glory. Wherefore I also, after I heard of your faith in the Lord Jesus, and love unto all the saints..."*

Once again, we have that seal or mark. It is called something different here, sealed, but it is still something that identifies us as Christ's. As Cain was identified with a mark for his protection— (which I am still trying to figure out why God would want that; and I have my theories why but they are just theories at this point)—we can see that when Nebuchadnezzar brought down the heat, even though neither he nor anyone else could see it, the ones that were marked in the spiritual world that Ezekiel saw in his vision were spared. In Ezra's and Nebuchadnezzar's world, they could not see that mark, but God knew how to spare them. That is all that counts, that is all that is important, and it is the same thing with the Holy Spirit.

They received the Holy Spirit of promise in Ephesians 1:13. Now, go to Ephesians 4:30, *"And grieve not the Holy Spirit of God, whereby ye are sealed unto the day of redemption…"* Sealed. Have you heard of being a *marked man*? Well, you want to be a marked man that Christ marks, who He has chosen to be one of His, not marked by the devil.

Another case in point, and then I will be done with this part.

II Timothy 2:19, *"Nevertheless the foundation of God standeth sure,* [steady is a better translation] *having this seal…"* HAVING THIS SEAL - how God has identified you by placing some of Himself as a down payment IN YOU. *"…having this seal, The Lord knoweth them that are his."* It has been the same message whether Old or New Testament. Different words are used but the same message. He knows how to identify those who are His. *"And, Let every one that nameth the name of Christ depart from iniquity* [that which is wrong].*"*

So, we have all these examples. There are more but this is enough to move on. In the material world you do not see the Holy Spirit marked, stamped, or sealed on anyone. If you could, like I said, I am sure Christians could make a pretty good dollar off it and they probably would. The Lord's mark is only visible in the spiritual world. The Holy Spirit's mark is a spiritual mark. It is not a physical mark. Ezekiel's vision was a spiritual mark, not a physical mark. Cain's mark was a physical mark, and anyone could see that. Why? Because it was not a spiritual mark, it was a physical mark. But I am telling you now, it was a physical mark that became spiritualized. Yes, you heard me right. It was a physical mark that became spiritualized, but not by God. Then by who? The presence he was under and that was Satan, not God.

You need to understand and accept the spiritual principle from the scriptures that we have here which has defined what is seen and what is not seen. If you do not come to this understanding folks, you will accept different *Christian Science Fiction* theories that are circulating in the Christian world. It is a tragedy and that is why there is so much nonsense out there. This is an important biblical principle that we must follow, to use as a guideline and a rule. When we get to Revelation 13, we cannot just make up what we think the mark can be, or should be, or could be by speculation and what we see the material world, what knowledge can produce now. No, let's stick with the verifiable Word of God and what marks have always been and how we can detect them before we go any further in trying to identify anything.

Now there are some that teach similar to what I teach concerning this topic, but they have a difficult time trying to come to a *clear* understanding (and I emphasize the word clear) of what this mark could be, what it always has been. You heard me right - what it always has been. Islam has not always 'has been'. Allah came before Islam and Allah is an element, the main feature of Islam, but Islam has not always been. So, to merely identify what Islamic jihad marks, pictures, stamps, seals, and emblems are is to have an incomplete understanding of what this mark is. Believe me, this mark, once identified, in conjunction with the true meaning of 666, will reveal clearly how Islam now is the final representation of all three of these distinguishing features that we see in the book of Revelation chapter 13.

Now, they have a difficult time coming to clear understanding of what this mark could be. For instance, in Revelation 13:16 which is *"to receive a mark in their right hand, or in their foreheads"*, they have concluded that this is written in a figurative language, which then would demand a figurative interpretation. For example, they generalize it using that concept of trying to understand what it is really saying: "With the mind he [the beast] thinks to do evil [that explains the forehead], and with the hand [explaining the hand] he does evil." That is one of their interpretations for Revelation 13:16. So his hand is going to react to what his mind is thinking and what it is telling him to do, therefore, whatever he is going to act upon, it will be done by his hands.

That is how they rationalize it. What I am saying is that is what happens when speculation is brought in to try to explain God's Word.

There are some that think, as I said earlier, that the Koran is 666. Others preach that the numerical value of the name of Allah equals up to 666. I do not disagree. Let me make that perfectly clear, I do not disagree with any of those explanations, but I am someone that needs biblical verification before I will entertain any outside source or opinion. Remember the line in the movie *Jerry Maguire*, "Show me the money"? Well show me the evidence, and not just any old evidence, show me the biblical evidence. I understand that sometimes we can only get about 90% of the way there, other times we get 100% of the way there and so forth, but that 90% better be a strong 90%.

So, with that, let's put our biblical detective hats on and go back to the beginning. To understand the mark of the beast, we must look at the mark of Cain and what it was. According to rabbinical literature, they believe it is the Hebrew letter *Tau*. Well, what did *Tau* look like? I am going to make some of the Christians that listen to me furious because where I am going is where most dare not go. So, let's go. Put on your seatbelts and let's move forward.

That which is now called the Christian cross was originally no Christian emblem at all...

"Where are you going? I do not think I like hearing what you are about to say. My cross is sacred to me. How could you offend it? After all, are you not the preacher that says, 'take up your cross'?"

First, it does not say cross in the Greek. The Greek word is *stauros*. It is not *xulon* which is a type of wood. It is *stauros*.

Did Jesus really die on a cross, the cross as Christians portray the cross to be? If He did, the wrong language was used, and I can prove that. So, what did He die on and was there a reason why He died on that, whatever it was? Absolutely.

*That which is now called the Christian cross was originally no
Christian emblem at all, but was a mystic Tau of the Chaldeans
and Egyptians—the true original form of the letter T—the initial
of the name of Tammuz—which, in Hebrew, radically the same
as the ancient Chaldee.*

Who were the Chaldeans? The Cushites. Remember Nimrod was one of the
sons of Cush; Semiramis, Tammuz, they all came from that area. After the
flood, that is where the pollution of false religion began. I have said before
when going over the moon-god history part of scripture, from that point on
it branched out east and west, especially after the Tower of Babel incident
when the languages became confused. They took their mystic evil religions
that they created with them and that is why we see the same kinds of gods in
all these other locations. They were just called different names depending on
the location. So, it started with the Chaldeans and the Egyptians after the
flood. Where would they get these ideas from? From their fathers. Cush got
it from Ham. Ham existed before the flood. He knew the stories. He was
closer to the Cain incident than they were after the flood. And it was
information that was passed on from generation to generation that everyone
had to remember, do not touch Cain, do not even put a hand on him, stay
away. He is literally a marked man by God, but not part of God.

*That mystic Tau was marked in baptisms on the foreheads of those
initiated in the Mysteries, and was used in every variety of way as
a most sacred symbol.*

"Are you saying this is the mark?" I am not saying anything yet. I am going
to lay down history and information and you can come to your own decision.
I have mine. I will let you know what my decision is with the information we
have, but I want to present enough of it, so you can come to the same decision
or maybe a different decision than I have.

*To identify Tammuz with the sun, it was joined sometimes to the
circle of the sun.*

Almost like a Celtic cross, by the way.

> *The mystic Tau, as the symbol of the great divinity, was called "the sign of life".*

Why was it called the sign of life? I know one of the reasons was because lo and behold a miraculous baby came out of Semiramis, and she claimed that it was a resurrected Nimrod, amongst other things, so it became the symbol that stated this is a sign of life. In other words, you could not end that type of life. It would be resurrected back again to accomplish what it needed to accomplish. You could not take that life away. It's kind of like what God did for Cain in a way, if you think about it.

> *There is hardly a pagan tribe where the cross has not been found.*

You can go to China, India, throughout all the Middle East, Africa, all the way to Mexico and find crosses that date back thousands of years, to a time before Christ.

> *There is hardly a pagan tribe where the cross has not been found. The cross was worshipped by the pagan Celts long before the incarnation and death of Christ. It is a fact not less remarkable than well-attested, that the druids in their groves...*

A type of asherah grove by the way.

> *...were accustomed to select the most stately and beautiful tree...*

Sound familiar? If not, I will be coving all those teachings on the moon-god history and the abominations the children of Israel did repeatedly in the Old Testament.

> *...their groves were accustomed to select the most stately and beautiful tree as an emblem of the deity they adored, and having cut the side branches, they affixed two of the largest of them to the highest part of the trunk, in such a manner that those branches extended on each side like the arms of a man...*

Hum. Is this story similar to what we find at Easter and what happened with Christ?

> *...in such a manner that those branches extended on each side like the arms of a man, and, together with the body, presented the appearance of a HUGE CROSS, and on the bark, in several places, were also inscribed the letter Tau.*

> *It was worshipped in Mexico for ages before the Roman Catholic missionaries set foot there. The cross thus widely worshipped, or regarded as a sacred emblem, was the unequivocal symbol of the Babylonian messiah for he was represented with a headband covered with crosses.*

The Babylonian messiah: put a headband on and put crosses all around it that circled the forehead.

> *This symbol of the Babylonian god is reverenced at this day in all the wide wastes of Tartary where Buddhism prevails.*

So even in those parts of the world.

> *Though it is not an object of worship among the Buddhists, it is a favorite emblem and device among them.*

Now it goes on and on, but I do not want to just stop there. I want to read another source. I think this is interesting. It is going to lead up to something eventually and we will see where it goes.

> *The cross is recognized as one of the most important symbols in the Roman Catholic Church.*

Now I am not going to dwell on the Roman Catholic Church. This author does, but I am not because I know the roots of this way before the Roman Catholic Church got their hands on it and I know where it extends after the Roman Catholic Church had established it as one of their sacred emblems.

So, do not get stuck on the Roman Catholic Church when I insert it here.

The cross is recognized as one of the most important symbols in the Roman Catholic Church. It is displayed on top of roofs and towers. It is seen on altars, furnishings, and ecclesiastical garments. The floor plan of the majority of the Catholic churches is laid out in the shape of the cross. All Catholic homes, hospitals, schools have the cross adorning the walls. Everywhere the cross is outwardly honored and adored in hundreds of ways. When an infant is sprinkled, the priest makes a sign of the cross upon its forehead saying, Receive the sign of the cross upon thy forehead. During confirmation the candidate is signed with the cross. On Ash Wednesday, ashes are used to make the cross on the forehead.

By the way, if the cross was so powerful a symbol in Christianity, whether Catholic or Protestant, how come exorcisms and exorcists constantly fail when crosses are placed on the human body, mostly the forehead? If it is such a powerful antidote to what has possessed you, then why does it not deliver the person from possessions? I am sorry; I have read hundreds of cases. I have studied this. I have a whole series of demonology ready to go, which I have never gotten to yet. Some things are the same, but it is different from the Spiritual Warfare Series. It is not just all about ghost stories either. Such a sacred emblem, such a tool. It does not work. If it was something that Satan and his demons or evil spirits feared, they would run for the hills in the presence of it. Is it that powerful of a symbol for Christ's purposes? Or is that just what you have been made to believe?

Let's read on:

Protestant churches, for the most part, do not believe in making the sign of the cross with their fingers. Neither do they bow down before crosses and use them as objects of worship. They have recognized that these things are unscriptural and superstitious, but the use of the cross has been commonly retained on steeples, on pulpits and various other ways as a form of decoration. The early

Christians did not consider the cross as a virtuous symbol, but rather as a cursed tree, a device of death and shame.

We find that, by the way, in Hebrews 12:2, ***"Looking unto Jesus the author and finisher of (our) faith; who for the joy that was set before him endured the cross, DESPISING THE SHAME"***. But after He came down off that cross, despising that shame, He sat at the right hand of the Father.

The early Christians did not consider the cross as a virtuous symbol, but rather as a cursed tree, a device of death and shame. They did not trust in the old rugged cross. Instead their faith was in what was accomplished ON THE CROSS and through this faith they knew the full and complete forgiveness of sin. It was in this sense that the apostles preach about the cross and gloried in it. They never spoke of the cross as a piece of wood one might hang from a little chain around his neck or carry in his hand as a protector or charm. Such uses of the cross came later.

"What does this have to do with the mark?" I am getting there. It is just going to take me a little while.

It was not until Christianity began to be PAGANIZED (or, as some prefer, paganism was Christianized) that the cross came to be thought of as a Christian symbol. It was in 431 A.D. that crosses in churches and chambers were introduced, while the use of crosses on steeples did not come until about 586 A.D.

Well, the cross came into use before 431 A.D. in a popular way, but I understand what this author is saying, it was really starting to have widespread use. Constantine reintroduced it. That is why I am not a Constantine fan. He was a fake and a phony. He was someone not controlled by Jesus Christ. I will cover that in the future.

In the 6ᵗʰ century, the crucifix image was introduced and its worship sanctioned by the Church of Rome. It was not until the second council at Ephesus that private homes were required to possess a cross. If the cross is a Christian symbol, it cannot be correctly said that its origin was within Christianity, for in one form or another it was a sacred symbol long before the Christian Era and among many non-Christian people.

According to a expository dictionary of the New Testament, the cross originated among the Babylonians of ancient Chaldea.

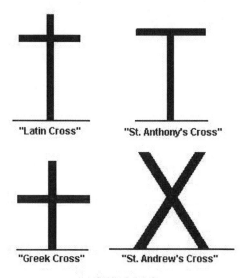

"Latin Cross"   "St. Anthony's Cross"

"Greek Cross"   "St. Andrew's Cross"

Daily Bible Study

Reintroduced by Cush, carried on by Nimrod and Semiramis, and eventually Tammuz; a practice they created that originated, I believe, before the flood going all the way back to Cain. I do not want to say too much yet, so I will just leave you with that, but once again after the flood it was reintroduced as a sacred symbol. You will see stars, you will see the moon quite often, and the sun, but most of Christendom that studies the ancient history of this time either rejects it or does not see how this symbol is inscribed on walls, paintings, even cave pictures or drawings. It is everywhere. You can find it in all parts of the world. Why? And why was there a fascination for the cross and different styles of the cross, depending on the area once again? Why? And

40

most of the fascination was among the pagan and heathens. Why? And why did it become sacred in the Christian world?

> ...the cross originated among the Babylonians of ancient Chaldea. The ecclesiastical form of the two-beamed cross had its origin in ancient Chaldea and was used as a symbol of the god Tammuz (being in the shape of the mystic Tau, the initial of his name) in that country, and in adjacent lands, including Egypt. In order to increase the prestige of the apostate ecclesiastical system, pagans were received into the churches, apart from regeneration by faith, and were largely permitted to retain their pagan signs and symbols. Hence the Tau or T in its most frequent form, with the cross-piece lowered, was adopted to stand for the cross of Christ.

It never was the cross of Christ, folks!

> In any book on Egypt that shows the old monuments on walls of the ancient temples, one can see the use of the Tau cross.

Left: you see variations of the cross.

These are just variations.

Below: An Egyptian illustration you can find on walls in Egypt. Here you have so much going on. The emblem at center is called an ankh - the ankh cross WAY BEFORE Jesus Christ.

This is a matter of ancient Egyptian history. Of course, you see the sun above it. I believe there it is the sun, possibly the moon, but the sun god being worshipped.

This one is kind of unique. See if you can spot it. Once you know what the ankh cross looks like, it is identifiable. The person sitting down on the left is probably a pharaoh and then the four servants following are carrying something. At least the first three are. What do you see there? The cross once again - the Tau cross, the ankh cross.

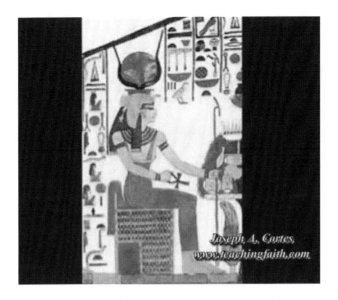

Here we have the two horns (which we will cover in the moon-god history part of this series) upholding either the sun or the moon. I believe this picture is the moon for various reasons, which I will not go into right now. This is Hathor the Egyptian goddess and she is holding the ankh or cross.

To the right is a bucket which was used for carrying holy water. It might be difficult to see, but in this picture, there is a one-inch band around the lower portion of the bucket. Throughout that band are those crosses once again.

Above is a limestone slab of the jackal, the Egyptian god of the dead. That god is depicted on the right-hand side. See if you can spot the ankh. I want you to become familiar with these pictures, and not just here in Egypt but other locations also. In the future, I am sure you will start to be able to recognize this symbol of the cross. It is everywhere - different variations of it, but it is everywhere. Now here also, of course, we see what I believe is either the moon-god or the sun-god that is once again being looked upon in an upward fashion, being praised and worshipped. We also see the cross again on the right-hand side and the left-hand side of the upper third of that slab. Then you move down you see the jackal holding the ankh cross. Right in the middle of that slab you can see another cross, almost a Greek-type looking cross. It looks like it is on some type of building or boat or pot. That is just another example of it.

Now this is obvious also. This is the serpent and the cross. Obviously, you can tell where the cross is located. It is held by the hand of this serpent-type god and obviously you see the horns and the moon.

On the left is a good illustration of the headband we read about earlier. This headband came into use a little bit later in history than the pictures we just looked at. It was popular to wear these headbands with crosses. The crosses would go completely around the head. And once again these types of crosses would look more like crosses you'd find both in Egypt, Greece, the Chaldean geographical area, even as far away as Mexico.

We have all these illustrations that go back thousands and thousands of years: the cross of Egypt, the Tau cross, the Grecian cross, all these mystic symbols. It is not peculiar to the Christian world. The Christians adopted paganism, or paganism adopted Christianity. I am not sure. Maybe a little bit of both happened. These cross symbols were revered amongst the Chaldeans, the Phoenicians, the Mexicans and every ancient people in both hemispheres. Not just one, in both.

As the cross symbol spread to various nations its use developed in different ways. Among the Chinese, the cross was acknowledged to be one of the most ancient devices. It is portrayed upon the walls of their pagodas. It is painted upon the lanterns used to illuminate the most sacred recesses of their temple.

The cross has been a sacred symbol of India for centuries among non-Christian people. It has been used to mark the jars of holy water taken from the Ganges, also as an emblem of disembodied saints. In the central part of India, two crude crosses of stone have been discovered that date back to the time centuries before the Christian Era; one over ten feet tall, the other over eight feet high.

The Buddhists and numerous other sects of India marked their followers in the head with the sign of the cross.

So it was a practice way back then, but where did they pick up these traditions long before Christ was on the scene who presumably died on the cross?

On the continent of Africa, natives plunge a cross into the River Gitche. The Kabyle women, although Mohammedans, tattooed a cross between their eyes.

That is strange.

In Wanyamwizi walls are decorated with the crosses. The Yaricks, who established a line of kingdoms from the Niger to the Nile, had an image of the cross painted on their shields.

When the Spaniards first landed in Mexico, they could not suppress their wonder as they beheld the cross, the sacred emblem of their own faith, the stone face raised as an object of worship in the temples of Anahuac. The Spaniards were not aware that the cross was a symbol of worship in the highest antiquity by pagan nations on whom the light of Christianity had never shone.

In Palenque, Mexico founded by the Votan in the 9th century before the present era, is a pagan temple known as "The Temple of the Cross. There inscribed in the altar slab, there is a central cross six-and-a-half by eleven feet in size. The Catholic Encyclopedia includes a photograph of this cross beneath which are the words 'pre-Christian cross of Palenque'.

In olden times, the Mexicans worshipped the cross as tota which means Our Father. This practice of addressing the piece of wood with the title "father" is also mentioned in the Bible. When the Israelites mixed idolatry with religion they said to a stock.

You find that in Jeremiah 2:27 - thou art my Father.

But is contrary to the scriptures to call a piece of wood (or a priest) by the title Father.

Ages ago in Italy, before the people knew anything of the arts of civilization, they believed in the cross as a religious symbol. It is regarded as a protector and was placed on tombs.

No matter where you go, these cross-like symbols were always regarded as protectors of something or another. Protectors. Where did they get that idea from? Where did they get this knowledge that these symbols could possibly protect them from something? Could it possibly date back all the way to Cain when he was marked, and he was given protection? Think about it. We will pursue that thought.

I am not drawing any conclusions yet, and do not try to figure out where I am going to go yet because I have more to introduce to you. That is why opinions do not matter much to me if you cannot back it up with Scripture and history. I have shown many times over biblical history has already been proven. Secular history goes side-by-side with biblical history and it declares God's Word to be true because when you put the two together, you can figure out what is truth and what is not truth, what is real and what is fabricated, what is fact and what is not fact.

Do not draw conclusions yet. Do not make that mistake because I must tie in not only this, but what I still have to present to give you the most complete picture using 6000 years of history to truly identify this mark. That is why I said earlier, I am not against some of the things like the Koran and Allah and all that as your identification point, especially the name of the beast, but you are missing quite a bit on how this mark was established, how it has been around since Genesis, and how it has been used over and over by different cultures as a sign of being protected by something, in the wrong way by the way. Do I believe it protects you against anything? No, I do not. Satan took it as his tool, created a method, a strategy to confuse and blind the world so that when the last days came they could not recognize it if it hit them in the face.

The Last Days Study Guide
The Mark of The Beast Part 2

1. What was Cain really saying when he lamented his punishment?
2. Why did Jesus instruct His disciples?
3. How are Christians marked today?
4. Why are jihad marks, pictures, emblems and such insufficient in understanding the mark of the beast?
5. What geographical locations are not included as being part of the 8th Beast?
6. What does rabbinical literature say the mark of Cain is?
7. When was the crucifix image sanctioned by the Church of Rome?
8. What pagan god did the Tau represent?
9. What was the cross regarded as in Italy?
10. What was early Christian opinion regarding the symbol of the cross?

The Mark of the Beast Part 3

I have been accumulating for some time now mountains of books, paperwork, pamphlets, you name it, anything that people have written or preached about the so-called mark of the beast or 666. Very few people ever refer to it as the name of the beast, but the mark of the beast or 666. I was going to present about 50 different sources with 50 different opinions, but I decided not to. Most of the sources and opinions are similar. Some of them have a little twist to it but really nothing based out of God's Word to back them up. Those of you who have been Christians for a while can identify with what I am saying. They make up all these different possibilities of what this mark could be. Believe me; they miss it by a mile and that is an understatement. They miss it completely. Many of these theories go back centuries upon centuries. Isaac Newton had his own opinion. The problem is we have people graduating from seminaries that have just been taught the same gobbledygook that has been taught for centuries concerning a group of about a dozen different possibilities of what the mark of the beast or anything concerning the last days could be. Then they must decide for themselves if the Christian Science Fiction theories could possibly be true and which ones cannot. Of course, they cannot prove any of it. That is why it is constantly changing. I have always based everything I have taught and the information I present to you on God's verifiable. I have many messages from people that state they are excited once again to read scriptures with a clearer understanding of what God's Word is saying and how I do not just go with the phrase that is so often heard, "Well, you just have to have faith. If you do not understand something, you just have to have faith". Listen, you do have to have faith. You do have to have trust and confidence in the Bible to start with. But God in His Word has substantiated everything. He has backed it up. He has given us the information to dig through to prove His

Word and to prove it to be true. But these Christian Science Fiction people are constantly changing everything, especially from the ones that are totally fanatical and out in left field saying, "This year Jesus is going to come back." Of course, that has been happening for 150 years. It goes farther back than that but let's just say for the last 150 years starting with the Millerites forward to our present time. A popular preacher made a prediction in 1980 that did not happen. Then we had the 1987 people and the 1989 people and so forth and so forth. Why? Because they really cannot back it up with God's Word. Of course, when they do that, they always add that little extra footnote that puts you in a bind because if you do not believe what they are saying, you are not having faith in Christ according to them, what faith is in Christ, which for them means, "Well, the Lord told me this and this and this. I had a vision. I had a dream. He spoke to me. He spoke to my heart." They probably ate some bad beans or something and had an awful nightmare or whatever. God has already spoken, and He has spoken through His Word. He does not need anything else. He did not say anywhere in His Word we would. And do not give me the beginning chapters of Acts. That has been twisted once again to put bondage over individuals that are not quite sure if what they are hearing is true or not. Acts 2:17 (in the latter days your young men, your young women, your old men shall prophesy) is used as a scapegoat verse. I will address it more fully later in this series, but that is not what that means. They twist such scriptures to give validity to their unsubstantiated claims. Well, take your information and put it somewhere where I cannot see it or hear it. I am not interested unless it is backed up with God's Word.

Now with that small introduction, let's pick up where we left off. Some of you might think I was stating that the cross is the mark. No, the cross is not the mark. Is there something about the cross that we need to know about the mark? Absolutely and I will lay the foundation down.

Revelation 13:17, *"And that no man might buy or sell…"*

Remember where John was speaking, where this is located, and who this was directed towards. "Well, isn't it the whole world?" No, it is not. I will have more to say about that, especially when I get into the seven churches in Revelation 2 and 3. Then you will have a better idea concerning why this is not really referring to the whole world. So, we will go back to that. For now, just take my word for it. It is directed toward the Islamic world and the nation of Israel though.

Revelation 13:17- 18, *"And that no man might buy or sell,* [buy or sell] *save he that had the mark, or the name of the beast, or the number of his name. Here is wisdom. Let him that hath understanding count the number of the beast: for it is the number of a man; and his number is Six hundred threescore and six."*

Now when you read this in the King James Version, or other versions, you are going to get the impression that it could be all three, or it could be two out of three, or all that is necessary is just one of the ways that identifies someone to this beast. *"And he causeth"*-Who? The Lion, Bear and Leopard Beast—which we already covered and which in our present 8ᵗʰ beast historical time is Islam. *"And he causeth all, both small and great, rich and poor, free and bond, to receive a mark".* So, it is referring to the mark. Then verse 17 it says, *"buy or sell, save he that hath the mark, or the name of the beast, or the number of his name."*

Now this is a big clue. It does not fill in all the information, but it is a big clue. No, it is not a chip somebody is going to put under your skin. No, it is not your retina and how computers or scanners can see your pupils or your eyeballs. No, it is not this and no, it is not that. This is a big clue. Remember I said we must put our biblical detective hats on again? You must approach certain parts of scripture with that biblical detective hat, go on a search and to try to find the truth and meaning of something.

I have been doing quite a bit of reading over the years and I cannot tell you how many I have read that say it is either going to be: 1) the mark; *or* 2) the name of the beast, it could be that; *or* alternatively 3) the number of his name. How many of you have read this as well? Now most people say it is going to be a mark, but a mark could come in various forms, various fashions. Therefore, it could be a mark, *or* it could be the name of the beast, *or* it could be the number of his name. **No.** It cannot be this or that or this. That is not what the original language says. I am sorry, it does not say that. It has to be all of it and this is a clue. It does not give us much information to go by, but it gives us a principle to follow to try to fill in the gaps of what this is referring to in verse 17. It all must be encompassed. There are no separate parts that could identify it independently and be 100% accurate that is what it is. All you could do is guess. Once I show you what this really defines the mark to be, you will be able to identify it here, there, and everywhere when you come across it, especially people in a different part of the world, not necessarily the United States of America. Once you read your history books, your art history books, view the collections of art in museums and so forth and see it, you will know it. It has been around an awfully long time, folks. It is not just going to pop up on the scene at some future period. It has been around. "So, what are you saying? because my Bible says in the King James that no man might buy or sell save he has the mark, or the name of the beast, or the number of his name."

Well, let's look at it. Below is verse 17 in the Greek (transliterated), starting halfway through the verse with *"he that hath the mark"*:

Ho		Ho	
to	charagme	to	onoma
the	mark	the	name

The Greek clearly states here how the latter part of verse 17 should be read. Some of you have become familiarized with this Greek word pronounced "ho" because I have used it before. *Ho* means "the". *"The"* what? *The mark.* Once again, *Ho - the name.* Followed by *ho* once again - *the beast.*

Ho			Ho	
tou	thēriou	ē	ton	arithmon
the	beast	then	the	number

So, right now we have: *the mark; the name; the beast.* Then it follows with a particle that should be translated "then". In the Greek, this would then be followed once again by *ho, the* - the what? *The number.* And finally, we see below this is *ho* again - *the name, he himself.*

Ho		
tou	onomatos	autou
the	name	he/himself

The Greek does not say the mark, <u>or</u> the name, <u>or</u> the number, giving you the possibility of one of three different ways of identifying what this mark of the beast is, what this 666 is, which is the common understanding of the mark. The term "or" is not in the Greek. No, it says *the mark, the name, the beast, then the number.* So in other words *A + B + C* to arrive at the identity of the beast himself. So, it should read: the mark, the name, the beast – not the mark or the name or the beast. No, it says: the mark, the name, the beast, then the number.

Why didn't scripture say the number, then maybe the mark and then the name; or the name and the number and the mark; or the number, the name, the mark; or number, mark and name, or any other variation? Because it is quite clear the mark must come first. So, number one - the mark; then number two - the name; then a third element; number three - the beast. So, the pattern then is to identify who 'he' or 'himself' is, because I can tell you right now it will lead eventually to Allah who 'he' or 'himself' is. I will show you how we get there so there is no confusion.

So, it does not read *"And that no man might buy or sell, save he had the mark, or the name of the beast, or the number of his name",* just one of the three; and if you can identify one of the three, then you know who it is or what it is. That is why there is so much guesswork, so much silly Christian Science Fiction, and so much nonsense that is written because they break the principle of following the clues that we have in Scripture and how we can identify it.

The mark - the name - the beast.

First, we must identify what this mark is. It has been a travesty in the Christian world to say this mark of the beast just means 666. That is an incomplete definition. I am sorry, it is a travesty what the Christian world has produced; that if you recognize what 666 is, you know the beast. And of course, there are a lot of differences from people, to places, to countries that have been identified with this 666. Back in the '80s, they thought Ronald Reagan was the 666 because of the number of letters he had in his name, first, middle and last. There have been scores of people who have been identified with the 666. The problem is: the mark, the name, the beast. If the beast is going to be more easily defined by the name, because all of this has some connection to the present day 8th beast which is Islam, how do we get there? It is one thing to call this or that the mark of the beast, but we must get to this number that identifies Islam. I am sorry; the Koran does not cut it. It is an element of it but that alone does not cut it. So that is our quest.

O course, I started with some history on crosses. Everybody thinks the cross was invented by Christianity. It was not. It was around thousands of years prior to Christianity ever being on the scene, thousands of years before Christ came on the scene. It was around, I believe, before the flood and I will get to that.

"Well, why are you bringing up this cross stuff if you are saying that is not the mark?"

Because to say something is the mark (the 666), to pick any one element of it by itself does not give you the complete definition. Subsequently, it will open many doors to speculation and I am not about speculating on God's Word. I have told you before, if I have an opinion on something in God's Word that I cannot totally back up, but I lean towards a certain opinion, I am going to let you know so you know it is coming from me and not from God's Word. You might agree with my opinion, and my opinion might be totally right, but you will know it is my opinion. This will not be my opinion. This will be biblical history alongside secular history to prove what this is in verses 17 and 18, *"for it is the number of a man; and his number is Six hundred threescore and six."* What is the number of man? An individual? That is what most assume. I am sure that is what you assumed. So, let's go back where I left off on the cross teaching.

> *In Palenque, Mexico founded by the Votan in the 9th century before the present era, is a pagan temple known as "The Temple of the Cross". There inscribed in the altar slab, there is a central cross six-and-a-half by eleven feet in size. The Catholic Encyclopedia includes a photograph of this cross beneath which are the words 'pre-Christian cross of Palenque'.*

> *In olden times, the Mexicans worshipped the cross as tota which means Our Father. This practice of addressing the piece of wood with the title "father" is also mentioned in the Bible. When the Israelites mixed idolatry with religion they said to a stock, 'thou art my father' but it is contrary to scripture to call a piece of wood or priest by the title Father.*

> *Ages ago in Italy, before the people knew anything of the arts of civilization, they believed in the cross as a religious symbol. It was regarded as a protector and was placed upon tombs.*

I mentioned this the last time. Everywhere you go for the most part (though not every case) people were worshipping all kinds of crosses, wearing them, making temples to them, worshipping these crosses way before Jesus Christ arrived 2000 years ago and died on the cross 32 to 33 years later. Most of them saw it as something of a protector, something that can keep them safe. Where did these people get this idea from? How did they reason? Of course, some of these people, including this author that I am quoting right now, will take it back to the Babylonian period, that Semiramis made it up or maybe Nimrod, but that is it. In some cases, they say possibly Cush who was Nimrod's father did, but for the most part they will just give Semiramis the credit. I am sorry, I am telling you right now, if she is the one that continued the practice, she is not the one that made up the practice or created the practice. It goes further back than that. No matter where you go—including Babylon, the Mesopotamian area during the Cush and Nimrod period (and Tammuz)—they saw this cross and variations of the cross as something that could protect them, something that could keep them safe. As these nations spread (especially after the Tower of Babel and the confusion of the tongues), they took these practices with them. They developed different crosses and different ways of practicing how they worshipped this cross and used this cross in their religious symbolism. Where did they get this from? It is one thing to say Semiramis, or Tammuz, or Nimrod, or Cush invented this. Prove it. No one can. So where did they get it from if they did not invent it? That is the question and it is a question a biblical detective wants to know. Don't you want to know? I sure do.

This has nothing to do with getting to heaven or about salvation. This is about learning what Christ sent through John, through over 20 chapters of information of what He wants us to know to prepare for His Second Advent. Just as the Old Testament was a preparation, not just for the First Advent but also the Second Advent, the second testament or the New Testament is a preparation for the final advent, His return and the conclusion of all things. He has given us this information. Once you have this information, you cannot convince me it is acceptable for most prophesy teachers or most people that are critical of prophesy teachers to say, "Well, it is something that really… if you know, great, but if you don't… well, so what." That is like telling Jesus when He is giving the information, "Well, I get it Jesus; but if I don't get it, what is the big deal?" Think about it. What an insult. What an insult to Christ. It is there for our benefit. It is there for our understanding, of what to expect as time gets nearer to what He says is going to happen and already has happened. You can see by using all of God's Word how much of it has been fulfilled and if that does not increase your faith and trust in God's Word, then I got news for you, probably nothing much will. So, don't tell me prophesy cannot increase and build faith. Taught correctly, it can. This ministry is not all about prophecy but do not tell me it cannot increase faith, because it can.

Back to this author:

> *Ages ago in Italy, before the people knew anything of the arts of civilization, they believed in the cross as a religious symbol. It was regarded as a protector and was placed upon tombs. In 46 B.C. Roman coins show Jupiter holding a long sceptre terminating in a cross. The vestal virgins of pagan Rome wore the cross suspended from their necklaces as nuns of the Roman Catholic Church do now.*

They were doing this before Christ.

> *The Greeks depicted crosses on the headband of their god corresponding to Tammuz of the Babylonians.*

> *Portecelli mentioned that the goddess Isis was shown with a cross on her forehead. Her priests carried processional crosses in their worship of her. The temple of Serapis in Alexandria was surmounted by a cross. The temple of the sphinx when it was unearthed was found to be uniform in shape.*

Wow. That is a little weird, isn't it? Why? Maybe I will have to get back to that.

> *Ensigns in the form of a cross were carried by the Persians during their battles with Alexander the Great.*

Which, was another beast in scripture; one of the four Daniel describes – and that was around 335 B.C., way before Christ.

> *The cross was used as a religious symbol by the Aborigines of South America in ancient times. Newborn children were placed under its protection against evil spirits. The Patagonians tattooed their foreheads with crosses. Ancient pottery in Peru has been found and is marked with the cross as a religious symbol. Monuments show*

the Assyrian kings wore crosses suspended on their necklaces as did some of the foreigners that battled against the Egyptians. Crosses were also figured on the robes of the Rot-n-no as early as the 15th century before the Christian Era.

The 15th century <u>before</u> the Christian Era. That is a long time before the Christian Era, crosses also figured on the robes of these people.

The Catholic encyclopedia acknowledged that the 'sign of the cross' represented in its simplest form by a crossing of two lines at right angles, greatly antedates, in both the East and the West, the introduction of Christianity. It goes back to a very remote period of human civilization.

"But since Jesus died on a cross", some question, "does this not make it a Christian symbol?" It is true that in most minds the cross has now come to be associated with Christ, but those who know its history and the superstitious ways it has been used—especially in past centuries—can see another side of the coin. Though it sounds crude, someone has asked, "Suppose Jesus had been killed with a shotgun, would this be any reason to have a shotgun hanging from our necks or on top of the church roof."

I think I would rather see that than the cross. Oh, I am going to offend some. Stick around and maybe you will know why if you listen long enough.

It comes down to this: The important thing is not what, but who it was that died, not what the instrument of death was.

He is right when it comes to the importance of Christ, but this author misses and marginalizes the importance of the cross and what we are to expect by understanding what we are supposed to understand in Revelation 13:16-17. You better know!

The important thing is not what, but who it was that died, not what the instrument of death was. St. Ambrose made a valid point when he said, let us adore Christ our King who hung upon the wood and not the wood.

Oh! not just the Catholics but even Protestant Christians. They have to have the wood for various reasons. If they were passionate in having 'The Christ' in their lives as much as 'the wood' this world would be changed overnight.

Crucifixion as a method of death was used in ancient times as a punishment for flagrant crimes in Egypt, Assyria, Persia, Palestine, Carthage, Greece and Rome. Tradition ascribes the invention of the punishment of the cross to a woman, the Queen Semiramis.

I differ. I think she strongly brought back what was already common knowledge that even predates Semiramis, predates her husband, predates Cush, and predates Cush's father Ham who was born before the flood but lived even after the flood (one of the few who survived in Noah's Ark). "So, are you saying this information probably came before the flood, that it was not invented but reintroduced back into the practices of the heathens before that? That they took something that maybe God established for a reason and twisted it? Is that what you are saying?" Maybe, maybe not, I will get to it.

Christ died on one cross, whatever type it was, and yet many kinds of crosses are used in the Catholic religion.

Not just the Catholic religion.

A few different types are shown...

Some of the types:

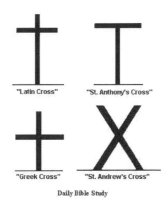

Daily Bible Study

Here we see the Latin cross on the top left. On the top right, the St. Anthony's cross which is really the Tammuz cross. The Greek cross which looks more like a plus sign on the bottom left. And then on the bottom right, the St. Andrew's cross.

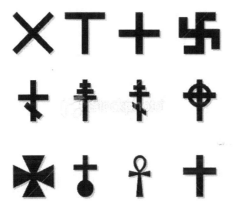

Now there are many, many different types of crosses. Some do not even necessarily look like a cross. Here we see the St. Andrew's cross once again, the Tammuz cross, the Greek cross, the swastika. "What! Is that a cross?" Well, if I have time in this part of the series, I will present that information to you. Many kinds of variations of crosses: the ankh, which we already covered on the (bottom row, second to the right); variations of the Latin cross; the bottom left, the Maltese cross and so forth. These are just a few. I have come across at least 50. I think it was more than 50 variations of the cross and things like the cross and how it was used.

If the Roman Catholic use of the cross began simply with the cross of Christ and was not influenced by paganism, why are so many types of crosses used? Says a noted writer: "Of the several varieties of the cross still in vogue, as national ecclesiastical emblems, distinguished by the familiar appellations of St. George, St. Andrew, the Maltese, the Greek, the Latin, etc., there is not one amongst them, the existence of which may not be traced to the remotest antiquity! The cross known as the Tau cross...

Which is somewhat like the ankh cross, but before that, the Tammuz cross.

... was widely used in Egypt. In later times, the Egyptian Christian Copts attracted by its form, and perhaps by its symbolism, adopted it as the emblem of the cross.

Now the Copts came after Christ, but we looked at images of wall paintings, pottery, and so forth from Egyptian history which demonstrated the ankh or cross was in use thousands of years before Christ was ever on this planet, way before He came and died for our sins, rose again from the grave, and sailed into the blue with the promise that He would be coming back. That ankh, that cross, that *Tau*, figured somewhere in the picture.

What was known as the Greek cross was also found in Egyptian monuments. This form of the cross was used in Phrygia where it adorned the tomb of Midas. Among the ruins of Nineveh, a king is shown wearing a Maltese cross.

The form of the cross that is today known as the Latin cross was used by the Etruscans, as seen on the ancient pagan tomb with wings of angels on each of the sides.

Among the Cumas in South America, what has been called the St. Andrew's cross was regarded as a protector against evil spirits. It appeared on the coins of Alexander Bala in Syria in 146 B.C. long before "St. Andrew" was ever born.

That is before Christ.

> *The cross which we show here today is called the Calvary cross, yet this drawing is from ancient inscriptions in Thessaly which dates from a period prior to the Christian Era!*

Now I do not have an example of that for you, but it is more like the Latin cross, like a little step version leading up to the cross.

> *The final question remains: Jesus died on one cross, what shape was it. Some believe it was simply a torture stake with no cross piece whatsoever. The word cross automatically conveys the meaning that two pieces of wood crossed each other at some point or angle, but the Greek word from which cross is translated in the New Testament, stauros, does not require this meaning.*

And I will probably get into more of it next time.

> *The word itself simply means an upright stake or post. If the instrument on which Jesus died was no more than this, it was not a cross as such at all. This would clearly show the folly of many types of crosses being Christianized, but we need not insist on this conclusion. The stake of Tammuz about the print of the nails in the hands of Jesus in John 20:25 would seem to indicate a cross piece, for on a single stake His hands would probably have been driven through one nail allowing room above His head for the inscription. These things would tend to favor what has been termed the Latin cross. Crosses shaped like a T or X can be eliminated since these would probably not allow sufficient room above the head for the inscription.*

More like a Tammuz cross or the St. Andrew's cross.

> *As to the exact shape of the cross of Christ, we need not to be concerned. All such arguments fade into insignificance when*

compared to the real meaning of the cross, not the piece of wood, but the external redemption of Christ.

Which I do agree on—but when it comes to prophesy, hold your horses. According to what Christ did, it might not be significant to argue against whether He died on a cross or not, and that is true because it takes away from the benefits that He provided for us by the spilling of His blood. We do not want to ever somehow displace that. That is the most important thing, especially as we understand what Christ did for us and how important that was. But what Christ died on is also important. I disagree with all these people. It is important. Unfortunately, it has been made unimportant and people have been establishing all types of crosses since Christ so they can identify with His suffering somehow, or to remember what Christ did for us on the cross. Do you need a piece of wood in various shapes to remember what Christ did for you? All you have to do in today's world is pick up God's Word and read the Gospel story. If you do not want to read the whole story, read the latter chapters in some of the Gospels. Do not stare at a cross and become 'cross-eyed'. Go to the record that gives us this information.

You might be asking by now, "So why are you dwelling on it?" Because I am trying to be a biblical detective to try to figure out the mark, the name, the beast, then the number. I am trying to follow an order here. First, we deal with the mark. "Are you saying the mark is the cross?" I have not said anything like that yet, so do not jump ahead.

The Last Days Study Guide
The Mark of The Beast Part 3

1. To who or what location was the apostle John directing Revelation 13:17?
2. It is believed that the mark of the beast could be a mark, or the name of the Beast, or the number of his name. How does the original language, Greek, read and how should it affect our understanding?
3. Other than Babylon, what other areas worshipped the cross before the time of Jesus Christ?
4. What does *starous* mean?
5. While the focus of the cross as traditionally understood should keep our hearts fixed on the eternal redemption of Christ, why is it important to have an accurate and factual understanding of it when applied to prophecy?

The Mark of the Beast Part 4

We have been camping out on the history of the cross, viewing different pictures, reading different sources of information. Again, I am not saying the 'mark' is the cross. I have never said that. What I intend to show is that the cross is not Christian and why eventually that is going to be important to know as we get to the mark, because that will be brought up again once we get there. It is not 'the' mark, but there is a connection. Just be patient. I must lay down more foundation. And yes, this Mark of the Beast volume of messages in *The Last Days* series is going to turn the world upside down. It is going to upset many in the Christian world if not most because it is different.

We see crosses all over the place. People wearing earrings, necklaces, ankle bracelets, rings, headbands, crosses on church steeples, crosses you hang up on a wall. They do not even have a clue about the background history on that cross that has become so popular to use, starting 1700 years ago with Constantine. Now Constantine did not start the use of the cross. He just made it popular. Its use started before that. The New Testament early church never recognized the cross as we know the cross today, as a religious relic. That is something that man created as some type of icon or relic to be adopted into their belief system thinking it would give them some type of protection from evil. In a sense, without saying too much, they were correct if they knew how to apply it—which cannot be applied any longer, since Christ's time—but they do not even have that down right. It is a moot point.

I want to share with you something that demonstrates the way the Christian world thinks about the cross. I read this article yesterday and I said to myself, "This is just a teenage kid from Fort Worth, Texas; good intentioned and probably a fine young man, but misguided and misled."

"Cross-Bearing Texas Teen Arrives in D.C. After Month-long Journey:

The Oasis Church is in Saginaw, north of Fort Worth. But early Friday the congregation gathered and waited anxiously in the pews to finish a journey 1400 miles away.

'Our country is in a serious moral decay,' the pastor told the congregation over the PA system as they waited. 'And that is what this journey is about.'

As the pastor paced back and forth delivering his message, images began flickering on a large projection screen behind him. The picture was shaky as the photographer moved the computer's camera into position. But between the blurs of trees and sky there were glimpses of The White House.

The church had gathered to watch a 19-year old finish a cross-bearing pilgrimage to Washington, D.C., The congregation of Oasis watched over the internet.

Finally, there was the face of the teen on the screen as he leaned against a 12-foot long cross."

They made a 12-foot long cross with a little wheel at the longest end and he drug that cross like Arthur Blessitt who has done it for decades, carry that long cross. "I took up my cross and I carried it around the world to get the message of the Gospel out there." You would think that if that was really an effective tool to get the Gospel out that the disciples would have come up with it. Or better yet, be instructed by Jesus Christ to "Go and make yourself a cross, a Tammuz-looking cross, and drag that along from place to place. Let's use props!" It is the fad now in the Christians world, in the pulpits. Let's use a prop! Forget the Bible; they will not stop and just listen. Let's use props to get their attention.

Listen, I came from a ministry which I did not agree with. They did certain things to get viewers to stop that would not normally stop to watch. God's Word does not need any additional help if it is preached correctly. The Holy Spirit will go to work to make that connection. **We do not need props!** We do not need 12-foot crosses! We do not need a 2-foot cross. We have the rightly divided Word (hopefully being preached). If not, listen to someone who does it. If you cannot identify with this ministry, please try to find one you can identify with.

> *"Finally, there was the face of the teen on the screen as he leaned against a 12-foot long cross."*

> *'I can't wait to get back home to all of you at the Oasis Church,' he told the congregation via the internet. 'And I just wanted to share this with you.'*

> *He began his journey in early June in Fort Worth. He has carried his cross...*

"He carried his cross." Oh, that is popular to say, "I have carried my cross. I have taken up my cross."

> *...along highways and back roads almost every day since.*

You might be asking, why are you being hard on this teenager. Well this teenager is a young man now at 19 years old. Unfortunately, he is guided by a pastor that knows diddly-squat about God's Word. God is not looking for gimmicks to get people's attention. He could create gimmicks far greater than man could ever come up with.

> *He began his journey in early June in Fort Worth. He has carried his cross along highways and back roads almost every day since.*

> *'I felt God put this in my heart, and it's something I felt so strong about, to just pick up my cross and carry it,' he said.*

Sorry my friend. God did not put it on your heart and your pastor should have been there to let you know that. Unfortunately, he is a spiritual fool also. And if that offends some… GOOD. You make my Jesus look ridiculous and that is not going to happen on my watch without me saying something.

Two small wheels on the bottom of the cross allowed the teen to carry his burden on his shoulders along the shoulder of the roads during the journey.

'I think it's awesome,' said an Oasis Church member. 'It's not for attention to himself.

What do you think is going to happen? What a naïve statement: it is not for attention for himself.

What he's wanting is to bring this country back to the founding principles it was formed on which is the cross of Jesus Christ.

I am sorry; this country was not founded on the cross of Jesus Christ. I don't know what history books you are reading, but… I don't even know what Christian history books you are reading to get that kind of information.

And that was his whole motivation for the whole thing.'

'I'm speechless right now, standing here in front of The White House,' he told a television photographer in Washington, 'I'm amazed that he gave me the strength to make it.

Good think you are young. "You are mocking this." Darn right I am.

And this nation's attention will be brought back to the cross and brought back to Jesus Christ and we will be one nation under God again.'

No, it will not. Not that way.

The teen's message brought a cheer from the small crowd gathered to welcome him to the nation's capital. And the congregation watching in North Texas cheered, prayed and sang along with the crowd in D.C. more than a thousand miles away.

'It's just overwhelming,' said another church member. 'It's overwhelming what he's doing.'"

Well, you might be emotionally wrapped up in the fact that he carried this cross 1400 miles and he made it, but I'm sorry, that did not do one darn thing for the cause of Christ. Now, I do not take anything away from this teenager. I think more than likely he is a good person and a fine young man. He is just misled and misguided. And unfortunately, there are too many pastors and preachers that are goofballs for Jesus that should know better – that should know better with God's Word, even in the minor sense.

With that, let's go to Matthew 16. I have been laying the ground work regarding the cross to eventually see how it is related in some way or fashion to the mark, but there is a lot more to fill in before I get to that point. And I am saying the cross is not the mark. So, I must sort all this out, don't I?

Matthew 16:21, *"From that time forth began Jesus to shew unto his disciples, how that he must go into Jerusalem, and suffer many things of the elders and chief priests and scribes, and be killed, and be raised again the third day. Then Peter took him, and began to rebuke him, saying, Be it far from thee"*—actually what he said was "pity thyself"— *"Lord: this shall not be unto thee. But he turned, and said unto Peter, Get thee behind me, Satan."* He knew who was influencing Peter to be a mouthpiece for Satan. *"Get thee behind me, Satan: thou art an offence unto me: for thou savourest not the things that be of God, but those that be of men."*

See, things that be of men create this idea that you need to create props, crosses, manmade devices to get people's attention. They might be good intentioned in the long run, but Christ does not need it. He made it very clear to his disciples what was going to happen. Peter wanted Christ to reject those thoughts and not to follow through on the thought to the point where Jesus would lose his life. And Jesus says, *"Get behind me Satan. You desire or savourest the things of this world not the things of God, but those that be of men."* Basically, what He was saying was, do not think like a man would think. (This is not his initial intention at this moment, but I am talking about this teenager right now.) You are thinking like a man and what man does to try to get people's attention, so people will listen to God's Word taught correctly. If you are a mouthpiece that preaches God's Word, a chosen one to preach God's Word, just keep on preaching. God will put you in the right places for people to hear the message taught correctly whether they are Christians already or new potential Christians that He is trying to draw into His family of believers. Now Satan does not want that to happen and he will come up with all kinds of tricks.

Now, it was clear what Satan was trying to do with Peter in trying to get Peter to be a mouthpiece to discourage Jesus from doing that. But Jesus would have no part of it.

Verse 24, *"Then Jesus said unto his disciples, If any man will come after me, let him deny himself, and take up his cross, and follow me."*

Of course, what you hear over and over is, "Have you taken up your cross yet?", and people mostly relate this to the burdens of their life, which has nothing to do with it. I have received questions such as, "What does in His likeness mean?" and "What is taking up the cross if it is not for my own particular afflictions and burdens? If it is not that, then what is it?" "Oh, I am carrying my burden, I am carrying my cross." The travesty is the message being relayed by verse 24, especially when you break it down in the Greek, is not being taught correctly and is becoming lost. So, people get these silly ideas that, "Oh, I know! I will build a 12-foot cross and show people that I am taking up my cross. I am bearing my cross and I am going across the country or across the world", or whatever other silly device they make to try and get the message out, "and show the world and show Christ that Hey! Look at me." And of course, "I don't do it to bring attention to myself…" But that is exactly what is happening, and Satan is laughing all the way because even he knows how silly it is. You are carrying the cross of Tammuz; an idea that Semiramis and probably Nimrod received from Cush, who received the information of a practice that started way before the flood from Ham, who lived before the flood—and for a reason, which I will get to. Silly fool. This is not what Jesus was referring to.

Tote	ho	Iēsous	eipen	tois	mathētais	autou
Then	The	Jesus; Jehovah is Salvation	commanded	the	disciples	themselves
Ei	tis	thelei	opiso	mou	elthein	aparnēsasthō
if	certain	desire	afterwards	of me	to follow	deny; forget one's self and interests
heauton	kai	aratō	ton	stauron	autou	kai
themselves	and	take upon one's self and carry what has been raised up	this	cross; wood, stake, upright pale	himself the same	and also
akoloutheitō	moi					
follow; join as a disciple	me					

Here is the transliterated Greek for Matthew 16:24, *"Then Jesus said unto his disciples, If any man will come after me, let him deny himself, and take up his cross and follow me."* I want you to give your attention to the correct translation of this verse. It will come across as broken English, but this is how you would read it if you broke it down word-for-word from the Greek.

"Then The Jesus (Jehovah is Salvation) commanded the disciples" What did Jesus do? What did Jehovah is Salvation do? He commanded. It is not really an option, folks. It is not a take it or leave it proposition. If you are going to be His disciple, you are going to have to follow His command. Period.

"Then The Jesus (Jehovah is Salvation) commanded the disciples themselves, if certain desire afterwards of me to follow" "Afterwards" or following what that

pertains to Jesus to follow? So, after something. Some will think, "Well, you are going to say after He said this." Yes, but after what else?

"if certain desire afterwards of me to follow, deny" It is not really "deny" per se, but I put deny there anyway because that is what it says in the King James Version. It is *"forget one's self and interests"*. Forget one's self and interests…. Wow! *"…forget one's self and interests themselves and take"*. In other words, this can go together with Luke 14. Remember it says in Luke 14 if you do not hate father, mother and all that? And I have told you that it is not saying you literally must hate your relatives. The Greek is very clear. You cannot put them first. Christ is the centerpiece. He is first and foremost. Your interests must be properly prioritized, and they are not first. Jesus is first, and all your interests follow. And if they fit in with what Jesus has planned for you, Great! And if they do not, you have got to lose it or put it on the shelf and maybe He will make it available for you at some time in the future.

"…afterwards of me to follow, forget one's self and interests themselves and take upon one's self and carry what has been raised up…" This is where we see in the King James version and in other versions the translation 'take up his cross'. That is not what it is saying and is where the translation is lost, folks, at these three Greek words: **aratō ton stauron**, *"take upon one's self and carry what has been raised up"*.

So basically, what this verse is saying is *"Then The Jesus (Jehovah is Salvation) commanded the disciples themselves, if certain desire afterwards of me to follow"*— which you cannot be a disciple of his if you do not have that desire to start with— *"forget one's self and interests themselves and* [Do what?] *take upon one's self and carry what has been raised up this cross…"*

The word "cross" is a bad translation for *stauros*. It never meant what we think of when we think of "cross" today. *Stauros* was wood, a stake, an upright pale. Used over and over in Classical Greek literature, you find stake and upright pale being referred to repeatedly for *stauros,* not cross as we would identify with what a cross is today. If we were going to put this in some type of understanding other than broken English, it would say, *"from this stake"*.

"...take upon one's self and carry what has been raised up from this stake or upright pale..."

Well, what was raised up from that stake or upright pale? Christ. Christ was raised from the dead. That upright pale or stake did not obtain the victory. Satan thought he had it for a few days, but Christ rose from the dead. If you do not believe Christ rose from the dead, then there is not victory over eternal death. The grave would have its sting, but the grave does not because He did rise again.

To follow *"...forget one's self and interests themselves and take upon one's self and carry what has been raised up from this stake..."* He is telling His disciples, take up yourself and carry what has been raised up. Carry what? The Gospel. Tell the story.

For *autou* (*staroun autou*), I put "himself" there, but it is really *"the same also follow or join as a disciple, Me."*

This is a command, folks. If you have the desire to be a disciple (if you don't, you are not one), and you know that Jehovah is Salvation because Jesus did die and rise again from the dead, then you are commanded as a disciple that has the desire, *afterwards of me to follow.* You are going to have to give up yourself and your interests in the capacity that God has called you in to be His disciple. Not all of you are going to be preachers or pastors. Most are not. But whatever God has called you in His Kingdom to do, what He wants you to be part of, guess what? a part of your life you are going to give up whether you like it or not. You are not exempt from that. He commanded what was going to happen and we all must *take upon one's self and carry what has been raised up from this stake, the same also a disciple*; one that follows Christ and joins as a follower of Jesus Christ and participates in what He commanded. Jesus is commanding that once He would be raised up from the dead, raised up from that stake that Satan thought he had the victory over, that pole, Join Me and carry what has been raised up. I want you to be My disciple. In other words, carry the Gospel message because I am alive. Satan did not have the last word. And they would carry the message forth that He is alive. What was prophesied came to pass and now we have a New Testament, a new message, a Gospel message of grace, peace, and forgiveness because the unblemished Lamb stepped in for us; and He only had to do it once for our benefit. This is the command, folks. It is not a command to build crosses and trot around the world or around the country to try to draw people to your feet or whatever it is with the mindset of, "Wow that is amazing that he is committed to doing something like that." Do you think that is really going to make a disciple? The instruction with this message and other passages is, Go make disciples. What are you going to do? Recruit a bunch of carpenters to build a bunch of crosses so you all can tote them around the country behind your back? What are you going to call yourselves? The Cross Gang for Jesus? Christianity has been made to look silly and it always starts with pastors behind the pulpit who have no business being there. That has become more and more obvious because they have different agendas than the Word of God.

The instructions we are commanded to follow if we want to be His disciple is "afterwards of me". So, whatever happens afterwards to Jesus, you are going to have to forget yourself and interests and *take up one's self and carry what has been raised up from this stake*, the message of the Gospel of the Good News. It is not a Tammuz cross the way you recognize it to be, as you have been instructed. As I [Jesus] brought the Gospel message **and lived it out** for your benefit, you are going to join Me and do the same by getting it out there that I rose from the dead, that I am alive and well, and I am coming back again; and in the meantime, My blood covered your sins and trespasses. Go to Jesus. He can make you clean by His precious blood and set you on a journey that will change your life from now to whenever He comes back or when you go to meet Him. It has always been the same message, but it has been twisted by stupid silliness, crazy doctrines and interpretations. The message has never changed!

If you go to Luke 14:27, the King James reads, *"And whosoever doth not bear* [take up] *his cross and come after me, cannot be my disciple."* Let me tell you how this verse should be translated: *Whoever that take up with hands that stake (or this stake, upright pale, or pole) themselves (or himself) and come (or to follow) behind Me, which you will be able with power and strength (or to be capable, strong and powerful) to be my disciple.*

In other words, *whoever that take up with hands,* that take up the cross—a different language being used but carries the same idea of something that you must pick up and carry forward that was on an upright pale or stake—*yourself and follow behind Me.* So, it is after the fact of what Christ did. It also says you will have the power, the strength; He will make you able with power and strength to be His disciple to make sure what He has commanded back in Matthew 16 to be fulfilled by you as a willing desiring servant and disciple of Jesus Christ.

Now you are not going to get that power and strength because you carry "your" cross or you carry "your" stake or pale…if that is what you want to do. If they are going to be copying anything, it shouldn't be copying a Tammuz cross. They should just get a 12-foot pole and carry that around with a wheel on the end. I do not recommend any of that, but if they want to be accurate according to what God's Word says, they are even doing that wrong.

I could go to another passage in Mark. Mark and Matthew are very similar, hardly any difference. Luke is just a little bit different. Luke gives us additional information. The most important information we find in Luke 14; that once you are His disciple because you desire to be one and you understand what the command was after what happened to Him, **He wants you.** He had to convince His disciples in the last chapter of the Gospel of John, Peter and a few others, not to go back to their former occupation before they met Christ, fishermen. He says I will make you fishers of men, not a fisherman catching fish. I will make you a fisher of men. Even after His death and resurrection, He had to convince Peter (being the one in the forefront in the John record) to forget his self-interests and put Christ first. That message has not changed. It is not a popular one any longer because everyone wants to put all their self-interests first and put Christ second. Actually, people's self-interests, which includes their family, their job, or whatever, are prioritized in such a way that maybe somewhere Christ ranks third or fourth, if He is that lucky.

Well, Christ commanded something different and it is not this silliness that you see preached about "the cross" and taking up the cross. Literally it is: *taking up upon one's self and carry what has been raised up from this stake or pole.* What has been raised up? There is only one thing that has been raised up and that was Christ! So yes, we are to preach the full Gospel, His death but also His victory, His resurrection. Do you want to be a disciple of His? He says, Join Me as a disciple. JOIN ME!

In Luke 14:25, *"And there went great multitudes with him: and he turned, and said unto them, If any man come to me and hate not his father, and mother, and wife, and children, and brethren, and sisters, yea, and his own life also, he cannot be my disciple."*

Now other translations clean this up a little bit but in the King James it is not saying you have to literally hate your father, your mother, your brothers, your sister's blah blah blah… No. That is not what it is saying. What it is expressing for the word *hate* here is loving one's relatives less than the Lord. In other words, loving the Lord more than your relatives. You got it? Similarly, the *forsaketh not* part of verse 33, *"So likewise, whosoever he be of you that forsaketh not all that he hath, he cannot be my disciple,"* does not refer to the abandonment of one's responsibilities or belongings but putting them in a proper priority. They come second or third depending on whatever your priorities are. <u>Christ is first and there is no watering-down of that.</u>

Most people that I talk to that backslide somewhere along their journey do so because of one reason and one reason only. They put Christ second, third, or fourth, if that high. Then, they try to justify it with certain reasons. But, once He slips into that number two position in your priority list, you have begun your backslidden track, period. I am sorry if that offends you. "Well, my family is important to me." "My job is important to me. If I don't have my job I don't know how I will pay my…" Don't complicate this. No one is saying not to be responsible to your job. Christ probably has you in that position for a reason and that reason is probably to support your family if you have one, your responsibilities (not necessarily all your desires; you create those things), including your responsibility in the capacity in which He has called you to participate in getting the rightly divided Word out to others. Most of the time that is going to require a financial commitment on your part which means you are probably going to have a job or some source of income. Again, don't complicate this.

Of course, I already told you how verse 27 should be translated. And then Jesus goes into the topic of counting the cost of building the tower, and a king that will be able to make war. After that He goes into verse 34, *"Salt is good: but if the salt have lost his savour* [if it becomes flat or strengthless], *wherewith shall it be seasoned?"* In other words, it is of no use any longer. Salt is good. We need salty Christians and the only way you are going to remain salty is if you put Christ first. That is it my friend. You will become tasteless. You will become flat. You will become strengthless. If we let Christ slip from that number one position, verse 35 makes the result really clear, *"It is neither fit for the land, nor yet for the dunghill; but men cast it out. He that hath ears to hear, let him hear."*

Do you think you are a salty Christian because you carry a cross behind you across the country? No. I have advice for the teenage boy. Find a ministry that can teach you correctly and put all your time and financial commitment (or whatever his desire that he thinks God is leading him to be part of a ministry) to good use, and, he is young enough that he is going to have to do some time under some leadership. Too many of these hotshot college kids come out thinking they are ready for the ministry without doing an internship, or as the world would call it, an apprenticeship somewhere under someone or some organization with authority that is rightly dividing the Word of God. Sorry. You are not ready. And I have not met one in my lifetime that was ready at that young of an age. That is not to say you should lose your enthusiasm for it if you feel the calling for it but if you are really called, you will understand that you have to be under some tutorship—and tutorship is not college, bible college or seminary. That is where you will go wrong and be led astray into the silly doctrines that are preached out there. Find a ministry or a church that can mentor you and develop you into a true disciple of Jesus Christ.

Now back to Matthew. I am not even going to get to Constantine and the Mark of the Beast, but this is part of the mark of the beast and when I preach the next few messages you will look back and say, "You know what? It is a good thing that we are starting to get an understanding of what this word *starous* truly means and how twisted it has become in its usage."

After Matthew 16:24, it goes on to say, *"For whosoever will save his life shall lose it"*. If you are not willing to take up yourself and carry what has been raised up—that is Christ Jesus and the Gospel message from that stake which He came off as a dead man and rose as a victorious Son of God, fulfilling everything that was required in the Old Testament for Him to fulfill—because you want to save your life, you have better plans for your life, then you are going to lose your life. And I am not saying not to follow through with some of your plans. Like I said, most reading this are never going to be a preacher or a pastor or anything like that, but that does not mean you do not have responsibility of getting the command that Christ said you need to be a part of fulfilled in your life. I have people that have situations and crisis's and circumstances that come up or come up periodically, and as soon as that happens, everything they were participating in suddenly takes the backseat. You know who you are. I may not know who you are, but you know who you are. You must question yourself, "This is how I was participating in the capacity that I was called to participate and for some reason, because of everything that happens around me, I am not doing it any longer." You did not even reduce it to handle all the other situations, you ELIMINATED IT. What is wrong with you? If you are a babe in Christ, I could see how you slipped into that mistake of putting these other things first. If you are a more mature Christian, what do you need, a spiritual 2X4? Well the answer is obvious. Yes, but get it together and say, "You know what? Enough with the distractions! I am going to get on the saddle again and I am going to do what Christ has called me to do at this point." And He will help you. Believe me;

I have been through it enough in my lifetime. He will help you far beyond any measure you can imagine, while you are still dealing with all those other distractions and circumstances. He will help you.

"For whosoever will save his life shall lose it: and whosoever will lose his life for my sake shall find it. For what is a man profited [all the hustle and bustle of life, all the things you are involved in of life], *if he shall gain the whole world, and lose his own soul? or what shall a man give in exchange for his soul? For the Son of man shall come in the glory of his Father with his angels; and then he shall <u>reward</u> every man according to his works."* The Greek word for works here is *praxis.* It means his vocation or office. What Christ has called you to be part of.

Listen to me carefully: When He comes back, you recent salt-less pretending Christians, is He going to be able to reward you according to your vocation or office? In other words, what you have been participating in? What is going to be your excuse? "Well, I was intending to do this, but You came back too soon. Can You go away for a couple of days and come back again? You will find me just full speed ahead participating in my vocation." He wants to reward you. Do you think He is going to be rewarding any salt-less individuals that become strengthless and useless? Too many of you find and create all kinds of different things to do in the Christian world including carrying crosses across the country and make up ways how you think you are saving yourself because you are doing what Christ wants you to do, telling yourself "He spoke in my heart" or "He spoke, and I heard in my mind". In these days He only speaks through His Word. Tell me from His Word where He is going to speak to you any other way? The Holy Spirit just confirms that. The Holy Spirit is not making up a new Gospel or an additional word that somehow slipped by and did not get recorded. Tell me! Give me the chapters and verses. I challenge you and you better know what you are talking about, not memorized garbage that has been perpetuated throughout the decades of "this is what this means". You better know why it means that.

I am not interested in making professing disciples. Christ is looking for disciples with the desire after He did what He did to follow Him—including, it is probably going to cost you something, and that something is including forgetting your self-interest that gets in the way of taking up and carrying what has been raised up from that stake, CHRIST. That is what the Gospel message is all about! And the challenge is still there. Will you follow Him the way He commanded? Or are you going to use some silly interpretation of what "take up the cross" means there. In His Likeness is He was the Gospel. Now He is asking you to participate in getting the Gospel to a lost and starving world that is lacking the Truth or never even heard it rightly divided. I will not have on my watch, what God has given me responsibility for, spiritual fools make God's Word a mockery and look foolish. Listen; it might still look foolish even after it is rightly divided, but if they choose to still think it is a foolish book from Genesis to Revelation, they are going to choose that after it has been rightly divided to them and not because of all the other tricks and gimmicks that are used to try and get your attention. There are tens of thousands of people who log onto our site. Very few become disciples of Jesus Christ the way Christ has commanded them, and they move on. Hopefully they can find somewhere else to be a true disciple. We do not use gimmicks. All we tell people is where you can find the rightly divided Word of God.

"Well, what does that have to do with the mark of the beast?"

I cannot fully explain the mark of the beast without laying down the foundation of the cross, the *starous*.

> An outstanding factor that contributed to the adoration of the cross image within the Roman Church was the famous vision of the cross and the subsequent conversion of Constantine. As he and his soldiers approached Rome, they were about to face what is known as the Battle of Milvian Bridge.

And this is where I will pick it up next time.

The Last Days Study Guide
The Mark of The Beast Part 4

1. What was happening to Peter when he told Jesus in Matthew 16 "Be it far from thee, Lord: this shall not be unto thee"?

2. Define *praxis*.

3. What is the proper translation of Luke 14:27?

4. Do you need to hate your family to be a disciple?

5. Who popularized the worship of the cross?

6. What is the Christian to take upon himself and carry?

7. What has become of the saint who does not follow Christ's command?

8. What is required to sufficiently prepare an individual for ministry?

9. Who cannot be Jesus' disciple?

10. Why do saints backslide?

The Mark of the Beast Part 5

I have been concentrating on Revelation 13:16, the mark of the beast, the name of the beast, the number of the beast. I have also been camping out on the cross and what the cross has meant throughout its history and where this idea of a cross came from. Most people think that the cross' history began with Christ. Sorry. As I have said, Jesus did not die on a cross. He died on a stake or a pole, or even possibly a tree - not on a cross, not on a Tammuz cross, a T-shaped cross, a Tau cross. Most historians that even dwell on this subject matter take it as far back as Semiramis and Nimrod, and Semiramis' son Tammuz. I contend that Cush knew the history prior to Nimrod (his son), Semiramis, or Tammuz. Cush was the father of the Mesopotamian Valley and the father of the false religions. His name literally means chaos. He is the father of chaos. He reintroduced chaos once again after the flood. Of course, his son Nimrod (and Semiramis and Tammuz) just enhanced what was already started. But where did Cush get this information from? I contend, which I have not really had the time to go into, that he learned from his father Ham (which existed prior to the flood) some type of information that gave them enough knowledge to establish false religions and false gods to not follow and serve the true God. I have covered that in earlier teaching and I will be come back to that, but I am not there yet.

In this message, we will cover Constantine and the cross. The early period of the New Testament church did not have a cross. Jesus did not give any instructions to make the cross. Now slightly before Constantine's period in history, around 300 A.D., the cross was already introduced but he took it to a whole other level and this is his story:

An outstanding factor that contributed to the adoration of the cross image within the Romish church was the famous "vision of the cross" and subsequent conversion of Constantine.

As he and his soldiers approached Rome, they were about to face what is known as the Battle of Milvian Bridge. According to the custom of the time, the haruspices (those who employed divination by such means as reading the entrails of sacrificial animals) were called to give advice.

So Constantine used divination to receive advice on how to win the battle he was about to face.

The use of divination was also practiced by the kings of Babylon. "For the king of Babylon stood at the parting of the way, at the head of the two ways, to use divination: he made his arrows bright, he consulted with images..." (Ezekiel 21:21). In the case of Constantine, he was told that the gods would not come to his aid [at the battle of Milvian], that he would suffer defeat in the battle. But then in a vision or dream, as he related later, there appeared a cross to him and the words, "In this sign conquer", a standard portraying a cross. The next day (October28, 312) he advanced behind this standard portraying a cross. He was victorious in that battle, defeated his rival, and professed conversion. Of course, such a seeming victory for Christianity did much to further the use of the cross in the Romish church.

It is admitted on all sides, however, that Constantine's vision of the cross is probably not historically true. The only authority from whom the story has been gathered by historians is Eusebius, who confessedly was prone to edification and was accused as a "falsifier of history". But if Constantine did have such a vision, are we to suppose its author was Jesus Christ? Would the Prince of Peace instruct a pagan emperor to make a military banner embodying the cross and to go forth conquering and killing in that sign?

The Roman Empire (of which Constantine became the head) has been described in the Scriptures as a "beast."

And people seem to forget this; that he was part of the Roman Empire, a beast, one of the four beasts.

Daniel saw four great beasts which represented four world empires - Babylon (a lion), Medo-Persia (a bear), Greece (a leopard), and Rome. The fourth beast, the Roman Empire, was so horrible that it was symbolized by a beast unlike any other (Daniel 7). We see no reason to suppose that Christ would tell Constantine to conquer with the sign of the cross to further the beast system of Rome!

Think about it. "Well, didn't the Medo-Persia beast also help the Jews go back to their homeland after the 70 years of bondage?" Sure. The king of the time gave permission for the Jews to go back. Only a very small portion of the population of the southern tribes of Judah and remnants of Israel went back to rebuild. They first worked on the temple, then took about a 15-year vacation, and then Nehemiah had to come around and stir them up and get permission to go back. He was the king's cupbearer and put his own life at risk to go back and rebuild the walls, which everyone partook, and everyone participated. So, it is not uncommon that God uses even beastly empires to fulfill His Word and what He has promised. God's Word made it very clear, so Daniel knew that they would return after 70 years of bondage and start rebuilding the Nation of Israel and Jerusalem—but, nowhere in God's Word does it say that the beast which was the Roman Empire, the Fourth Beast, would participate in protecting Christianity, keeping it safe. They were under a lot of persecution. Eventually what happened was most of that persecution went away, but it came with a price. It resulted in a watered-down message, a message of cooperation, an ineffective message that lead to the Dark Ages. But that is another story and I will have much to say about it when I get to Revelation chapters 2 and 3.

The fourth beast, the Roman Empire, was so horrible that it was symbolized by a beast unlike any other. We see no reason to suppose that Christ would tell Constantine to conquer with the sign of the cross to further the beast system of Rome!

You cannot find it anywhere in God's Word. At least in God's Word you can find that even though the Jews were in the Medo-Persian Empire Beast at the time, that after 70 years they would be given the opportunity to get out of that bondage, which they did, but that did not change the attitude of what God's Word thinks concerning that beast, the Medo-Persian Empire. It too would be destroyed.

But if the vision was not of God, how can we explain the conversion of Constantine? Actually, his conversion is to be seriously questioned. Even though he had much to do with the establishment of certain doctrines and customs within the church, the facts plainly show that he was not truly converted - not in the Biblical sense of the word. Historians admit that his conversion was "nominal, even by contemporary standards."

Probably the most obvious indication that he was not truly converted may be seen from the fact that after his conversion, he committed several murders - including the murder of his own wife and son! Constantine's first marriage was to Minervina, by whom he had a son named Crispus. His second wife, Fausta, bore him three daughters and three sons. Crispus became an outstanding soldier and help to his father. Yet, in 326—very shortly after directing the Nicaean Council — he had his son put to death. The story is that Crispus had made love to Fausta. At least this was the accusation of Fausta. But this may have been her method of getting him out of the way, so one of her sons might have claim to the throne! Constantine's mother, however, persuaded him that his wife had yielded to his son. Constantine had Fausta suffocated to death in an overheated bath. About this same time he had his sister's son flogged to death and his sister's husband strangled - even though he had promised he would spare his life.

These things are summed up in the following words from The Catholic Encyclopedia: "Even after his conversion he caused the execution of his brother-in-law Licinius, and of the latter's son, as well as of Crispus his own son by his first marriage, and of his wife Fausta...After reading these cruelties it is hard to believe that the same emperor could at times have mild and tender impulses; but human nature is full of contradictions."

Constantine did show numerous favors toward the Christians, abolished death by crucifixion, and the persecutions which had become so cruel at Rome ceased. But did he make these decisions purely from Christian convictions or did he have political motives for doing so? The Catholic Encyclopedia says, "Some bishops, blinded by the splendor of the court, even went so far as to laud the emperor as an angel of God, as a sacred being, and to prophesy that he would, like the Son of God, reign in heaven. It has consequently been asserted that Constantine favored Christianity merely from political motives, and he has been regarded as an enlightened despot who made use of religion only to advance his policy.

Such was the conclusion of the noted historian Durant regarding Constantine. "Was his conversion sincere - was it an act of religious belief, or a stroke of political wisdom? Probably the latter. He seldom conformed to the ceremonial requirements of Christian worship. His letters to Christian bishops make it clear that he cared little for the theological differences that agitated Christendom though he was willing to suppress dissent in the interests of imperial unity. Throughout his reign he treated the bishops as his political aides; he summoned them, presided over their councils, and agreed to enforce whatever opinion their majority should formulate. A real believer would have been a Christian first and a statesman afterward; with Constantine it was the reverse. Christianity was to him a means, not an end."

Persecutions had not destroyed the Christian faith. Constantine knew this.

Despite all the persecutions that happened, it wasn't destroyed. We really do not have the true count, only estimations, but scores of Christians were persecuted. The church was never stronger than during those persecutions, than during those afflictions. It became weaker when the political and religious combined. This author just touches on it, but in some cases, they went as far as putting Constantine almost on the same level as Jesus, having almost the same level of authority not only here but eventually in the heavens that Jesus has. In a sense, they put him in the same category, which amounts to idol worship. Christianity became political and the political world adopted Christianity.

Persecutions had not destroyed the Christian faith. Constantine knew this. Instead of the empire constantly being divided - with pagans in conflict with Christians - why not take such steps as might be necessary to mix both paganism and Christianity together, he reasoned, and thus bring a united force to the empire? There were similarities between the two religious systems. Even the cross symbol was not a divisive factor, for by this time it was in use by Christians, and "to the worshipper of Mithra in Constantine's forces, the cross could give no offense, for they had long fought under a standard bearing a Mithraic cross of light.

So, he found a common denominator between the pagans and the Christians. Now like I said, he did not introduce the cross to Christianity. About 30-50 years prior, depending on which historians you want to believe, the cross was starting to be introduced into the religious world of Christianity, the Church. So, Constantine came up with an idea and claimed that he had a vision from God that would lead him to victory; and since victory would be obtained for all of Rome, both the Christians and the pagans that practiced paganism, why not find a unifying symbol that they could rally behind - because it was used in both societies. If you really think about it, to come up with a scheme of that kind sounds more like the work of the devil than God.

Constantine was no Christian, folks. He was a crafty Satan-controlled individual (king) that combined political paganism and Christianity into his own little trinity grouping where they could all get along, so he could pursue and advance his Roman Empire.

The Christianity of Constantine was a mixture. Though he had his statue removed from pagan temples and renounced the offering of sacrifices to himself, yet people continued to speak of the divinity of the emperor. As pontifex maximus he continued to watch over the heathen worship and protect its rights. In dedicating Constantinople in 330, a ceremonial that was half pagan and half Christian was used. The chariot of the sun-god was set in the market-place and over it the cross of Christ. [In other words, the best of both worlds.] Coins made by Constantine featured the cross, but also representations of Mars or Apollo. While professing to be a Christian, he continued to believe in pagan magic formulas for the protection of crops and the healing of disease. Yet, the concept by which the Roman Catholic Church developed and grew-the concept of mixing paganism and Christianity together as a united force-is clearly linked with Constantine and the years that followed in which the church became rich and increased with goods.

A story that greatly influenced cross worship within the Romish church - even more than that of Constantine's vision - centered around his mother Helena. When almost eighty years of age, she made a pilgrimage to Jerusalem. Legend has it that she found three crosses buried there - one the cross of Christ and the other two the ones upon which the thieves were crucified. The cross of Christ was identified because it worked miracles of healing at the suggestion of Macarius, bishop of Jerusalem, while the other two did not.

Says an article in The Catholic Encyclopedia: "A portion of the True Cross remained at Jerusalem enclosed in a silver reliquary; the remainder, with the nails, must have been sent to Constantine

. One of the nails was fastened to the emperor's helmet, and one to his horse's bridle, bringing to pass, according to many of the Fathers, what had been written by Zacharias the Prophet: 'In that day that which is upon the bridle of the horse shall be holy to the Lord'. "

Of course, you can find that verse in Zachariah 14 and it is just another example of the twisting of scripture to give him the edge he needed over the Christians; to place it in that 'super-spiritual' realm that Christians no longer argued against. Scripture says, "***Not by might, not by power, but by my Spirit sayeth the Lord***" – that includes any icons or relics, including any crosses that were dug up.

First, Jesus was not murdered on a cross—never was—He was never murdered on a cross. If I do not prove it in this section of the Mark of the Beast, I will prove that in the future. He did not die on a cross.

This same article, while attempting to hold to the general teachings of the church regarding the cross, admits that the stories about the discovery of the cross vary and the tradition (which actually developed years later) may be largely based on legend. That Helena did visit Jerusalem in 326 appears to be historically correct. But the story of her discovery of the cross did not appear until 440 - about 114 years later! The idea that the original cross would still be at Jerusalem almost 300 years after the crucifixion seems very doubtful. Besides, laws among the Jews required crosses to be burned after being used for crucifixion. What if someone in our day did find the actual cross of Christ and could prove it to be such? This would be of great interest, of course; but would there be any virtue in that piece of wood? No, for the cross has already served its purpose as did the brass serpent of Moses. We recall that "Moses made a serpent of brass, and put it upon a pole, and it came to pass, that if a serpent had bitten any man, when he beheld the serpent of brass, he lived" [That is in Numbers in the Old

*Testament]. Lifting up the serpent in the wilderness was a type of the way Christ was lifted up in death. But after the brass serpent had served its intended purpose, the Israelites kept it around and made an idol out of it! Thus, centuries later, Hezekiah "did that which was right in the sight of the Lord ... he removed the high places, and brake the images and cut down the groves, and brake in pieces the brazen serpent that Moses had made: for unto those days the children of Israel did burn incense to it"[**You can find that story in II Kings 18**]. Hezekiah did "right" - not only by destroying heathen idols - but even that which God had ordained, for it had served its original purpose and was now being used in a superstitious way. On this same basis, if the original cross was still in existence, there would be no reason to set it up as an object of worship. And if there would be no power in the original cross, how much less is there in a mere piece of wood in its shape?*

Even as the pagan Egyptians had set up obelisks, not only as a symbol of their god, but in some cases the very image was believed to possess supernatural power, even so did some come to regard the cross. Had it not helped Constantine in the Battle of Milvian Bridge? Had not the cross worked miracles for Helena? It came to be regarded as an image that could scare away evil spirits. It was worn as a charm. It was placed at the top of church steeples to frighten away lightning, yet because of its high position, was the very thing that attracted lightning! The use of the cross in private homes was supposed to ward off trouble and disease. Many pieces of wood - supposedly pieces of the "original" cross - were sold and exchanged as protectors and charms.

What I am seeking to highlight is no matter where you turn the cross has a fabricated history that served a purpose; whether for paganistic purposes that became a part of religious worship or whether it served the purpose of a protection device due to legends passed on before the flood and beyond. That necessitates us going back even further in history to before the flood and where that might have come from, but also after the flood. And of course, depending on who, where, and for what reasons, Constantine used Christianity as a pawn (I believe for political reasons) to try and unify the empire without all the internal bleeding that was going on, that was causing all the friction and conflict between pagans and Christians, and Christians and the beast, the governmental part of the beast. He wanted all of that to come to an end and he used any means to unify all parties involved. This is just a general short history of that whole fact.

There were very few people in Rome that did not believe in something, folks. It is not like today where you have a certain percentage of our country that is Atheistic and do not believe in any type of god. At least that is what they think. In those days in the Roman Empire, that was not the case. Everyone believed in something. Most believed in paganistic religious practices that they followed and there was conflict between them and the Christians. And of course, the conflict was also because the Christians would not bow down to the emperor, the Caesar. They had some vicious, evil, wicked Caesars during Rome's early Christian history who sought out and destroyed like the roaring lion, as Satan is, to see who they could devour and eliminate, namely the Christians. But they were not successful. The Christians did not get weaker, they got stronger.

But about 30-50 years before Constantine's vision, Christians were starting to get weary. The further they were from the disciples' period and the disciples of the Apostles, they began to allow the introduction of some paganistic practices and bringing in the cross is just one of those things. There were other practices that they started adopting as well and there was a lot of "you have to do this and that," which I do not have time to go into now. That caused the Christian Church to become weakened. Then they saw the opportunity that presented itself and said, "Well, we are already using the cross now for the most part, and, since Constantine is saying he saw this vision and he is going to put (what they thought was) the cross of Christ on his shield and declare that Christianity will no longer be persecuted..." they took advantage of it. You can read the history yourself. I am not going to give you that much of it because I do want to move on and finish this Mark of the Beast section of the series. The history is there to be read. It is not that hard to find. Christians became *weary in well-doing* and they started to adopt some paganistic practices even before Constantine's vision. When Constantine's Satan-inspired vision came on the scene, it served to provide a method to attract Christians. They got on the same page as Constantine. Since they now had a common denominator and they could get on the same page as Constantine, the pagans did not have a problem necessarily with Christians - especially after Christians started adopting more paganistic holidays, festivities, festivals, relics, you name it. It was one big happy family starting to form all under the name of Jesus Christ or whatever pagan practice the pagans were allowed to follow. And of course, Constantine sat in the seat of authority and he just administered both. He was the mediator to make sure it all worked out. After the Nicaean Council, the church would go into a very dark period. Eventually, it would find its self in the Dark Ages. But it would come back. It would come back.

Satan has never changed his plans from day one, my friend. He began trying to mimic something that I believe God used to send a message. He took that same image and twisted it, put paganistic definitions to it, and thereby changed its meaning with the purpose of making the connect. This is why I had to lay down some of this history on the cross. Even though what I have been presenting to you is very general, it will help you to know where I am eventually going with this. It will enable you to look back and see how I got there. We cannot look at the Mark of the Beast without understanding how the cross plays a role in it. It is going to shock many of you and it is going to make you cringe. It is not the Mark of the Beast, but it has some association with the Mark of the Beast. Throughout history, from a certain period onward, in many different places around the world some form of a cross has always been there. Why? And how did Satan adopt it, twist it, and eventually incorporate it into something that would be, according to God's Word, identifiable in history, both biblical and secular? That is, for the ones that can see it and put it all together accurately, what the true mark is really going to be. What it already is. Ninety-nine percent of the Christian population does not even realize what it is. People are already being marked. That is why this message is important to keep alive. That is why your participation in this ministry is so important.

The Last Days Study Guide
The Mark of the Beast Part 5

1. What method did Constantine use to receive advice or guidance?
2. Why is the legitimate conversion of Constantine in doubt?
3. What type of cross did Constantine's forces worship under?
4. What was the noted historian Durant's conclusion regarding Constantine's conversion?
5. Who influenced cross worship in the Romanish church more than Constantine?
6. Who was the father of all false religions and what does his name mean?
7. What period followed the weakening of Christianity?
8. What avenues did Constantine employ that we can see today regarding Islam?
9. Is the cross the mark of the beast?
10. Who is responsible for the paganizing of Christianity?
11. When was the Church at its strongest?
12. What is the T-shaped or Tau cross also known as?

The Mark of the Beast Part 6

Open your Bible to Revelation 13:16.

"And he [the beast] *causeth* [or literally, to make] *all, both small and great, rich and poor, free and bond, to receive a mark in their right hand, or in their foreheads: and that no man might buy or sell, save he that had the mark, or the name of the beast, or the number of his name."* Or you could read it, "And that no man might buy or sell save he had the mark, then the name of the beast, then the number of his name." *"Here is wisdom. Let him that hath understanding count the number of the beast: for it is the number of a man; and his number is Six hundred three score and six."*

When you read this verse, the only way you are going to figure out what the mark is, is to know the name of the beast. Those of you that have been following this teaching know who the 8th Beast is, who was also the 7th, and it is Islam. It is the area around the Middle East and how it affects Israel. The 8th Beast is Islam. So, we know what the name is. Does he have another name that could identify the mark? Possibly. We will look at it.

Since we know the 8th Beast is Islam, the name of the Beast has to be something connected to Islam. We can figure that out from previous teaching. So, the number has to be associated with this Beast. That is the only logical conclusion if you accept everything else leading up to this message. If you do not come to that conclusion, then you do not believe anything I have presented to you thus far. So, why do you continue to listen? So, I am assuming you do believe who the 8th Beast is and it is Islam; and the name of the Beast is something related to Islam. So, the number must be related to Islam and this name of the Beast also. Like I said, that is the ONLY logical conclusion. If you do not identify the Beast correctly, you are going to miss the mark. No pun intended. That is what has happened in the Christian world. They have not identified the Beast correctly and especially in the last 200 plus years of naming who this Beast is. It has been everything except Islam and the things associated with it. So, if you do not identify the Beast correctly, you are going to miss the mark. PERIOD!

Throughout man's history, he has either been marked by God or marked by the devil. You only have two choices in life, be God's or you belong to the devil (knowingly or unknowingly). If you are not of God, you are of the devil. You either belong to God through Jesus Christ or to the devil. Those are your only two choices. There are no other options.

You can find early in the Scriptures that Cain (Gen. 4) was marked by God; but in his case, because he refused salvation by the blood. Why? Because he refused to present the proper trespass and sin offering for forgiveness as his brother Abel did. Obviously, they were instructed, probably, by their father way before the Mosaic Law ever came around. He refused. He decided to follow his way – being influenced by Satan no doubt – than God's way. He murdered Abel. Then God called him on it. He did not have any remorse. He was more concerned about someone finding him and murdering him too. So, God placed a mark on Cain that no one was to touch him. We see in the Scripture that there are unseen spiritual marks and there are also physical marks that are seen. I believe the spiritual mark that we can find in the New Testament is the unseen mark of the Holy Spirit. We do not need anything else if we have been sealed by the Holy Spirit. However, in the Old Testament there are also seen marks, marks that you can see. Obviously, Cain is one example. Satan did not mark Cain. Satan influenced Cain. Cain carried out, whether knowingly or unknowingly, the desires of Satan. He was being controlled by Satan. But once he pleaded to God for his safety, for whatever reason, God decided He would grant him that and He marked him. So, God marked Cain with a visible mark. Listen; if it was invisible, the people that may have wanted vengeance over what he did to Abel would have killed him – but, it was not invisible. And, obviously the word got around that God has marked him. He has protected him. He has spared his life, at least his physical life in the here and now. They were not to touch him or else there would be consequences. I will continue with more of that line of thinking later in this message if I have the chance; if not, by the next message.

Now we have also looked at some of the history of the cross—not the *stauros* or the *xulon*, the two most famous or most often words used in the New Testament that somehow got translated "cross". BAD TRANSLATION. It was not that. *Stauros* was either a stake or a pole or some type of beam. The best translation for *xulon* could be either tree or wood. Sometimes *stauros* was even translated as tree or could be. So, we covered some of the history of the cross and I told you I was just going to generalize it. I did not get into all the sexual symbolisms of the cross' history. And believe me, there is a lot of it dating all the way back to the Babylon mystery religion that was formulated by Cush, Nimrod, Semiramis and Tammuz.

The point I am trying to make is that Satan also used the cross as an identifying mark. He picked it up from somewhere. Now, he twisted it but there is not a place in this world from ancient times onward where you cannot find some type of version of the cross being worshipped as an icon or some type of symbol, something that they would wear, or something that they would carry with the intention of it serving one of two purposes: 1) for safety and protection against the unseen world and possibly even the seen world; or 2) to mock God. Where did they get these ideas from? It goes back WAY BEFORE Christ; it goes back thousands of years before Christ. Is it something that possibly started when God marked Cain? Could it be related to something as simple as that? I say yes. But Satan being Satan twisted it to serve his purposes, to form his doctrinal philosophy so-to-speak and convince mankind it would protect them. That can be seen throughout Scripture. He is always trying. He even tried to twist Scripture to convince Jesus to follow him and bow down to him during His 40 days and 40 nights experience in the wilderness. It is nothing new.

I have said in all the previous messages on this portion of the series on the Mark of the Beast that the cross is not the mark. I will show you how it might tie in, so you understand how Satan twists things. Believe me, when I tie it in you will say, Oh yeah! I see it. But I have said from the very first message when we started looking at the cross in general that it is NOT the mark found in Revelation 13:16. But nevertheless, you need to know the history and see the importance of why Satan always uses something or another including the cross, which God possibly used or had a purpose for way back, to lead man astray.

Nations throughout this world, no matter where you go, from their earliest beginnings have been influenced to mark themselves, whether knowingly or unknowingly, to pagan traditions and doctrines. Without question, anyone that studies ancient history will find that. If you train yourself to look for these things, you can see it for yourself. I am not coming up with anything new. It has been there all along. The cross as it has come to be known is a mark.

I want to point out something and I want this to make an impact. Never forget this no matter what the subject matter is. Satan is the greatest copycat. He is the greatest copycat of all time. He is the master copycat. I am sorry, but he is just not as creative as some might think. Whatever God has established and set in motion, Satan copies, no matter what it is. But not only did he copy it, he changed it to serve his evil purposes. Then, and he's good at this, he puts the stamp of "religious" on it. He copies it, then twists it, then puts the stamp of "religious" on it. That is how he has been able to deceive nation after nation throughout the millenniums. No matter what you are studying, you can see his evil grip on whatever the subject matter is and twisting it for his evil purposes. Satan is nothing more than a counterfeit copycat. Write it down and remember that! What I have just said can be proven just by looking through God's Word. If you do not believe me, take that principle and start searching through God's Word. You are going to find what I just said to be true. You can find Satan over and over duplicating and twisting what God set in motion.

Now with all that in mind, let us read Revelation 13:16-17 once again. *"And he* [this Beast and his beastly kingdom] **maketh** *all, both small and great,* *rich and poor, free and bond, to receive a mark in their right hand. Or in their foreheads: And that no man might buy or sell, save he that had the mark, or the name of the beast, or the number of his name."*

A lot of preachers preach with much drama that this is going to be something that is done in the future for the very first time. No. This is nothing new. Can we find it in other areas of God's Word? Like I said, SATAN IS THE MASTER COUNTERFEITER. But you believe this will be the first time this has happened to mankind, when it does happen, because that is what you have heard over and over. I am telling you, the mark is not something that is going to happen in the future. It has already happened. By the next message you will see that to be true without any doubt. Yet, we have a bunch of Christians like a goose in a new day honking all kinds of nonsense of what to expect in the future. You silly fools—and I am speaking to preachers—you will be accountable for your nonsense because you drifted away from God's Word. And I am sorry, but you do it knowingly because what I am preaching is nothing new. It has been here all along. Yes, certain times had to come and go for certain things to be revealed, but it has been in the Bible all along. It is nothing new. In fact, if we looked at God's Word hard enough without being so influenced by spiritual stupidity that has been preached out there, it could be easily seen. But we have been spiritually blinded by spiritual fools and it is time we take the blindfolds off. That is why I said, when we can achieve getting a million volumes of *The Last Days* series out, we will change the mindset, the conversation, and how people look at these last days and everything that surrounding it including Revelation 13:16-17. **You need to take this seriously**.

Exodus 13:4, *"This day came ye out in the month Abib* [the first month in the Hebrew year]. *And it shall be when the LORD shall bring thee into the land of the Canaanites, and the Hittites, and the Amorites, and the Hivities, and the Jebusites, which he sware unto thy fathers to give thee, a land flowing with milk and honey, that thou shalt keep this service in this month."* And it continues with what is going to happen in verses 6 and 7, and then we get to verse 8, *"And thou shalt shew thy son in that day, saying, This is done because of that which the LORD did unto me when I came forth out of Egypt."* In other words, you are to remind them what God did to free the Israelites from the bondage of Egypt. Verse 9, *"And it shall be for a sign..."* Sign; it can mean sign, but it can also mean a distinguishing mark, a mark, a mark of certain importance for a reason. *"And it shall be for a mark unto thee upon* [Where?] *thine hand, and for a memorial between thine eyes..."* That sounds familiar; doesn't it? *"...that the LORD's law may be in thy mouth: for with a strong hand hath the LORD brought thee out of Egypt. Thou shalt therefore keep this ordinance in his season from year to year."* From year to year...Go to verse 14. *"And it shall be when thy son asketh thee in time to come, saying, What is this?"* What is what? This mark upon thy hand and the other one on his forehead. *"What is this? That thou shalt say unto him, By strength of hand the Lord brought us out from Egypt, from the house of bondage".* Verse 16, *"And it shall be for a token upon thine hand, and for the frontlets* [the highest portion of the forehead] *between thine eyes: for by strength of hand the LORD brought us forth out of Egypt."*

There is nothing new in Revelation 13. It just shows you what Satan has copied, because he is a counterfeiter, and how he is going to use the 8th Beast to copycat what God used for a purpose for the right reasons, for his wrong reasons. So, can we gain from this some clues about what he might be doing and how this mark of the beast is to take place? Absolutely.

Deuteronomy 6:4. *"Hear, O Israel: The LORD our God is one LORD: And thou shalt love the LORD thy god with all thine heart, and with all thy soul, and with all thy might. And these words, which I command thee this day, shall be in thine heart. And thou shalt teach them diligently unto thy children, and shalt talk of them when thou sittest in thine house, and when thou walkest by the way, and when thou liest down, and when thou risest up."*

That was then. See; I do not buy this nonsense. Maybe some of you have heard not to share the Lord Jesus Christ's Gospel message with others. You do not want to impose on their time. I do not believe you should be rude with it. I think there is a place, a time and a purpose for when those opportunities can happen. But some of you, because you do not want to be rude, you use that as your excuse - especially to family members in some cases, but not necessarily just family members.

We have so much more to be teaching diligently, not just to our children but to anyone that wants to listen to the rescue plan Jesus provided with His precious blood. Shouldn't we talk of Him when we are sitting in our house as verse 7 says? Or when walking by the way? "Well, it is just not me." Oh, that is just your excuse. Get over it! Listen, you talk about a lot of foolish things that probably do not mean anything in comparison to what Christ means to you in your life and what He has done for you, and that He is willing to do for anyone else that would have faith and trust in Him. You talk about the silliest things to people all the time. I know I do, sometimes not wanting to. They just suck me into their conversations. How much more will you desire to share? Now, share is an overused word which kind of gives me the *heebeegeebees* because Christians have made it sound something like, "Ewe, I do not want to be a part of that because they only share about their emotional experiences" when it does not really mean much to anybody. I mean share the meat of God's Word. I want the meat. I am sure others do too, especially if they need it.

"...diligently unto thy children, and shalt talk of them when thou sittest in thine house, and when thou walkest by the way, and when thou liest down, and when thou risest up." Jesus should be on your mind when you lie down to sleep and when you wake up, when you are walking around talking amongst people that you know, or even those you don't know. You need to ask yourself if you have that attitude. If not, you need to ask yourself why not. Like I said, I am not saying to go out there and be rude or be some of these people that go around with their big posters saying, do you know Jesus? Pray that God gives you the opportunity to participate in all the aspects here in verse seven that you possibly can. That is why we give you these informational cards for this ministry. You do not need to get into deep conversations, but you can at least direct them to a ministry that can maybe answer some of their

questions or provide the information they have been starving to hear and are just waiting for someone to deliver it. Excuses…

Deuteronomy 6:8, *"And thou shalt bind them for a sign upon thine hand, and they shall be as a frontlet* [literally, a band] *between thine eyes. And thou shalt write them upon the posts of thy house, and on thy gates."* Verse 12, *"Then beware lest thou forget the LORD, which brought thee forth out of the land of Egypt, from the house of bondage. Thou shalt fear the LORD thy God, and serve him, and shalt swear by his name. Ye shall not go after other gods, of the gods of the people which are round about you."*

Now, no one really knows what that 'band' looked like. Of course, traditions have developed; what we see Jewish people wearing now. Here are several pictures of that:

This little box would be placed on top of your forehead and the straps would tie around your head. You would also place one of these around your bicep area so that it could touch your heart. Those are called Tefillins.

The Tefillin are two perfectly square black boxes made of a leather of a kosher hide with black leather straps. The straps and the boxes must be dyed black with a special dye. Each weekday morning (Sunday through Friday), Jewish men are required to wear Tefillin. One Tefillin Box (the "Head Tefillin") is placed upon the head, above the forehead, so as to rest upon the cerebrum. The other Tefillin box ("Hand Tefillin") is tied on the left arm so that it rests against the heart, and the suspended leather strap is wound around the left hand, and around the middle finger of that hand.

If for some reason it was impossible to wear Tefillin in the morning, one may still be put on later in the day, but not after sunset.

Tefillin are not worn on the Sabbath or on most Jewish holidays. On the fast day and on that day only, they are put on during the afternoon instead of the morning service.

All kinds of rules and regulations - which you do not find in Scripture, by the way. And you do not find the design like you are seeing in this picture. This is what traditions have produced.

The English term for the Hebrew word Tefillin is "Phylacteries," although most Jews tend to use the Hebrew term (Tefillin).

Putting on Tefillin is the first Mitzvah Jewish males assume upon their Bar Mitzvah (the 13th Jewish Birthday).

The text inserted into the two Tefillin boxes [the one that is worn on the frontlet and the one that is worn on the arm] *is hand-written by a duly qualified Scribe on a special consecrated parchment, and consists of four sets of biblical verses*

Some of those verses I already read to you; for instance, verse 8, *"And thou shalt bind them for a sign upon thine hand, and they shall be as frontlets between thine eyes".*

> *The head Tefillin has four compartments. Each contains one of four scrolls upon which one of the four different sections of the Torah relating to Tefillin are inscribed. The hand* [when I say 'hand' it is really an arm one] *Tefillin has only one compartment and contains all these four sections of the Torah inscribed on one scroll.*

Joseph A. Cortes
www.teachingfaith.com

In this next picture, you can see how it is worn by an individual. Here, I believe, it is a soldier.

You can see the frontlet on the top of his forehead, the head Tefillin and the specially dyed black strap going around it. Inside that frontlet on the head Tefillin are those four compartments with those four different verses.

As you look at his bicep you see there is another arm or hand Tefillin. This Tefillin is all four verses but instead of being in four different compartments, it is written on a single parchment.

Technically, this is the way they do it. I have researched this out and spent some time doing it. No one knows for sure how it was done both in the Exodus story and Deuteronomy, but this is how it is done today and how it has been done for a while. Then if you follow the straps, they work their way down the forearm to the wrist and it attaches to the third finger of the hand. So that is termed the hand Tefillin, and then there is the head Teffillin.

Do you see what I am saying about how Satan copycats and twists things to use for his purpose in Revelation 13:16? He causes the mark in the right hand and in their forehead. He is nothing more than a counterfeit copycat.

I would now like to go to one more chapter, staring with Deuteronomy 11:16, *"Take heed to yourselves, that your heart not be deceived, and ye turn aside, and serve other gods, and worship them; And then the LORD's wrath be kindled against you* [literally, be burning up against you], *and he shut up the heavens, that there be no rain, and that the land yield not her fruit; and lest ye perish..."* This is what Elijah referred to in king Ahab's court. If you are not going to turn and serve the true God and destroy your false gods and false idols, God will shut up the heavens and it will not rain again until Elijah says it is going to rain. Of course, they did not heed to that and He did shut up the heavens. *"...and that the land yield not her fruit; and lest ye perish quickly from off the good land which the LORD giveth you. Therefore shall ye lay up these my words in your heart and in your soul, and bind them for a sign..."* The same word is used here as earlier; bind them for a mark, a distinguishing mark *"upon your hand, that they may be as frontlets between your eyes."*

We have several different locations giving the same set of instructions. Like I said, I do not think it was like the pictures that I have shown you. No one knows for sure what it was. We know it was something that you would wear on your frontlet and on your hand (or on your arm with it extending down to the hand with the bands). What was it? It was for a reason. The reason was for instruction to your children, to let them know what God delivered them from and to remind them not to serve any other gods. And of course, Satan went to work as the counterfeiter that he is to twist that message and to put his own mark as you can see in Revelation 13:16-17. He is a copycat. There is nothing new. And when we get to the mark of the beast we will see him copycatting something else that God had already set in motion a long time ago. It did not last, it only served a purpose, but Satan never forgot the purpose that it served, and he twisted that and he (as you will see) introduced all kinds of cross worship. This was for a reason, folks—which I will tie in through the next messages.

Deuteronomy 11:19, *"And ye shall teach them your children, speaking of them when thou sittest in thine house, and when thou walkest by the way, when thou liest down, and when thou risest up."*

They are going to teach their children about how God delivered them from Egypt and not to worship any other gods. And we are too afraid to share the Good News of the Gospel of Jesus Christ? Too embarrassed in some cases? Or flat-out unwilling because of stupid stubbornness? SHAME ON US!

"Well, you are making me feel guilty."

GOOD! There is not that much effective preaching any more that makes you stop and listen and examine what you are hearing to be true coming straight from God's Word. Have we been delivered not just from a territorial geographical area such as Egypt, but from eternal damnation? How much more do we have to share with other about Christ who delivered us when we walk around, sit around, even before we go to bed and we wake up. You cannot even compare the two. You just cannot.

Verse 25, *"There shall no man be able to stand before you: for the LORD your God shall lay the fear of you and the dread of you upon all the land that ye shall tread upon, as he hath said unto you."* I feel for my enemies or non-enemies that do not recognize who goes before me and who goes before you. They do not know who they are dealing with. Until they do, they are cursed because it goes on to say in verse 26, *"Behold, I set before you this day* [two choices] *a blessing and a curse"*—a blessing and a curse, *"And a curse if ye will not obey the commandments of the LORD your God, but turn aside out of the way which I commanded you this day, to go after other gods, which ye have not known."*

Remember, other gods can mean being in your way – which is not God's Way. It does not necessarily have to be an idol or an icon of some thing or another. It could be **your way**; pursuing your own desires wherein getting what you want becomes more important than following God. There is no room for that. You do not want to be in that position because that is a position that a curse would find itself in, not a blessing.

Under the New Covenant, we are marked, and we are sealed by the Holy Spirit. It is our promise. It is a promise given to us in the New Covenant over and over. It is the promise that Christ gave to those who trust in His ownership and deliverance, folks. We wear it internally because He plants His Holy Spirit in us. We wear it internally and He sees it in the spiritual world. We do not need to be tying bands or anything around our head or our arms any longer and neither do the Jews. They just have not recognized that yet (most them that still deny that Jesus was the Son of God). We do not need to wear anything that is visibly seen. We have an invisible seal of the Holy Spirit and it is only a partial down payment too. There is more to come. A lot more! Like I said, we wear it internally and Christ sees it; God sees it in the spiritual world.

But there is something else also. Satan in the physical world is constantly twisting anything that God will possibly use or has used in the past (because most things have already been fulfilled) and for his own evil purposes. As I said earlier, Revelation 13:16-17 is no exception. It all has been done before. God has done it His Way. Then Satan is going to do it his way; and he is going to do it his way through the beastly empire, the 8th Beast, through Islam and anything that is associated as we will see in the next message concerning this mark. Hopefully what I am preaching to you will give you eyes to see, FINALLY, what God's Word has always declared.

108

He sees this mark we have, the Holy Spirit, which is in us. Why? Because He put it there in us in the first place… if we have trust and confidence in Him. But guess who else sees it? Satan, his fallen angels, and demons—and they are not all the same. Satan, fallen angels and demons, being in the spiritual world, also see what Christ sees, what God sees, what They implanted in us. Because Satan, fallen angels, and demons are spiritual beings also, they see. But I preached this in the Spiritual Warfare series: they see it and they tremble. THEY SEE IT AND THEY TREMBLE.

I would rather wear God's mark than Satan's. One is a blessing and the other is a curse. Which mark do you plan to wear? That is, if you have not already received that wonderful gift of the Holy Spirit because of your confidence and trust and faith is in Christ Jesus. If you choose the latter, the curse, your destiny is bleak and that is an understatement.

Satan and his demonic evil army of angelic beings that fell with him, they know what we are wearing. They know what we have been marked with. They know who are His that have also been marked. But I have got news for you: I would much rather wear the mark of Christ, because demons, and fallen angels, and Satan himself must bow down to it and not vice versa.

Glory to God for those of you who are wearing the right mark!

My whole point in this message is to make you realize that Satan is the master counterfeiter, the grand counterfeiter of all time. He is a liar, a murderer, a thief, etcetera, etcetera. He has not come up with anything new. He has just taken what God has established along history's timeline and twisted it for his evil purposes; and we see that all the way to the end of these last days, the end of time. Do not be caught wearing the wrong mark.

And GLORY TO GOD if you are wearing the right mark.

The Last Days Study Guide
The Mark of The Beast Part 6

1. How far back in history does the cross go?
2. Was Cain marked by a physical mark?
3. Who is the 8th Beast?
4. Can anyone precisely identify the mark of the beast if they do not or cannot identify the beast in Revelation 13 correctly?
5. List two reasons why people in history and even today wore a cross in some fashion or form?
6. Were there marks established by God?
7. Satan has always had his Plan A. How does he accomplish it?
8. How is the Christian marked today?
9. What does *xulon* mean?
10. What was the purpose of the Teffilin?

The Mark of the Beast Part 7

Open your Bible to the book of Job. It is in your Old Testament right after the book of Esther. Some of you are probably wondering what I am doing in the book of Job. Most of you know the story of the testing of Job. In chapter 1 verse 1 we find, *"There was a man in the land of Uz, whose name was Job; and that man was perfect..."* I preached on this before: *he was complete, not wanting in any respect.* That is what *perfect* literally means; *not wanting in any respect.* *"and upright, and one that was fearing* [or in awe of] *God, and eschewed* [or departed] *from evil."*

Now, this is a person that took God seriously and he gave Him honor, which belongs to God only. He was in awe of God, The Almighty. There was no doubt about it and I will prove it hopefully in this message. Now Job, like I said, was complete, not wanting in any respect, including physical things. He had livestock. You can read that in verse 3. He had seven sons and three daughters. He had a wife. He was living the dream, but he was protected of God. God put a hedge around him and Satan knew it. One day when the sons of God, the angels, were meeting in the heavenlies, Satan brought this up to God. So, God took the hedge off him and allowed Job to be tested, and he was. He lost all his livestock. In other words, he lost his wealth. All his sons and daughters died. He faced himself and had to endure a physical disease so horrible that he was scraping the boils, the open wounds, off with pieces of broken pottery. He was in a mess. All of you know the story. But here we have Job being tested.

Now before I go any further, I also want to point out that I believe Job lived in a time somewhere between Abraham and Moses. I know there are all types of opinions from theologians about when Job possibly lived and who wrote

Job, but I have concluded and believe that he lived somewhere between Abraham and Moses. I lean closer towards Moses than I do Abraham for various reasons. One of those reasons is either Moses or Solomon is the accepted opinion of who wrote the book of Job. Now, I do not believe it was Solomon as far as I can throw a 100-pound anvil. I just do not believe it. And besides what you read from those that want to categorize Job as a poetic writing, it is not all poetic, folks. The writing style is very similar to the first five books we find in the Old Testament written by Moses when you analyze it. This leads me to believe, when compared to everything else that was written that we find in the Old Testament, there is a good chance Moses jotted this information down somewhere, sometime. Now without getting into it that much, we do have a clue in that direction. Remember when Moses got kicked out of Egypt for slaying an Egyptian? Where did he go? To Midian. And he spent 40 years of his life there prior to returning to Egypt. Well guess where Uz is located? It is adjacent to Midian. How convenient. Isn't it ironic? Of course, we know the Moses story about the burning bush. Here Moses is doing what he is doing, married into a family, going about his life for 40 years herding sheep, or whatever he was doing besides that. Have you ever considered the other possibilities that perhaps could have taken place at that time to prepare Moses for the journey back after the calling, after he was told to go back through the burning bush experience? Did the burning bush just happen and then Moses says "okay, I am going" and just packs up his bags and leaves? Or, did he have some type of preparation period where he was gaining knowledge and confidence in God; that He should be trusted for who He is, what He said, and the promises that still needed to be fulfilled, which he knew were not fulfilled yet because his people (once he came to recognize who his people were) were still in bondage?

See, I do not believe it was just 40 years of nothing out there in Midian except herding sheep around, fetching water, and producing children. Even Paul after being called by Christ spent time on the back side of a desert preparing for what was yet to come. I am sure he got a crash course in a hurry. Of course, it did not hurt that he had the training and the knowledge of the Torah and the Jewish traditions. Like I said, something had to happen. I am just throwing things out there for you to contemplate. But when you start piecing things together, how much of a coincidence is it that where Moses finally spent 40 years of his life it was adjacent to Uz that we find in Job? And because the writing style is so like what we see in the first five books, could Job (as an old man in my opinion) have met up with Moses, somewhat like a mentor; someone that he could share his story of what God not only did for him prior to the hedge being lifted, but also after all the experience of troubles and woes. I know once the Spirit of God exists it can do anything it wants, and it does. But who better to prepare Moses about the hardships that he would face, including dealing with a bunch of rebellious Hebrews once they were eventually delivered by God out of the land of bondage, Egypt? Who could better prepare Moses in the flesh-tutoring than Job? Who? I believe that Moses had a preparation period, folks. Someday when I can get back to this type of history in this book, we will look into it further. I am convinced Moses had a preparation period.

Back to Job; back to the mark of the beast. I have been talking about people being marked, whether marked of God or marked of the devil. These are the only two choices. Can we find that kind of mark, a type of mark here in the book of Job? Absolutely, without a doubt. Just like we found a mark in Ezekiel 9 where some were spared from the abominations that were about to happen in Israel. They were spiritually marked by God in that case but so was Job. I think possibly even a physical mark, but I cannot really say 100% that is God's Word. But I can say with absolute confidence that he was spiritually marked by God in His Word. I will show you that in a minute.

I marveled at Job throughout my Christian life by not only what he went through, but what he also had to endure when his wife said, "Why don't you just curse God and die. Get it over with; enough of this suffering. It is not going to get any better from this point on, so why don't you just end it all." Just when he is finished hearing that news coming out of her own demon-inspired lips, guess what, here comes his friends. We find his friends throughout the chapters giving Job their accusative advice. Who needs friends like that? Job sure did not. You must hand it to Job: even though he thought he could still reason with God, in some cases thinking that God was dealing unfairly with him, he overcame all those things. Then when God finally intervened at the end, God not only blessed him again, healed him from his physical disease, but gave him another wife, more sons and daughters, and the wealth to boot. When he went through this horrible tribulation, it was not just a few days my friend. This lasted longer.

I always marveled at this individual in the Old Testament. It is sad that more is not preached on this individual and the riches of God's Word that we find between the first chapter and the last chapter. I believe some of the ways to pull those riches out (if you have a clear understanding what this Word is declaring and how it can be verified throughout God's Word) is through the spiritual aspect of psychological warfare that takes place. Satan knows that he has no business marking you any longer because you are God's.

For instance: Chapter 13. How many messages, books, or sermons have been written about this? We read in verse 15, *"Though he slay me, yet will I trust in him"*. Really! Really! *"Though he slay me, yet will I trust in him: but I will maintain mine own ways"*. *I will prove my own ways before him.* In other words, Job thought he could reason, "Look, I did all this Lord and now you are paying me back this way!" Like I said, Job slipped in and out of faith throughout these chapters, but he got it all together again with God's assistance when God said enough is enough when intervening in the latter part of this book. We do not find any of his friends giving him good advice to bring him to the point where he would say, *"Though he slay me, yet will I trust in him"*. Just the opposite. They were trying to find some fault and sin in him for the reason why he was being persecuted by Satan. *"Though he slay me, yet will I trust in him"*. I always marveled at this statement, not from the point of view that most people preach this from, but the point of view that after going through everything that he went through he can still make this declaration, *"Though he slay me, yet will I trust in him"*. What does he base that on? Up to this point we find nothing much here, except that he was an upright man. That would convince me that somewhere during this period of his life up to this point he experienced all the necessary things to build up that kind of trust and confidence in God. He did not have God's Word as we do now. Here is a man that is not living where you normally would find this kind of attitude, this type of trust or faith like we would find in what we call Israel today. No, we just do not see it. Furthermore, Israel was not in Israel at that time period. They were in Egypt. So, he had to find somewhere from some source the knowledge that he could put his trust in God. So, I always marveled. Yet that is not all I marveled, even though that is an amazing statement if you read through the book of Job, after what he has been through and how he can actually say, *"Though he slay me, yet will I trust in him"*. Then he goes and says in verse 16, *"He also shall be my salvation: for a hypocrite shall not come before me."* Or literally, *a godless one shall not come before me.* *"He also* [take out *shall be*] *is my salvation* [literally]*"*. *He also is my salvation.* How did he know that? He knew it somehow and he makes other declarations in God's Word that gives us a little bit more information.

Some people read through God's Word and never ask enough questions. I have books bigger than the Bible with nothing but questions that I have come up with. I recommend if you decide to read any one book of the Bible, all the books of the Bible from front to back, or any order you want to, accumulate a bunch of notepads and start writing questions on each chapter or verse(s). I guarantee if you are anything like me, you are going to have an encyclopedia of questions for just this one book. I guarantee you have not exhausted all the questions that you can ask. One does not just read the Bible to read it. Read the Bible so it can build faith and trust in God and what He has said and declared, but also to learn, to gain knowledge and wisdom about what He wants us to know. It is there for a reason.

Go to Job 19:25. Here another strange statement. At least to me it is. *"For I know that my Redeemer liveth, and that he shall stand at the latter day upon the earth."* Think about that. He is suffering miserably. He lost family, seven sons and three daughters killed, livestock, his wealth, the way he would finance his wellbeing in life destroyed. His wife has turned on him. His do-nothing friends that were worthless. *"Though he slay me, yet will I trust in him"*. Then he comes here and says in verse 25, *"For I know that my Redeemer liveth..."* Really! your Redeemer liveth. *"and that he shall stand at the latter day upon the earth."*

Forget the word *day* in the translation: it is added by the translator. Look at the word *latter*. In the Hebrew, it is a period still yet to come at the end of time. In other words, Job is saying, "All you good-for-nothing friends with all your advice, you are forgetting the big picture. What I am experiencing in the flesh is not the final last word on my life or anyone else's. That is still yet to come."

Like I said earlier, Jesus is going to get the last laugh and we will be right behind Him laughing along with Him. Satan will not have the victory. Christ made sure of that 2,000 years ago. The outcome is still yet to happen when all is concluded and fulfilled. But from where did Job get all this faith-building confidence and trust in what God can do and what He still is yet going to do at a time period still yet in the future, in the latter time, whenever that time will take place? Doesn't anybody ever stop and ask these kinds of questions? How? Do not just tell me the man had faith. Tell me what it is based upon. Now that is not the message. I am trying to give you a glimpse, a sneak peak of what is still yet to come in the Ephesians series when I get to it again. I just thought I would throw that in because now I am going to get to the mark.

Go to Job 31:35, *"Oh that one would hear me! Behold, my desire is, that the Almighty would answer me, and that mine adversary had written a book."* I am not going to dwell on the latter part of that verse, but I want to focus in on *"Oh that one would hear me!"* Job at this point is so sick of listening to his friends' advice that he is reaching out... though not only in this statement. But this statement is unique. Circle the word *desire*. I will be introducing a little bit of a Hebrew lesson, so you understand what exactly is being said here because that is not what the Hebrew actually says. One way you could read this is, *Oh that one would hear me! Behold, my sign, the Almighty will answer me.* What! Let me give you another translation which I believe is closer to the literal translation. *"Who giveth to me a hearing?"* It is a question. *"Who giveth to me a hearing? Lo my mark...* "(I will come back to that in a second.) "*Lo my mark, the mighty one...* "Who is the mighty one? We just read about it in Job 19. His Redeemer, the one that he is trusting back in Job 13. **Who giveth to me a hearing? Lo my mark, the mighty one doth answer me.** You're probably thinking at this point, "Wait a minute. Now you really got me confused. What do you mean *lo my mark*? What mark?" Good question, what mark? Circle the word *desire*. The Hebrew is *Tav*. **Behold my tav.**

Let me read you something:

> *There are two "t" sounding letters in Hebrew: Tet (ט) which is a dull "t" made by placing the tongue against the pallet.*

You can practice that if you want at home. And...

> *Tav (ת), though originally a cross shape* [letter], *has two pronunciations and forms in the later, classical Hebrew.*

I will have a lot more to say about that next time.

In other words, the further back you go, you can see it in two different shapes, which I will point out next time.

> *Different pronunciations today: the Tav is pronounced "th" by some and "s" by others, best seen in the word covenant. Some call it brit (ברת) - some call it bris (ברת). It is the circumcision/ covenant ceremony for a son held eight days after birth when the sign is "marked" (+, X, or ת)...*

'*When the sign is marked*' - I will have a lot more to say about this next time. What sign? Either the "X" sign or the "+" sign in the classical Hebrew or ancient Hebrew.

> *It is the circumcision covenant ceremony for a son held eight days after birth when the sign is marked as a sign of who he is...*

Listen closely to the next statement:

...and who he belongs to.

From the Hebrew point of view, he is marked for life. God is in the marking business, folks. That is why I took some time in the last teaching to point out that Satan has been a copycat. He is a counterfeiter. He copycats anything that God has set in motion and he tries to put his evil twist on it. This *Tav* is extremely important, especially when we get to Revelation 13. I will point out how it all connects, which is one of the reasons why I spent time discussing the cross - another counterfeit, another copycat version of what Satan twisted and uses for his evil purposes—and it dates back way before Christ died supposedly on a cross, which He did not, but that is another subject.

Exodus 12:1, *"And the LORD spake unto Moses"*. Remember plague after plague has happened now and the first born was going to die except... and I will tell you the exception here in a minute. *"And the LORD spake unto Moses and Aaron in the land of Egypt, saying, This month shall be unto you the beginning of months: it shall be the first month of the year to you. Speak ye unto all the congregation of Israel, saying, In the tenth day of this month they shall take to them every man a lamb, according to the house of their fathers,* [every man a lamb, according to the house of their fathers] *a lamb for a house: And if the household be too little for the lamb, let him and his neighbour next unto his house take it according to the number of the souls; every man according to his eating shall make your count for the lamb. Your lamb shall be without blemish, a male of the first year: ye shall take it out from the sheep, or from the goats: And ye shall keep it up until the fourteenth day of the same month: and the whole assembly of the congregation of Israel shall kill it..."* Shall kill it! Hum, that is interesting.

Let me read you someone's commentary on this. They put some flesh and blood on it.

The Israelites understood the importance of the blood. They knew that the blood makes atonement for the soul. They were told to put the blood on the doors and the posts of the doors. On the tenth day of the month, in the first month of the year, each family brought into their home an unblemished perfect lamb. Home at the time may have been a tent. [If they did not have a physical home, it could have been a tent.] In that home they kept the lamb until the fourteenth day. Imagine the scene, a beautiful little lamb and children together for all those days. Mother might suffer, but the children would have loved it. They would have come to love the lamb. Imagine the trauma where on the fourth day the whole congregation, including the children, had to ritually slaughter the lamb and smear the blood on the doors. Then they cooked the lamb and ate it from the head to the legs and the insides.

Talk about being politically incorrect, folks. Try to get away with that now.

However, those who obeyed God were spared death. God said, When I see the blood I will pass over you. The blood marked their home for life.

Now, whether this author gets it or not, when I read this, something dawned on me: *marked for life*. Huh, isn't that interesting.

Verse 7, *"And they shall take of the blood, and strike it on the two side posts and on the upper doorpost of the houses, wherein they shall eat it."*

I am even guilty of saying years ago that they were just making like the sign of the cross (like the shape of a "T"), but the more I thought about it, even though I even heard it that way, it really does not make much sense. If you understand what is being said there, it leads to something and it is not the sign of the cross. And of course, everyone that usually preaches on this verse says this was a sign of things to come; how Christ's blood would be smeared and spilled on the cross that He died on. Come on! You may have heard this over and over too. I cannot be the Lone Ranger here. I know you can find it and can read it for yourself if you do not want to take my word for it. Just read commentaries.

In any event, once they went through this set of instructions we find here in verse 7 and went through the act of following through on them, then we find in verse 8 that they had to eat the flesh, and the unleavened bread, and so forth; and, if it all was done properly, something happened. What?

In verse 12 we find, *"For I will pass through the land of Egypt this night, and will smite all the firstborn in the land of Egypt, both man and beast; and against all the gods of Egypt I will execute judgment: I am the LORD."* Then in verse 13, *"And the blood shall be to you for a token..."* NO, that is not what it says in the Hebrew, folks! Check it out yourselves. *"And the blood shall be to you for a MARK upon the houses where ye are: and when I see the blood..."* What is going to happen when He sees the blood? *"I will pass over you, and the plague shall not be upon you to destroy you, when I smite the land of Egypt. And this day shall be unto you for a memorial; and ye shall keep it a feast to the LORD throughout your generations; ye shall keep it a feast by an ordinance for ever."* FOREVER.

Now we know verse 13, *"And the blood shall be to you for a token,"* says *for a MARK.* So, the sign they were going to make on that doorpost (whether it was a tent, or a home, or whatever they were living in) would be marked by blood and that blood would be a signature, a mark, meaning something - and it is not the cross of Jesus Christ as so often is preached. It is a type, but it is not that. Christ did not die on a cross. I can go to the brazen serpent and make more of a connection with that than this, even though that has been preached over and over. *"And they shall take of the blood and strike it on the two side posts and on the upper doorpost of the houses, wherein they shall eat it."*

Going back almost to the beginning of the book of Genesis, the *Tav* would look like an "X" or a "+" sign, say for instance as an alphabet letter. If that is what is taught that it would have looked like back then, what would it look like shortly after this period when they were instructed to mark the doorposts? What does the *Tav* look like today?

ה This is the *Tav*, my friend.

Let's look at it again in case you are missing the visual. Exodus 12:7, *"And they shall take of the blood..."* Whose blood? The lamb's blood. *"...and strike it on the two side posts and on the upper doorpost of the houses"*.

Would Christ eventually die that way? I believe so and His blood was spilled. That blood became our mark if we believe in Him to seal us now in the New Testament period with the Holy Spirit. But back then, the blood of the lamb would be smeared on this occasion and remembered as a memorial, as an ordinance from generation to generation, forever. You smear it once down the doorpost, you smear it across, and you smear it down. Shortly after that instruction, this "+" and "X", the way the *Tav* used to be (and it still looks like that today by the way), now looks like this ה. Coincidence? Not if you tie it in with verse 13, *"And the blood shall be to you for a mark"*. For a mark.

There is plenty of marking going on folks, both Old and New Testament. That is why I am so frustrated with the silly Christian Science Fiction theology out there; doctrines that are just made up science fiction theories to try to come up with some type of explanation for what Revelation 13:16-18 is saying. All they must do is look in Scripture and follow the instruction, the clues. I said when we first started this first message on *The Mark of the Beast* that we must become biblical detectives, didn't I? I know some of you have been frustrated because it is taking a while to get to the mark, but I had to lay this down. Believe me, I am just as frustrated as you because I wanted to give you much more material. This could have been 20 messages, but I am giving you enough for now to lay down the foundation of where we are eventually going to go.

My friend, the *Tav* was a mark.

> *The cross shaped Tav [I showed you that earlier. Either the "+"
> looking sign or the "X" looking sign] was the first letter, and when
> encircled, it became a Tet.*

121

So imagine the X and then put a circle around it.

A cross within a circle (⊕) represented the four corners of the earth or universe, perhaps originally derived from the two cross sticks. As far as we know it always meant life.

It always meant life. Hum.

A further confirmation of this early meaning is found in ancient Chinese [of all languages] *which drew a cross within a square to symbolize enclosed space. Being enclosed meant protection and life.*

Where did all these ancient civilizations get this from? I am telling you right now, it is as old as the mark of Cain. Now the mark of Cain was a physical protection, not necessarily a spiritual protection mark. Cain never showed any remorse as far as we can tell through Scripture, but God protected him physically from being harmed.

"Do you think these particular marks that you have been referring to have something to do with Cain?"

Absolutely, absolutely. God marked Cain. God did not mark Cain with an evil purpose or intention behind His marking. He spared him his physical life. I do not believe there is any repentance or remorse in Cain, so spiritually I think he was doomed. I have no evidence that tells me anything different. But we see marks that God has always used throughout history that eventually Satan would steal. The counterfeiter that he is would take it and twist it and change the meaning and definitions from one area of the world to another, especially after the dispersion following the Tower of Babel incident.

Let me read on:

A further confirmation of this early meaning is found in ancient Chinese which drew a cross within a square to symbolize an enclosed space. Being enclosed meant protection and life. This cross-in-a-circle sign⊕ suggests a predictable, circular heavenly motion (○) joined with a linear order on earth (+).

The + sign there in this case, not the X.

Just as a 'You are here' X sign on a shopping mall directory orients a person, this mark was a symbol of orientation and protection, according to the stability of the heavenly order, giving a feeling of order, meaning and hope for humans.

The Tav is a mark. It marks one's place. It speaks of ownership. It is a brand, 'X marks the spot'…

No pun intended. X does mark the spot.

…whether referring to a city, circumcision, cattle brands, signature on a clay slab or name carved on a knife. Tav (X or +) is one of man's oldest signs…

I am telling you it dates back all the way to the mark of Cain.

… and although the custom of the mark of the X for a signature is ancient, we still use the phrase "put your John Henry here." The Hebrew verb "to mark" is taveh (תוה). The heh sign of life (ה)…

…is added to that *Tav* mark I just showed you. Does this explain Cain's mark? Was it a literal X or a + sign that eventually became ת ? The *Tav* is nothing more than the smearing of blood on the header and the doorposts. It was a sign that something would eventually come, who would die, and would only need one death because it was a perfect sacrifice - no animals necessary any longer. Christ was the perfect unblemished sacrifice that paid our price just as it was promised, to fulfill all that needed to be fulfilled for our benefit.

I took us to Job to show you that marking is nothing new. What became new a few hundred years ago was the number 666 and how we are supposed to be looking for a 666. Citizens of the United States of America that are against

Obamacare are freaking out now because anything that Obamacare might eventually produce for us for our wellbeing, we will have to implement it in our own lives or else not be able to have health care, especially the senior citizen, and they will put in a chip. And, of course, everybody thinks that a chip is the mark of the beast somehow, whether it is a card-carrying chip or in-the-body chip, or whatever and putting in a chip will be forced upon us because (in the language nobody read) in that Bill was something to that effect. But anyway, I am sorry, you are fearing over the wrong and unfortunately mistaught belief systems that the number 666, or a chip, or this or that is the mark of the beast. It is not. It never was. It never will be. So, stop running in fear with your superstitious silly nonsense of the number six. I am fed up with the Christian Science Fiction nonsense. Do you know why everybody is fearful of the number six? Do you the biggest reason? Because in Revelation 13 it reads as 666. In the Greek, like the Hebrew, the words can also mean a numerical value because they do not have a separate numbering system, so the world has been fearful of the number six ever since. Some have even put forth a good argument for why it isn't 666 but 616 if you want to go by the numerical system. Superstitious hogwash! When I get Revelation 13:18, which reads *"Here is wisdom. Let him that hath understanding count the number of the beast: for it is the number of a man; and his number is Six hundred threescore and six,"* I am going to point out how it ought to read and why it is not 666 at all. Only the spiritually foolish will be looking for that. I am with Job, *"Oh that you would hear me".* The literal translation is: *"Who giveth to me a hearing, Lo my mark."* God the Father, you can't not listen to me. Why? I have the mark of Jesus Christ. It is a spiritually unseen mark, but no less of a mark. I have the mark of Jesus Christ - my Mighty One, my Redeemer. He did answer for me and for you, and for anyone that wants to recognize what that powerful blood that He spilled did for mankind, to bring the rescue plan to us so no one has to live his eternal life in damnation but can have everlasting life with our Savior, Jesus Christ.

I am with *"Oh that one would hear me. Behold my mark."* I am sure some of you questioned when I was talking about Ephesians 6 [the Spiritual

124

Warfare Series], whether I have that much confidence that when the devil sees my breastplate of righteousness he does not see me as a person, he sees Christ in me who he knows he cannot defeat. Well, I do. He is in me and I am in Him, and guess what Satan? You better take a long look at my mark because it is the mark of victory. It is the mark of victory and it is high time now that Christians start realizing that and stop running in fear.

1. Where did Moses flee after murdering the Egyptian?
2. What did Job actually say in Job 31:35?
3. What are the two "t" sounding letters in Hebrew?
4. What is the Hebrew verb for "to mark"?
5. Give examples for why the concept of marking individuals is not new.
6. What purpose did the blood on the Israelites doorposts serve?
7. What have Christian Science Fiction authors and promoters who claim the mark of the beast is 666 failed to do?

The Mark of the Beast Part 8

Open your Bibles to Revelation chapter 13. We are going to be looking at verses 16 through 18.

How many of you have ever read Isaac Newton's *Observations upon the Prophesies of Daniel and the Apocalypse of St. John*? That is a long title for a book. My guess is that most of you have never even heard of it. I do not think you can even find it in a bookstore, but you could probably find it online or purchase it online. Do not waste your money though. Isaac Newton is one of those individuals that was trying to figure it out before prophetic timelines had been fulfilled to even have any understanding of what scripture was really referring to, especially concerning the 7th and 8th Beast, and what happened in 1948 and 1967, this last 100 years. So, he is just another individual that tried to figure out how to decipher the prophesies and, of course, he came up with all kinds of theories, mostly based out of the notion that the Catholic church was the antichrist, or at least the false prophet. Then he starts naming all the different individuals, mostly in his time period by the way. So, like I said, do not go out and purchase it. You would be wasting your time and money. "Then why did you read it?" Because I must read everything. I am trying to present you the truth, and unfortunately by doing that you have to read all the other *stuff* that has been written or preached to decipher the truth and see how it lines up with God's Word.

I want to show you just a portion, a little section, from the Observations and it concerns the verses that we are looking at in Revelation 13:

Obſervations upon the

rich and poor, free and bond, to receive a mark in their right hand or in their foreheads, and that no man might buy or ſell, ſave he that had the mark, or the name of the Beaſt, or the number of his name ; that is, the mark ✚, or the name ΛΑΤΕΙΝΟC, or the number thereof χξς, 666. All others were excommunicated.

It is in Old English, so the 'F' looks like an 'S'. It reads: *…rich and poor, free and bond, to receive a mark in their right hand or in their foreheads, and that no man might buy or sell, save be that had the mark, or the name of the beast, or the number of the name…*

And, of course, Newton in his *Observations* would love to put his little commentaries after the verses. Now it is not part of the verse, but Newton's explanation of what this verse is referring to is written right behind it, which is *"that is, the mark* ✚*"*. You'll see it looks like a Maltese cross. Now in Newton's day, there was a great backlash against the Catholic church. A lot of it was rightly justified because the Catholic church is a whole other creature, which I will cover later in this series. But still, the Catholic church is not what Newton thought it was, namely, the false prophet or even (possibly) the antichrist. It was neither of those things. And of course, Newton thought the mark was the cross.

This is why I spent so much time on the cross, because so much has been written about it, so much has been preached about it, so much has been said about it. And, it was not to be worshipped as an icon. As I've said, what if Jesus was shot with a pistol? Would you wear a pistol around your neck? Or, what if He was killed with a guillotine? Would you wear a guillotine around your neck or see it on top of some steeple somewhere? But, we make jewelry out of the cross; necklaces, earrings, bracelets, all kinds of signage including what we see on top of steeples. I could go on and on.

So after the verse Newton gives his suggestion of what that mark is. "That is, the mark" he says, designating the Maltese-type cross and then he goes on to the name—which I will not go into because he isn't even close. Then we read, "...or the number thereof 666. All others were excommunicated."

That was not the mark. I am sorry my friends, it just is not the mark you find in Revelation 13:16-18. Now I will get to the problem with 666 in a minute, but if you look at some of the older Bible scrolls or manuscripts, there is a controversy. I have mentioned before that some have determined that it is not 666. Of course, they are still looking for a numbering system, so they interpreted it as six hundred and sixteen or 616. There are some that even say it is 665 or six hundred and sixty-five. The problem is, and as we have seen with so many prophesies that we've looked at previously, they could not be interpreted until an appointed time. This particular verse is no exception.

Now I am convinced the Bible translators did the best they could do with the information that they had, but this is the issue: They took the Greek words that we find in these verses and made—and listen carefully—and made one of two choices in translating it. That is right; they looked at these verses and made one of two choices and that choice was to go down the numerical route. That is why you have the 666, that is why you have the 616 or the 665, or any other numbering system that is possibly out there. Like I said, they made one of two available choices. They chose to translate these verses with a numbering system. "Well, isn't that the way you are supposed to translate it?" Like I said, one of two choices. They could not see at the time the other translation alternative as a possibility—which incidentally, would have eliminated a lot of future confusion, from the time period of the King James onward. It would have eliminated a lot of Christian Science Fiction theories that developed from their translations. They were trying to see something using one of two choices they had available to perceive it. Since they could not see it through the other choice, which I have not mentioned yet and I will, they chose the numbering system. They chose incorrectly is what I am saying.

Go to Matthew 2:1, *"Now when Jesus was born in Bethlehem of Judea in the days of Herod the king, behold, there came wise men from the east to Jerusalem..."* I said before in a previous teaching that it was about a year later after the fact. *"Saying, Where is he that is born King of the Jews? for we have seen his star in the east, and are come to worship him."*

Highlight "have seen" in that verse. What does that mean? It means to perceive with the outward senses. These individuals were seeking Jesus because the signs lined up in the heavenlies and they could see what the heavenlies were saying because of what they knew previously about what to expect. What they saw in the night skies was just confirmation. So, they perceived it with their outward senses; "Aha, this is the time period we have been waiting for." That timeline was fulfilled, and they knew how to read what they were seeing, what they were perceiving with their outward senses. You must know the timelines of both biblical and secular history to see, to perceive with your outward senses and also at the conscious level, what you are analyzing, what you are seeing for yourself that just leaps out of God's Word and says, "There it is!" Take the King James translation for example. When the King James was being put together, Islam was not perceived or recognized as the 7th or the 8th Beast at that time. Not that Islam was not already in existence because it was, but no one could perceive it until certain timelines and certain prophesies were fulfilled (between 300 to 400 years later); as opposed to now where we can say "Aha, there it is!" and it leaps out from God's Word for us and be convinced because the verifiable truth is there as fact. Islam was not recognized as the 7th or 8th Beast when these translations were put together. So, with *that* in mind, they chose to go down a numbering system route to translate these verses. "Are you telling me there is another way to translate them?" Absolutely, and to tell the truth, it has only been in the last almost 70 years that we've been able to see it clearly and without a doubt.

Revelation 13:16-18, *"And he causeth* [literally *he maketh* or *to make*] *all, both small and great, rich and poor, free and bond, to receive a mark* [or *to give them a mark*] *in their right hand, or in their foreheads:* [the right hand could also mean the right arm] *And that no man might buy or sell, save he that had the mark, or* [then] *the name of the beast, or* [then] *the number of his name. Here is wisdom. Let him that hath understanding count the number of the beast: for it is the number of a man; and his number is Six hundred threescore and six."*

Verse 18 is the key verse to figure out who or what the mark of the beast is. Verses 16 and 17 play a role in that too, but really pay attention to the 18th verse as I lay it out to you.

Hode	*este*	*sophia*
Here	to be	?

Let's start with the first three words: *"Here is wisdom."* The Greek is *Hode este sophia.* What does it mean? "Doesn't it mean Here is wisdom?" Yes and no. Now, it says 'Here is wisdom' in the King James, right? Well, let's just keep the English translation of *here* [*Hode*]. *Este* literally should read *'to be'.* And of course, the King James follows with *wisdom;* but what type of wisdom? What is this referring to?

Sophia is an old Greek word. I challenge you to look it up in your Greek dictionaries or Lexicons. They are not going to give you this kind of information. You must dig deep into Greek literature to get an understanding of how they would communicate back in those days and all the rich meaning of the words they used to describe something, including the styles or ways in which they would use words to present their point or deliver their message about the subject matter. *Sophia* is an old Greek word that was used when individuals would try to figure out complex problems that required wisdom. This is where the word *philosophy* comes from. For example, the Greek word *philosophia* literally means the love of wisdom. So, if you were philosophizing or trying to use philosophy to try to find an answer to your complex problems, you were pursuing the avenue of common sense, in a lot of cases, but other avenues also to get to a point where the problem no longer seems complex to you because you have broken it down. In other words, you peeled it apart like an onion and you worked the problem from the inside out. Instead of looking at the exterior and saying, how in the heck am I going to solve this, you went inside the problem and worked outwardly to figure out how to make this complex problem into a simple solution and how to deal with it. Unfortunately, Greek dictionaries just do not get that. I do not know why they would not include all the rich meaning of how *sophia* played an important role for the people of that time, specifically the Greek language of that time. For instance, to say 'here is wisdom', *Hode este sophia (here to be wisdom)* was the colloquial way of that time of saying: *here is a riddle* or *here to be a riddle*. Wow, a riddle! That is right: *here is a riddle;* or *here to be a riddle.* Why is that important? Well, it sure turned out to be the greatest riddle of all time. How many people have tried to figure out what these six hundred three scores and six means, what this mark of the beast means? How can we identify it? What is all this? We know the name of the Beast. It has Islam in its association (which we will delve more into later), but the 666 is what has been the confusing part. It has been a riddle and the reason why is because when this was translated it was not yet the time for it to be revealed. It was not even time 1,600 years previously when John received the message. Many things had to be fulfilled first before this riddle would gain some understanding of where it applied and what it was referring to. *Here is a riddle*, without question, the greatest riddle of all time.

Some of you may be questioning, "This is a riddle?" The reason why you do not think it is a riddle is because Christian Science Fiction theories have given you all these speculations for what it might be in the future. My reply is, yes, this is a riddle because a riddle is nothing more than a phrase or sentence that can be interpreted more than one way. Grammatically we call it an amphiboly in our language; where something can be interpreted more than one way. Now if some want to dismiss that this is a riddle and maintain that it is an actual number that we find here in Scripture, then you would have to count this number. Once that happens, you then would conclude that eventually the number would reveal who the Beast would be. Right? And what the number means, right? That is what you were counting on before you ever listened to me, and, the reason why you are counting on it is because of Christian Science Fiction theories.

Oh, I know, Christian Science Fiction teachers are waiting for some future time in a seven-year period to finally have the answer revealed to them. That is their poor excuse to dig in. Really, it is lazy Christianity at its best. "We do not want to think too hard about it, so it will be explained in the future in that seven-year period." Right? Lazy Christians. I am not even blaming the Christians sitting in the pews. That takes me back to *Woe to the Shepherds* and pastors that have an obligation to keep digging in. You never get to the point where there is nothing more that is needed to be known about any subject matter, my friend. The only thing that we need to be convinced of, that is set in stone is Christ came, He died for our sins, we benefit from it, and if we live in Him and He is living in us, we are guaranteed eternal life. That will start when we go meet Him or He comes back for us, but everything else you must keep searching the scriptures on. Pastors unfortunately think if they put a few years in some seminary somewhere, they have learned all they need to know. That is why Christianity is in such a sad state it is, my friend, institutionalized preachers produced by systems of learning that really puts the cap, the closure on their ability to learn if they choose to do so.

I can hear you saying now, "If this is not counting a number, then what the heck is it?" Good question. What the heck is it?

Let's continue reading in verse 18. We are at *here is a riddle* or *here to be a riddle*. By the way, you can find many examples of *sophia* in the Greek. The understanding of how to apply a certain type of wisdom to reveal the riddle was part of the school of learning. So why not bring that to the forefront? Well, we are now. *"Here is a riddle. Let him that hath understanding"*. Let him have understanding. Of course, I have said, and I said it previously, when you are finally at the period that enough prophesy has been fulfilled and you can clearly verify that, then you are at the point and the place where you can have the understanding. You got it?

"Here is a riddle. Let him that hath understanding count". Circle that word *count*. This is the second most important word thus far in this verse. The Greek word is *psephizo*. You can find this in a Greek dictionary. It means to cast a pebble into an urn. For instance, that is what you would do if you went to vote for something; you would cast a certain type of pebble into an urn, depending on what or who you were voting for. It was like the ballot box so-to-speak. That is how it was used for counting purposes and this is how the translators not perceiving yet translated it because they did not have this sign that could be seen with outward perception. So, they decided to use a counting system, a numbering system. However, when not referring to a number or numbers, the most common way *psephizo* was used simply means *to reckon or to decide*; not used in a sense when you went to count something [1, 2, 3], but when you went to reckon something or when you had to come to a decision about something...of course, based on the wisdom that you can obtain because of your understanding of the riddle. You get it folks? So, *to reckon or to decide*.

Now, let's circle the word number. *"Here is a riddle. Let him that hath understanding decide or reckon the number".* Is that what it is saying? The Greek word is *arithmos* and it means a number. I do not argue that point at all. If you want to translate it number go right ahead, that is what the translators did. It means a number but **only** when referring to numbers. Do you get it? Only when it is referring to numbers would you then decide or reckon that it was the number. The translators not having that perception that was eventually visible many centuries later chose to use 'number' to translate *arithmos*. Remember I said at the beginning of this message, they had one of two choices. Here is the catch. When referring to **people**—by the way which you can with this Greek word *arithmos* and everything that came before it— it must be accurately translated multitude - MULTITUDE. You get it. Not number, but multitude. This changes the whole outlook, the whole definition, the whole perception in this entire verse by just looking at three important words, *sophia, psephizo* and *arithmos*. If you do not understand that, you will never have understanding about this 18th verse and you will have to rely on Christian Science Fiction theories.

There were only two ways that Greek verse could have been interpreted. The translators opted for the numbering system route. Because they made that decision, it created a lot of confusion. One translation worked off another and voilà, we have a vast array of confusion. And not that the translation was intentionally bad, to tell you the truth. I just think the perception was not there then to see the truth because it was not unveiled yet. The book of Revelation is an unveiling of the truth. I cannot stress enough the importance of what we saw in Matthew 2:2; those travelers could recognize the signs because it finally was perceived by their outward senses, "Ha, there it is! We know the king of kings is now here, so let's go find Him." The same thing must happen in God's Word especially concerning prophesies that still have not been fulfilled yet. You will either recognize that fact, or you are going to remain arrogant because you refuse to see the other option as a possibility and try to figure it out on your own, coming to a false conclusion.

The verse reads in the King James, *"Here is wisdom. Let him that hath understanding count the number of the beast: for it is the number of a man"*. Of course, everybody is looking for the "number of a man" and thinking that it is six hundred and sixty-six, or have a phobia of the number six, "Oh! Do not give me the six, anything but a six!" That is superstitious nonsense based on bad interpretation. Sorry, it is not the "number of a man". It is the same Greek word as before, *arthimos*. I want you to write this down: *"Here is a riddle. Let him that hath understanding determine or decide the multitude of the beast: for it is a multitude of man"*. And, of course, the latter part of that verse: *"and his number..."* should read *"and this multitude..."*

The correct translation of Revelation 13:18 thus far is: *"Here is a riddle. Let him that hath understanding determine or decide the multitude of the beast: for it is the multitude of man; and this multitude is..."*

Is it six hundred and sixty-six, or six hundred threescore and six, or is it something else? Everything else has been something else up to this point, hasn't it? I am telling you it is something else. You do not have to run in fear of the number six any longer. Six is not Satan's number. Whoever tells you that has no understanding of God's Word concerning the numbering system. They have just gone on hearsay and stupid doctrines that were developed because of the misunderstanding of 666.

"So, what is it saying? Are you saying it is not 666?" Absolutely. Do you want to know what it says?

The Last Days Study Guide
The Mark of The Beast Part 8

1. What two choices did Bible translators face when they attempted to translate Revelation 13:18?
2. What should the word *sophia* be more accurately understood as?
3. How did the men from the east verify what they had heard regarding the Messiah?
4. What does *psephizo* mean?
5. What is the book of Revelation of Jesus Christ?
6. Why are most Christian's in the dark when it comes to the accurate understanding of Revelation 13:18?
7. When referring to people, how should *arithmos* be translated?

The Mark of the Beast Part 9

First, I want to read a message I received.

> *"Thank you for your faithful teaching in rightly dividing the Word of God. Your translation of Revelation 13:18 sheds new meaning as one considers to determine what the mark of the beast might be. Based upon your translation of the original Greek language, verse 18 should read,* **"Here is a riddle. Let him that hath understanding determine or decide the multitude of the beast: for it is the multitude of man and this multitude is..."**

I did not finish verse 18. Now hopefully I will.

> *The three key words are: riddle, determine or decide, and multitude. Since the beast is Islam and the multitude is also Islamic, it points to the followers of Islam, Allah and Muhammad. That is for sure. Therefore, the mark or sign has to be also related to Islam as you have previously attested to. We cannot wait for the final piece of the riddle to be revealed by you. Thanks, and we are all eyes and ears. God bless."*

God willing, I will get that far but before I do I want to read something.

> *The understanding held by most with respect to the mark of the beast or "666," is that this "mark" or "number" is the identifying sign of the Antichrist and his followers.*

That is what they assume.

Many also believe that Mark will somehow be tattooed on or physically implanted into the antichrist minions.

Yet, beyond these basic notions, few have given the matter much thought. For those who seek the answers however, the Bible does provide some crucial information about this mark. First and foremost, according to scripture, the mark is essentially used as a means to distinguish the followers of the Beast from the followers of God. By accepting the mark of the beast, one displays a dedication to antichrist...

This is where I disagree with this author. He still has the notion that antichrist has yet to come. You cannot find that anywhere in Scripture. That is unless you make up a possible scenario and convert it into what you believe is true doctrine, or what I have called for what it is, Christian Science Fiction. There is a spirit of antichrist and that has been in the land since shortly after Jesus left the first time; and, it is going to be a prevailing force until He comes back. But "'A' Antichrist", no. I would follow *'the mark of the beast, one displays a dedication to'* with "the Beast and his false prophet, Muhammad"—which worshipped the moon god and just created a different way of presenting it, and that is now why the driving force behind it is Islam.

By accepting the mark of the beast, one displays a dedication to **[my correction follows]** *the beast, and his false prophet, and Allah and, at the same time his opposition to God of the Bible.*

The Scriptures also tell us that those that take the Mark will be subject to some unique benefits, as well as some extreme punishments. For instance, the Book of Revelation speaks of a time where the only ones allowed to buy or sell will be those who have taken the Mark of the Beast:

And, of course, everyone assumes that it will be a worldwide situation. Are you sure?

"And that no man might buy or sell, save he that had the mark..."
(Rev. 13:17). Conversely, we learn that these same people will be
subject to God's divine punishment for taking the mark.

I will have more to say about that later if I have time.

With the advent of modern technology, some students of prophesy
have assumed that the mark may somehow be related to a type of
invisible barcode system, or perhaps the microchip implant with
the numbers 666 encoded into it. Although, these scenarios do not
seem very realistic or practical, when one considers the fact that
most of the world's population, particularly many of the remote
areas in the Middle East, have yet to see a credit card or a barcode
scanner for that matter.

Still other problems crop up that seem to render technology-based
scenarios implausible. To begin with, there is the obvious difficulty
associated with implanting untold numbers of people with a
microchip or marking them with some type of barcode.

I am not even too sure that the hardline Islamists would even allow a barcode
on or a chip in their body.

Still other problems crop up that seem to render the technology-
based scenarios implausible. To begin with, there is the obvious
difficulty associated with implanting untold numbers of people
with a microchip or marking them with some type of barcode.
Further, if the microchip tracking system became a reality, it is
conceivable that one could approach a person who was sleeping—
or in an otherwise vulnerable position—and literally force the
mark upon them, thus labeling them as a follower of the Beast
without the individual ever having a choice in the matter.

"Well, that is why they will not be able to buy or sell, so therefore they would
have no choice if they want to keep on existing." I know the other side's

argument. They will have to succumb and get the mark.

The Bible makes it clear that those who take the mark will be cast into hell. Considering this, it does not stand to reason that God would allow this fate to befall those who were forced to take the mark and therefore rob them of the opportunity to exercise their free will and refuse it.

That is actually a very interesting thought that raises a question. What if someone pinned you down and forced you to take the mark and you could do nothing about it? What would happen then? Are you damned to hell because you have that mark, whether an implant or tattoo (whatever kind of system it is) somewhere on your body, on your head, your hand, or whatever according to Christian Science Fiction doctrine? Think about it.

I do not think you have to worry about being forced down against your own will and somebody implanting the mark on you because I do not think that is going to happen. I know it is not going to happen. I do not think it is a chip or an identification number. I do not think it is any of those things. Why? Because we can see more than the translators could see and Scripture gives us an option when rightly dividing the Word. That does not mean the translators were not inspired by the Holy Spirit. Somebody asked me, "Well then is Scripture reliable because you said it is the inspired Word of God. If it is the inspired Word of God, why didn't the translators get it right?" As I said before, the time was still sealed for the prophetic events recorded in Daniel's day, that He said would happen, but Daniel had no understanding of how that was going to happen. When that time period came, 1948 and 1967 for instance, the knowledge then was released. It is like the curtain just opened and you could see all the information behind it. The translators did not have that option. That does not mean they were not inspired. In fact, if you think about it, the inspiration was for it to not be translate correctly otherwise God's Word would not be reliable, because it says until the time of the end it was to be sealed. Just take the 1611 King James people, that time was not yet when they put the Holy Bible together or any other translation prior to the King James or after. It was sealed until a set time. That is why it is important to really understand what these verses are saying. Remember I told you the translators had two choices when translating verses 17 and 18. They could go the numerical way - *arithmos*. Or, they could look at it in a different way. Well, if they would have gone with Option B, they really would have no idea what to translate because the time was not right. It was not the time for this to be understood, period.

Revelation 13:17 and 18, *"And that no man might buy or sell, save he that had the mark, or the name of the beast, or the number of his name. Here is wisdom. Let him that hath understanding count the number of the beast: for it is the number of a man; and his number is Six hundred threescore and six."*

Let's look at the accurate translation:

HERE IS A RIDDLE. LET HIM THAT HATH UNDERSTANDING DETERMINE OR DECIDE THE MULTITUDE OF THE BEAST: FOR IT IS A MULTITUDE OF MAN; AND THIS MULTITUDE IS *CHI XI STIGMA.*

Here is a riddle. That is how it should be read because that was an option there for the King James people. Instead of Here is wisdom, "here is a riddle", because they were trying to figure out what exactly this 666 is. They did not know. *Here is a riddle. Let him that hath understanding...*

I said you can either use determine or decide, either one fits, so: *Here is a riddle. Let him that hath understanding determine or decide the multitude of the beast.* There were two ways this could have been translated: Either "number"; or when it is referring to people, "multitude" *of the beast.* So instead of "number of the beast" it should be *multitude of the beast* - a group of people or an association of people that are aligned with the Beast, in other words.

Here is a riddle. Let him that hath understanding determine or decide the multitude of the beast: for it is... Again, <u>not</u> "a number" because it is the same word here; and still the meaning is **multitude** because it is still talking about the followers of the Beast. *...for it is the multitude of man; and this multitude...*

And now here we are at the Greek - *chi xi stigma*. Of course, it reads 666 in the King James Version and any other version at this point. And man has been running in fear of the number six or this complete number of six hundred and sixty-six since these translations were put together. Some people will not even use six at all because they tie it to Satan and his antichrist in some way. That is where I left off at: *chi xi stigma*.

So what is the 666? Remember, if you are using a numerical system it would add up to 666, but what if there is another option for the *chi xi stigma*. Remember: it is a riddle - a riddle that would not be able to be understood until a set time, as stated in Daniel 12, and be unsealed so the riddle could be understood. Remember that.

chi xi stigma

Look at the left-hand side of this picture. Now with the Greek text, the characters on the left-hand side appear to be positioned vertically rather than horizontally. That changes things, by the way. I do not really have time to go into it and show you the two different ways it could be looked at, but just take my word for it. The image in the center and the one on the right helps us illustrate a possible riddle-solving meaning that we can place on this *chi xi stigma* shown on the left. I want you to take close note to what you see there on the left. Memorize this in your mind as we move forward. So, on the left you see the Greek text for this image.

Now that center image is Arabic. Do you see that 'w'-looking letter, ﷲ? Let's just call it a letter for now. It is right next to the "✕", right next to the first letter. (Actually, it is the last letter in the word because the Arabic reads right to left too.) I want you to become very familiar with these two letters. I want you to <u>train your eyes</u> because you will be surprised. It is not as prominent here in the United States yet, but I have seen it used in several different places here and I guarantee you once you train yourself to look for these things you will see more and more of it even in this country. In other countries such as Europe, especially Western Europe, you see it all over the place. Train your eyes on that squiggly-like looking 'W'; and there looks like an 'I' right next to it.

Again, the center image you see there is in Arabic and is commonly seen throughout the Islamic Empire. Do you know what the whole thing spells out? In the name of Allah. Now, it is followed by two cross swords and I told you in Arabic, it reads from right to left. So, that middle image would actually be read from right to left with the crossed swords being the last symbol there in that image.

The image on the far right was taken (of all things) out of the Codex Vaticanus which I have talked about before. It is a little bit different than the image of the Greek text on the left. The Codex Vaticanus, if they got anything right—and a lot of things they did not—this is the one thing they did. That is taken from the Codex Vaticanus, but the symbols that it resembles, if you look at it closely, is the exact Arabic image there in the center which says, "in the name of Allah". A little bit flipped but still the same.

I want you to notice the similarities between the center image and the right-side images, but I also want you to look at the left side image there in the Greek. Do you see the middle symbol or letter in the Greek text? Just invert that. Kind of go counterclockwise, to the left, and compare that with the center image of that squiggly 'W'. You have something very similar. What a coincidence, huh! Also, if you take the right center image.

Now below is a better illustration.

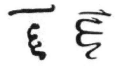

xi

Remember that I told you to make this mental image in your mind- the one on the left that we just saw previously and the one on the right. Now the one on the left (the Greek), if you invert that to the left, you have a similar image again of what we just saw on the center Arabic image and the image from the right (Codex Vanticanus) that I showed you in the previous picture. Note the similarity.

Above we have four different variations of the phrase "in the name of Allah". You can Google this. You will see many different phrases. They are pasted everywhere; from wallpaper, to tattoos, to drinking cups, to jewelry, you name it. It is becoming more and more popular. This phrase and all these different variations you see above, all the four images there in the picture say, "in the name of Allah".

Now take the last two bottom images. Put on hold everything else that you saw previously. Remember it reads right to left. That squiggly 'W' reads, "In the name of Allah". Look at the one in the right corner, the same thing. The upper images also say, "in the name of Allah" designated by a squiggly 'W'. **I want you to memorize that.** I want you to start recognizing it, making a mental image in your mind.

"Well, what does that have to do with anything?" "Why do I have to care?" Why did you want to know what these verses translated correctly would say or mean? I am going through with this exercise because obviously you have the desire to know what to be looking out for. Not to mention how God's Word could be shown off to a doubting world and how what He said thousands of years ago is now taking place. You can see the evidence, not only through timelines, which we will cover, even in these images that read "in the name of Allah". The whole thing reads: "in the name of Allah, most Gracious, most Wonderful" as it appears in Arabic.

"But how can you get this out of the Greek text?" Before I get there, regarding "in the name of Allah", here is something else I want you to remember: bismallah or bis-mal-lah or bis-ma-allah. There are different ways of saying it. In Arabic, you can see bismallah in these images. Some of you were trying to guess what the mark is and were saying bismallah because you have probably heard it somewhere else before and that it is a possibility. I do not want you to just know what the possibility is; I want to give you some of the facts. I will not be giving everything out. I just do not have the time. I will come back to it hopefully in the future, but I want to give enough information that you can see this is not a coincidence.

In this next image is once again the Greek Bible text, the one made most popular by Hinds & Noble Interlinear Version that also gives you an English translation beneath the Greek text. Of course, they say it is 666. I am not saying they are wrong, but a 666 number is not what we are supposed to be looking for.

We already know somewhat what the riddle is referring to: *"Here is a riddle. Let him that hath understanding determine or decide the multitude of the beast: for it is the multitude of man"*. It is not the number of the beast or the number of a man. It is *"the multitude of the beast; for it is the multitude of man; and this multitude is…"* THAT [$X\xi\varsigma'$].

But since it was not yet time to reveal what THAT really means, can we look at something else to try to come up with what truly God was saving for the last period of time that Daniel referred to, that things would be unsealed, to give us understanding?

The sideways Allah, as you can see in that center symbol in that image, and the crossed swords (we will come back to that crossed sword a little bit later) are clearly identifiable. No doubt about it. Take what Hinds & Noble did (and others by the way, in their versions) and invert it. Guess what you see there? Kind of strange. You see Allah in there, don't you? Can you see where? In the second image, in the center image inverted, you see Allah? Of course, on the right is just another clear example of "in the name of Allah" that we see here which was inverted in the center image that was taken from the Hinds & Noble Interlinear Version.

Despite some of these slight variations, there is no mistaking the uncanny likeness between the Greek and Arabic characters and symbols. A picture paints a thousand words, folks. Common sense would seem to dictate that the odds of what you see there happening could not be sheer coincidence. The odds are beyond calculation. So, with what we have seen and what I have shown so far, the question is: Could the true meaning of the mark of the beast have been hidden in plain sight all along until a set time?

Presuming that the mark of the beast is in fact in the name of Allah, certain questions come immediately to mind; the most obvious being how could this go undetected for nearly 2,000 years?

I already told you, because it was sealed.

Unfortunately we can only speculate as the combination of events that make up the initial concealment of the mark, but there is a certain area that seems plausible.

Let me just read this author's scenario.

As chronicled in the book of Revelation, the Apostle John was given a vision of the future in which he was told by an angel to write down what he saw. In this vision, rather than being shown the Greek letters that present the number 666, John may have actually been shown Arabic words and symbols that he cannot understand but nevertheless faithfully recorded to the best of his ability.

Allowing for this possibility, it seems likely that the scribes who were later commissioned to copy the original text would have been unable to recognize the foreign Arabic words and symbols as recorded by John. Faced with these odd looking characters, they might have done exactly what many people in their position would do which is to assume a mistake or perhaps some poor penmanship on John's part.

Now I do not necessarily agree with all that, but it is interesting to read anyway, to give another option.

Thus in an effort to make sense of these markings, they may have chosen to slightly modify them into the Greek characters that they most closely resembled. While all of this is purely conjecture, it most definitely merits careful consideration and also begs a further question: Is it possible that God, in His all-knowing wisdom, allowed this to happen, realizing the meaning behind these symbols would remain undetected until the end of time.

Not possible. If you believe God's Word to be true, there is no doubt that is what He did.

When one considers the manner in which prophesy has been revealed in the past, this possibility makes sense on many levels. It has been said that when God wants to bring understanding into the forefront, He enables ordinary men and women to discover what has been hidden. Throughout the ages we find this process at work. As the time of fulfillment nears, elements of the Bible prophesies are understood.

We have proven that.

For instance, when it came time to discern the timing of Christ's birth, the wise men from the east determined from the scriptures that the moment had come.

I have already taken us to Matthew 2 and we looked at that.

Could it be that the current generation has been called to understand the prophesies concerning the beast and its mark...

Not "could it be"; it *has been* called. We are living in a time period that even the Old Testament saints and New Testament saints wished they could have been in - the forewarned people; not the silliness and all the silly doctrines that have been created to try to explain what these verses mean, but what the truth is. **You have been called. You have been chosen. You have been given the commission of unveiling the truth, just like I have.** Do you realize what an honor and privilege that is? You should be waking up every morning saying, "Thank you Jesus for letting me stand in such a crucial time, the time that we see the conclusion even at the door and your return even closer." But yet, many do not treat it that way. Why would they! The majority are waiting for all this other Christian Science Fiction nonsense to happen.

> *Could it be that the current generation has been called to understand the prophesies concerning the beast and its mark, as this same generation will witness their fulfillment. While it is not inconceivable that someone might have discovered the correlation between these symbols and characters at some point earlier in this history, it most likely would have escaped detection of the necessary insight into looking into Islam and Allah.*

First, until the 7th and 8th Beast arrived on the scene, no one could even guess it could be Islam. So the earliest possibility of that happening is 632 AD but that is pushing it. And, of course, that leaves out all the fulfilled prophesies that still had not happened yet in 632 AD or even 1232 AD. None of this could have been figured out and seen for what it was because the curtain had not opened yet. It was hidden behind the curtain until certain dates and those dates were 1948 AD and 1967 AD, folks, the two most important key dates outside of 688 AD and 691 AD.

Now this author goes into antichrist nonsense. It is a shame because he gets some of it right, but then he falls back into the Christian Science Fiction doctrine and he has nothing to base it upon. That is what is aggravating and why I do not recommend much.

> *The Bible tells us that the beast...*

This author actually said, "the antichrist", which I have corrected. I scratched it out in my copy and put *"that the beast and false prophet"* because if Muhammad had never come on the scene as the false prophet, none of this would be taking place to start with.

> *The Bible tells us that the beast and the ~~antichrist~~ false prophet will require all people to receive the mark...*

First, put a big question mark on 'all'. That is reserved for a latter time. Scripture does not say that. It says, *"that no man might buy or sell, save he that had the mark, or the name of the beast, or the number of his name"*. But who? Where? What people? So, this is where I differ again.

> *The Bible tells us that the beast or the false prophet will require all [not all] people to receive the mark. Assuming the mark is the name of Allah, what might this indicate? In our search for the answer to this question, Revelation 13:16 is a good place to begin. This verse tells us that all [once again, not all] must receive the mark in their right hand or in their forehead. Does this mean then "in the name of Allah" would literally be stamped on the forehead of man like a tattoo, perhaps encoded onto a microchip and implanted into the followers of the beast? Again, these options remain somewhat unrealistic for the reasons that we noted earlier. In view of this as we search for plausible answers, we are wise to return to the most untainted source, which is the original Greek text of the Bible. By doing some research, we find the Greek word which has been translated 'a mark' in this verse actually refers to a badge of servitude.*

That is correct. So, if you go back to verse 17, *"And that no man might buy or sell, save he that had the mark"*, that should be translated (and write this down in your margins): **badge of servitude.** I am writing it down in mine. Even though I knew it, I did not write it down. You never know who might read my Bible in the future, and at least they will have the correct translation. Badge of servitude… of WHO? Of course, this author says, and this is where I disagree, that it is the followers of antichrist. No; it is the followers of Muhammad and Islam.

> *Thus the Greek word seems to suggest something that is worn rather than permanently tattooed.*

Something that is worn rather than permanently tattooed or implanted like a microchip.

Further, it is worth noting that the phrase 'right hand' comes from the Greek dexios which means also, and can be translated 'the right side'.

This implies that the mark or badge of servitude might also be displayed on the right arm and is therefore not necessarily limited to the right hand. Nevertheless, assuming the mark to be some sort of badge that displays the name of Allah...

In other words, the ones that are serving Allah, whatever piece of identification they might be wearing, probably clothing or wristband, armband, whatever, would identify who they are serving – in this case, Allah.

Nevertheless, assuming the mark is some sort of badge to display the name of Allah, what might we expect it to look like?

Well, let me show you.

I want you to look at all those people with a Hitler-like salute. (I will address Hitler in the future. He was the Little Horn.) You see children there. Notice the child with the knife… probably in front of his father? If you look at the right part of his headband, can you identify what it says? You should be able to now with everything I just covered. How about the center bottom photo? It is clearly defined. In all of them, you can see "in the name of Allah". Their badge of servitude on their forehead and on their right side is clearly seen. Not so much on the right side because you probably cannot see it, but there are other images you can find. You clearly see there who they are serving, who they are honoring by what they are wearing –just as John saw it according to Scripture as he was being told the information 2,000 years ago. That badge displays the name of Allah. We do not have to speculate at what it might look like. We can see it for ourselves and these are just a drop in the bucket of images that you can find. Go to your libraries. Try Googling it. Let's go to the next image. Maybe we will have something else there.

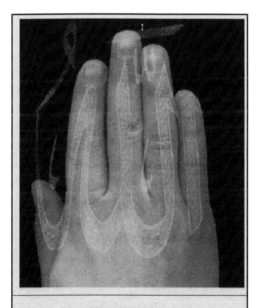

If We contemplate in the shape of
the fingers at the back of the
right hand we will find out
Amazingly, That it draws the
name of ALLAH

Oh, yeah, this is very interesting. Let's just read what it says on the image there:

> *If we contemplate in the shape of the fingers at the back of the right hand, we will find amazingly that it draws in the name of Allah.*

This is not some Christian understanding of what is being seen there in that picture. This is an Islamic point of view – what they see, as far as what Allah has created, even their right hand, so they never forget who they should honor, worship and follow, and that is Allah.

> *Yet once more we note the widespread use of the Shahada within the Muslim world. As we know, the Shahada is essentially a declaration of allegiance or servitude to Allah and is commonly recited as follows: there is no god but Allah and Muhammad is his prophet. The inscription of this declaration is already worn as a badge by millions on the forehead or right arm. It can be seen on Muslim demonstrators and Jihadists everywhere.*

Everywhere. You can see that imprinted on foreheads, people wearing headbands. I just showed a few images worn by Islamic people, moderates to fanatical Jihadists; and most of these images (and there are many) "in the name of Allah" is easily identifiable. Maybe not to the Western world, but for much of the rest of the world (in Europe, Indonesia, definitely in Africa, definitely in the Middle East, some parts of China, the lower portions of Russia, all the 'stans') it is easily identifiable to them already; but yet, we are like a goose in a new day. That is why I wanted to get the Last Days e-book series out to at least a million people, a million copies, and hopefully they share with others. We need to change the conversation away from these silly Christian Science fiction doctrines.

HERE IS A RIDDLE. LET HIM THAT HATH UNDERSTANDING DETERMINE OR DECIDE THE MULTITUDE OF THE BEAST: FOR IT IS A MULTITUDE

OF MAN; AND THIS MULTITUDE [not 666] IS *IN THE NAME OF ALLAH.*

Another way of saying "in the name of Allah" is bismallah.

"Here is a riddle. Let him that hath understanding determine or decide the multitude of the beast; for it is a multitude of man; and this multitude is in the name of Allah or bismallah." Remember bismallah? You will see it more and more as time goes on because it is becoming more and more popular as a catch phrase. And, it is more than just a catch phrase. Remember I told you a few messages back in The Mark of the Beast, Satan, the Beast, Islam is attempting to always duplicate God's program. He just came up with his own mark or name and he, duplicating what God has done in the past, has put it on the foreheads of his followers and on their right side. That is clearly seen without any doubt. I mean you can see it places, on headbands, bound on foreheads by Jihad fighters, containing an Arabic script. It can be as little as the crescent moon which identifies them to the moon god, or "in the name of Allah," or the whole Islamic creed. What is that again? There is but one god Allah and his messenger is Muhammad.

Why is bismallah an important element of this whole teaching session? Because to the Western world it means nothing, but you will start recognizing it because you will start hearing more and more if you know how to listen for it, if you know how to read it, if you are able to do that.

The Arabic phrase shown above is pronounced as Bismillah ir-Rahman ir-Rahim, and is a beautifully poetic phrase...

I do not think it is. And, of course, this is an Islamic point of view that I am reading.

... which offers both deep insight and brilliant inspiration. It has often been said that the phrase Bismillah ir-Rahman ir-Rahim contains the true essence of the entire Qur'an, as well as the true essence of all religions.

Muslims will often say this phrase when embarking on any significant endeavor, and the phrase is considered by some to be a major pillar of Islam. This expression is so magnificent and so concise that all but one chapter of the Qur'an begins with the words Bismillah ir-Rahman ir- Rahim.

The common translation:

"In the name of God, most Gracious, most Compassionate"

Also, you will see it "in the name of Allah". It is hard to even read this information, but I must, so you can be aware of it knowing, oh oh trouble is ahead. "Do you believe that?" Oh absolutely. You might need to review it over and over.

The common translation:

"In the name of God, most Gracious, most Compassionate"

fails to capture either the true depth of meaning or the inspirational message of this beautiful phrase. So, let's look deeper into the meaning of these wonderful words.

The common translation of bismillah is "In the name of Allah", which is actually an idiom, an expression that really does not make much sense on a literal word-by-word basis.

The phrase 'In the name of' is an idiom having a connotation of: with the blessings of, under the governance of, as an instrument of, in devotion to, in adoration of, on behalf of, with the support or for the glory of. In each of these cases, the idiom 'In the name of' indicates that one is submitting to, honoring, or glorying that which is referred to.

Of course, that is Allah.

Now, let's take a deeper look at the Arabic roots of this magnificent word bismillah.

Magnificent to them.

The term bismillah is a combination of three words:

1) The particle bi [the first part of that word] which can mean by, for, with the aid of, through or by means of and points toward that which happens next.

2) The next word in the phrase is ism [...] which indicates the means by which something is distinguished, whether by use of an identifying mark, or by being raised up high so that it may be distinguished, and would include a name, reputation, light or vibration, and points toward the very essence of something, the inherent qualities and signs of the existence of something, the underlying realty of something.

3) The ending of the term is the word Allah, which is the Arabic name of the One.

Now we have the full word bismallah:

The Semitic roots of the word Allah extends back several thousand years to the Canaanite and Aramaic Alaha. These roots point towards unity, oneness, the eternal power which includes all of existence and of non-existence. In modern English this would generally be translated as God...

Of course, meaning from the Islamic point of view, god or Allah is to be worshipped, honored and adored.

Using these basic roots, the term bismillah might be translated as:

- By means of the very essence of God [Allah]

- For the glory of our Creator [Allah]

- With the light of the One

Of course, that *light of the One* again is Allah.

- With the guidance of The Divine [Allah]

- As an instrument of the One

- In harmony with the Divine Presence

Whose presence? Of Allah's presence.

The central idea here is that whatever we do, every step that we take, every breath that we breathe, is done for, because of, and through the essence of the One who has created us [Allah].

To say bismillah is to humbly offer one's self as a vehicle for the glory and majesty of The One.

And that is the Beast's point of view, which is even difficult to read. That is what they live and breathe for. Satan has done his job.

These two terms rahman and rahim refer to attributes of the One. While they are often translated simply as Merciful and Compassionate, the roots of the words points to a deeper meaning.

Both rahman and rahim are derived from the Semitic root [r-h-m] which indicates something of the utmost tenderness which provides protection and nourishment, and that from which all of creation is brought into being. And indeed, the root [rhm] has meanings of womb, kinship, relationship, loving-kindness, mercy, compassion, and nourishing- tenderness.

Makes you want to puke.

Thus, both rahman and rahim point toward that which emerges from the source of all creation, while also conveying a sense of tenderness, loving- kindness, protection and nourishment.

The term rahman is a very emphatic statement, and then the sentiment is echoed by being immediately followed by the use of another form of the same root word. Such repetition is a joyful celebration of this Divine attribute, much the same as saying "The one [that of course being Allah again] *who is the Supreme Loving-Kindness, oh such Loving-Kindness.*

Uh! Hard to get through that.

The term rahman describes the aspects of the source of all creation which is endlessly radiating, endlessly nourishing, regardless of who or what is receiving the endless flow of blessings.

Rahman conveys the idea of fullness and extensiveness, indicating the great quality of love and mercy which engulfs all of creation without regard to any effort or request on our part.

...rahman describes the quality of abounding Grace which is inherent in and inseparable from the Almighty [Allah].

On the other hand, the term rahim describes that aspect of the source which is issued forth only in response to the actions and the behavior of the recipient. It is in this manner that God [Allah] *takes ten steps toward us when we take even a single step toward God* [Allah].

Rahim conveys the idea of constant renewal and giving liberal reward in response to the quality of our deeds and thoughts.

...rahim expresses the continuous manifestation of the Grace in our lives and its effect upon us as a result of our own activities.

Rahman points toward the Beneficent One whose endless outpouring of love and mercy are continually showered upon all creation, while Rahim points the Merciful One whose love and mercy are manifested in that which is received as the consequence of one's deeds.

So, the phrase ir-Rahman ir-Rahim is a recognition and honoring of the very source of all existence, the source of all blessings, the source of all compassion, the source of all mercy who gives endlessly to us and who also responds according to our moral integrity, our harmony with all creation and our love of Allah.

I did not think I was going to make it through that.

There is no way for any one translation to capture the many facets of this beautiful phrase Bismillah ir-Rahman ir-Rahim. Here are some poetic renderings that attempt to capture some aspects of the meaning without being literal translations:

With every breath that we breathe, may we act on behalf of the Divine Presence, the Source of all that we receive.

With every step that we take, may we be instruments of the One Light which guides us, the Source and Nourisher of all of creation.

Every moment of this life is filled with your eternal radiance my Beloved. You are the Beneficent One who endlessly showers all of creation with nourishment and blessings, and the One who generously rewards those who live in harmony with Your Divine Will.

Bismillah ir-Rahman ir-Rahim; that is to say Bismillah.

I want you to remember this: *To say bismillah is to humbly offer one's self as a vehicle for the glory and majesty of The One. To say bismillah is to humbly offer one's self...* (Remember that badge of servitude I was talking about earlier?) *...as a vehicle* [an instrument] *for the glory and majesty of The One* [Allah]. That is why it is called Bismallah or Bis-ma-allah. You got it, folks?

"Well, you know, that is good information to have but where do you really see it?"

One of the most obvious places you can see it in the Western world if you do not read a lot like I do is through music. I will give you just one example. Remember the rock group Queen? I think it started back in the late '70s or somewhere in the '70s. Its leader Freddie Mercury had a very popular song. It is used in movies. Young kids still listen to it 30+ years later. That song is called *Bohemian Rhapsody.* Have you ever looked at the lyrics of that song? You can hear the song here: http://www.youtube.com/watch?v=R3_0Pky8vVg Listen closely. This is just one of many examples that I could have pulled. I want you to listen for bismallah, and then I will read what the lyrics actually say. See if you can hear bismallah.

Now let's look at the lyrics. I am not going to show all the lyrics in this song. It is kind of a stupid sick song. I will just read the actual lyrics that apply to the teaching. Bismallah came up several times, folks. This is nothing new. Satan knows what he is doing. He has a plan and Christians have been gooses in a new day honking away with their Christian Science Fiction theories and do not even know what they are being indoctrinated with. They do not even know what their children are being indoctrinated with. Like I said, this is just one example. I was going to do a demonology series and I am going to have to wait to teach on it—but in that series I put together at least 50 songs that became so popular that had nothing more than Satanic meanings behind them. It is nothing new.

What you heard in *Bohemian Rhapsody* was:

> *I'm just a poor boy, nobody loves me*
> *He's just a poor boy from a poor family*
> *Spare him his life from this monstrosity*
> *Easy come, easy go, will you let me go?*
> *Bismillah! No, we will not let you go!*

Now they spell it b-i-s-m-i-l-l-a-h which could be spelled that way also.

> *(Let him go!)*
> *Bismillah! We will not let you go!*
> *(Let him go!)*
> *Bismillah! We will not let you go!*
> *(Let me go!)*
> *No, we will not let you go.*
> *Let me go!*
> *Never, never let you go!*
> *Let me go!*
> *Never let you go!*
> *Let me go!*
> *No, no, no, no, no, no, no*
> *Oh mama mia, mama mia*
> *Mama mia, let me go*
> *Beelzebub has a devil put aside*
> *For me, for me, for me*

Yes; and what they did not realize is it is in the form of bismallah. This is just one of many examples, folks.

Rev. 13:18: *"Here is a riddle. Let him that hath understanding determine or decide the multitude of the beast: for it is a multitude of man; and this multitude is* [not 666, not *chi xi stigma*] *in the name of Allah."* Another name for saying it is bismallah. I showed several different examples. It is time the world sees Revelation 13:17-18 rightly divided because now is the time to do so. That is what it is saying.

162

The Last Days Study Guide
The Mark of The Beast Part 9

1. What are the some of the basic notions Christians have about the number 666 and why are they wrong?
2. Why is a barcode system impractical as an option for the mark of the beast?
3. What is one communicating when they take the mark of the beast?
4. What is the Shahada?
5. When Muslims say bismallah, what are they saying?
6. Other than within Islam, where else can bismallah be heard?
7. In comparing Islam with the facts regarding Jesus Christ, how has Satan counterfeited the way of salvation?
8. What is the mark of the beast?

The Mark of the Beast Part 10

Revelation 13:17, *"And that no man might buy or sell, save he that had the mark, or the name of the beast, or the number of his name..."*—or, the multitude of his name. *"Here is wisdom. Let him that hath understanding count the number of the beast: for it is the number of a man; and his number is six hundred threescore and six."* Or what people have come to know as 666.

Translated correctly verse 18 should read:

> HERE IS A RIDDLE. LET HIM THAT HATH UNDERSTANDING DETERMINE OR DECIDE THE MULTITUDE OF THE BEAST: FOR IT IS A MULTITUDE OF MAN; AND THIS MULTITUDE IS *CHI XI STIGMA* (Χξϛ′).

If you read *Chi xi stigma* as a number, it is 666. But I said no, you cannot read it as a number. Part of *chi xi stigma* if you do not read it as a number says "in the name of Allah" or bismallah, which is correct but not complete because we dealt with bismallah; we only dealt with *xi* and *stigma*:

I will review these two in a moment, but we really have not looked at *chi* yet. What is this X-looking symbol? Now, do not get me wrong, it is a mark. I am going to tell you it is a mark that goes all the way back to Cain. That is right, Cain.

Genesis 4:15. *"And the LORD said unto him, Therefore whosoever slayeth Cain..."* Cain had already murdered his brother and he is concerned because he will be a fugitive knowing that others will seek their revenge on him. *"And the LORD said unto him, Therefore whosoever slayeth Cain, vengeance shall be taken on him sevenfold. And the LORD set a mark upon Cain, lest any finding him should kill him."* Remember that? Then I went to the cross teaching and we came back to this *chi xi stigma* and the verses related to it.

Now since God marked Cain, Satan has twisted and used that mark for his purposes and it is a seen mark. God uses marks. Most of the time, it is unseen except in this case with Cain. Nations throughout the world from the earliest beginnings have been influenced to mark themselves knowingly or unknowingly to pagan traditions and doctrines. Why? Where did they pick up this tradition, and, how far back does it go? I have said in previous teachings in this section of The Mark of the Beast that Satan is the greatest copycat. He copycats by twisting what God sets in motion, twists it for his purposes, and generation after generation makes people, no matter where they are, believe it is something holy or something that whoever and whatever they are following is something that would please the gods, or whatever false god they were worshipping.

Now we have looked at this *chi xi stigma*. I have covered this because some of you have asked me what *stigma* means. It means *scar, mark, or badge of service*. Now *chi xi stigma* or what you see there that the translators used as six hundred threescore and six is the only place in God's Word you will even find these Greek letters together, only in Revelation 13:18. It has puzzled scholars and translators for centuries.

The translators took the Greek words we find in these verses and made a choice when they were trying to translate it. As I already preached, they only had one of two choices that they could have made. Because they still did not have a clue how to resolve this riddle, they chose to use the numbering system translation of *chi xi stigma*. Therefore, that changed the whole verse around. It reads (if you use a number system) that you have to *count the number...for it is the number* and I said no, no, no. Understanding the other available translation option it reads: *"Here is a riddle. Let him that hath understanding determine* [not number] *or decide the multitude* [not the number but the multitude] *of the beast: for it is* [the translators put number there, but it should be multitude] *a multitude of man; and this multitude is… "*and, of course, then they put the number 666, which you already know, because they chose the number route. The Greek word translated as 'count' in Revelation 13:18 is not count because we are not counting. We are not using a number system. We need to decide to use Choice B when translating this verse and it means to *determine or decide or reckon.* Remember that? Now the word *arithmos* means a number when referring to numbers, but when referring to people, it must be accurately translated multitude, which I have done.

They could not figure out the riddle then. Why? Because it was not yet the set time for it. It was not at the "time of the end". I do not even care if you had put Daniel and John together in the same room, they still would not have figured it out because it was still a riddle. Once the time came and went, God's set time when this could be figured out, then we could look at the alternative because we can figure out it does mean something else. And, of course, I already covered what it does mean.

I am sorry; unfortunately, the people that do lean towards this translation of what this verse says have taken shortcuts. It does mean "in the name of Allah" or bismallah but it is not complete. So, that is what I am going to cover in this teaching, the complete and accurate translation of *chi xi stigma.* Before I even get there though, remember the cross teaching I taught on? I am going to go back to it somewhat. I am going to read you something:

> *The history of the cross, and its worship and use as a religious symbol by pagan nations long before the time of Christ, shows us plainly that it is not a symbol that Christians should attach any reverence toward.*

"What does this have to do with what you are trying to teach about the *chi* (or X) symbol? What does that *chi* part mean?" Well, that is marking something. There is no doubt about it. That is why we need to go back to the cross. The Unger's Bible Dictionary, a very popular dictionary still in use today, says:

That the cross was widely known in pre-Christian times as an emblem has been clearly shown by independent investigators. Indeed, it was a well-known heathen sign.

So how did it become Christianized?

The vestments of the priests of HORUS, the Egyptian god of light, are marked ✝.

The cross symbol is what Unger's Bible Dictionary is referring to. By the way, if you just turn ✗ counter-clockwise with your imagination you get the same thing.

At Thebes, in the tombs of the kings, royal cows are represented plowing, a calf playing in front. Each animal has a ✝ marked in several places on it. Rassam found buildings at Nineveh [where Syria is located today] marked with the Maltese cross. Osiris, as well as Jupiter Ammon, had for a monogram a ✝. The cross is found marked on Phoenician monuments at a very early date."

In his fascinating historical book The Two Babylons, [I read portions of it to you] Alexander Hislop tells us a great deal about the history of the "cross". Notice what he says about this ancient object of worship:

I have read some of this before, but it is worth reading again. "What does this have to do with the mark of Cain?" We are getting to that.

There is yet one more symbol of the Romish worship to be noticed, and that is the sign of the cross. In the Papal system, as is well known, the sign of the cross and the image of the cross are all in all. No prayer can be said, no worship engaged in, no step almost can be taken, without the frequent use of the sign of the cross. The cross is looked upon as the grand charm, as the great refuge in every season of danger, in every hour of temptation as the infallible preservative from all the powers of darkness. The cross is adored with all the homage due only to the Most High; and for any to call it, in the hearing of a genuine Romanist, by the Scriptural term, "the accursed tree," is a mortal offence. To say that such superstitious feeling for the sign of the cross, such worship as Rome pays to a wooden or a metal cross, ever grew out of a saying of Paul, "God forbid that I should glory, save in the cross of our Lord Jesus Christ"—that is, in the doctrine of Christ crucified—is a mere absurdity, a shallow subterfuge and pretence. The magic virtues attributed to the so-called sign of the cross, the worship bestowed on it, never came from such a source. The same sign of the cross that Rome now worships was used in the Babylonian Mysteries, was applied by Paganism to the same magic purposes, was honored with the same honours. That which is now called the Christian cross was originally no Christian emblem at all.

That is from *The Two Babylons*. Let's continue:

The cross that is so adored…dates back to ancient pagan worship — the "mystery religions" stemming out of ancient BABYLON!

The pagan /so-called Christian "cross" is a perversion of the mystic "Tau", the last letter of the Hebrew alphabet.

We already have covered all this. It is a good review.

The "Christian" cross has no direct connection with the "Tau", which was in the form of a capital "T" in English, but puts the cross-beam down the stem of the letter, as a small "t" shape. The Jews refer to it as cherev, or the "sword". It is an ancient pagan phallic symbol of the male penis, a symbol of pagan sex worship and the abominable rites of Baalism and the pagan temple prostitution carried out in worship of Astarte ("Easter")!

Or also Ishtar, or another name for it you have heard me use quite a bit is Asura.

The major "crosses" of history, such as the Latin, Greek, and Maltese crosses, all have the crossbar in the middle or upper part of the upright pole. The archaeologist Layard found the Maltese cross as a sacred symbol in ancient Nineveh of the Assyrians, close kin to the Babylonians. Layard identified the cross symbol he found with the sun, thus showing it was a sign of sun worship.

The pagan cross was worn suspended from the necklaces of the vestal virgins of pagan Rome, even as Roman Catholic nuns wear it now, seemingly in imitation of their predecessors. The pagan Egyptians did the very same thing. A scholar who studied the ancient Egyptians and nations of Africa, found that the people of many tribes "frequently had a small cross suspended to a necklace, or to the collar of their dress. . . showing that it was already in use as early s the 15th century before the Christian era.".

That is even before David's time. It is around the time of the Exodus story, way back in the Old Testament in the Bible. That is how far back. It goes further back than that, but according to this author in his research that is what he found.

Says Alexander Hislop, in Two Babylons, regarding the early history of the "cross", and its widespread use as a religious symbol in antiquity:

"There is hardly a Pagan tribe where the cross has not been found. The cross was worshiped by the Pagan Celts long before the incarnation and death of Christ. [...] It was worshiped in Mexico for ages before the Roman Catholic missionaries set foot there, large

stone crosses being erected, probably to the 'god of rain'. The cross thus widely worshiped, or regarded as a sacred emblem, was the unequivocal symbol of Baccus, the Babylonian Messiah, for he was represented with a headband covered with crosses.

I showed the picture of that before.

The cross was anciently used by the Chinese on their pagodas, painted on lanterns to illuminate the recesses of their sacred temples. In India the cross was used to mark the jars of sacred water taken from the Indus and Ganges Rivers. In southern India it was used as an emblem of disembodied saints. The Hindus regarded the cross as sacred to their god Agni. Buddhists and other sects in India mark the heads of their devotees with the sign of the "cross".

In 46 B.C., Roman coins depict the god Jupiter or Zeus as holding a long sceptre which ended in a cross. This was the symbol of Jupiter, the chief of the gods. In ancient Egypt, the goddess Isis (Ishtar or Semiramis) was shown with a cross on her forehead. Her priests carried processional crosses as they worshiped her.

Monuments show that ancient Assyrian kings wore a cross suspended on a necklace or attached to their collar. Of course, their descendants, the modern Germans, are identified with the famous "German cross", and the Nazis in the Third Reich used the Swastika — a form of the cross — as their symbol of power and might!

Another scholar in his research in Mexico:

...describes the wonder and amazement of the Spanish Catholic priests and missionaries when they encountered the "cross" as an emblem of worship among the Aztec Indians!

This noted historian writes:

"Yet we should have charity for the missionaries who first landed in this world of wonders; where. . . they were astonished by occasional glimpses of rites and ceremonies. . . In their amazement. . . They did not inquire, whether the SAME THINGS WERE NOT PRACTICED BY OTHER IDOLATROUS PEOPLE. They could not suppress their wonder, as they behold the cross, the sacred emblem of their own faith, raised as an OBJECT OF WORSHIP in the temple of Anahuac. They met with it in various places; and the IMAGE OF A CROSS may be seen at this day, sculpted in bas-relief, on the walls of one of the buildings of Palenque, while a figure bearing some resemblance to that of a child is held up to it, as if in adoration".

In Palenque, Mexico, founded by Votan in the 9th century before the present era, is a pagan temple known as "the temple of the cross". Inscribed on an altar there is a cross six and one half by eleven feet in size. As these Indians had no contact with the Spanish until the 16th century of the present era, some 2,300 years later, obviously their "cross" predates the time of Christ by some eight centuries, and could not have been "Christian" in origin!

The early Mexicans worshiped the cross as "our Father", or "Tota". The Scriptures condemn the practice of addressing a piece of wood, or a "stock", as "our Father". God says through Jeremiah, the prophet, "As the thief is ashamed when he is found, so is the house of Israel ashamed; they, their kings, their princes, and their priests, and their prophets, saying TO A STOCK [In Hebrew meaning stick, wood, timber, stake, post, log], "Thou art my father; and to a stone, Thou hast brought me forth: for they have turned their back unto me, and not their face" (Jer. 2:26-27).

Is this prophecy and condemnation of a pagan custom or rite, which had crept in amongst the people of Israel, not a description of ANCIENT PAGAN PHALLIC CROSS WORSHIP?!!

He is asking a question. No doubt.

> *Jeremiah 10 also speaks of this pagan custom. Notice! God Almighty declares, concerning the customs and practices of the heathen nations around Israel, the ancient pagans:*

> *"Thus saith the LORD, Learn not the way of the heathen, and be not dismayed at the signs of heaven; for the heathen are dismayed at them. For the CUSTOMS of the people are VAIN: for one cutteth a tree out of the forest, the work of the hands of the workman, with the axe. They deck it with silver and with gold; they fasten it with nails and with hammers, that it move not. They are UPRIGHT AS THE PALM TREE, but speak not: they must needs be BORNE, because they cannot go. Be not afraid of them; for they cannot do evil, neither also is it in them to do good. But they are altogether BRUTISH AND FOOLISH: THE STOCK IS A DOCTRINE OF VANITIES" (Jer. 10:2-8).*

> *We have often referred to this passage of Scripture in the past to refer to the pagan custom of the Christmas "tree"...*

Which I thought was not a proper use for that. They wanted to interpret it as a definition for Christmas trees, but that is not what it is referring to, folks. So, in a sense I do agree with this author but not completely.

> *We have often referred to this passage of Scripture in the past to refer to the pagan custom of the Christmas "tree", which pagans used to deck with silver and gold, and place in their homes every year at the winter solstice. However, this passage could also refer* **[because this author has not given up the possibility of that also]** *just as easily to the pagan CROSS, the "STOCK", made out of WOOD, and "carried about" by pagan priests at the head of pilgrimages, parades, and processions.*

If you don't know the history of that time, they would cut these pieces of wood and deck them with all kinds of decorations. They would carry around these pieces of wood and then they would plant them in the ground like an asherah grove practice.

> *Notice the similarity! Jeremiah clearly is speaking of an object made of wood, which is often adorned, and carried about in processions. Normally, decorated trees are put in one place and left there for the duration of the holidays. However, the pagan objects which are carried about in processions were WOODEN CROSSES!*

Now he is on the same page. These were not Christmas trees. I am sorry to burst some of your bubbles - and you'll have to rewrite some of the books that you bought. They were literally carrying around dead wood, decking them out, decorating them, and planting them down after they were done with all their processions. Then they would bow down to it. That is what Jeremiah was referring to.

> *However, the pagan objects which are carried about in processions were WOODEN CROSSES! Roman Catholic priests still do this ancient custom today! Says Unger's Bible Dictionary, "It was only after superstition took the place of true spiritual devotion that the figure of the cross was used or borne about as a sacred charm".*

> *As an instrument of death, of crucifixion, the cross is also very ancient —and very pagan. In the Cross in Tradition, History and Art, we read:*

> *"The cross was used in ancient times as a punishment for flagrant crimes in Egypt, Assyria, Persia, Palestine, Carthage, Greece, and Rome. . . Tradition ascribes the invention of the punishment of the cross...*

To who?

...to a WOMAN, THE QUEEN SEMIRAMIS".

How did this ancient PAGAN symbol creep into and become a part of the established Christian church?

Good question!

How did it become a part of mainstream Catholic and Protestant religious orthodoxy?

Good question! Another author:

It was not until Christianity began to be PAGANIZED that the cross came to be thought of as a Christian symbol. It was in 431 A.D. ...

I read sources even further back than that.

...that crosses in churches and chambers were introduced, while the use of crosses on steeples did not come until about 586 A.D. In the 6th century, the crucifix image was introduced and its worship sanctioned by the Church of Rome. It was not until the second council at Ephesus that private homes were required to possess a cross. Such use of the cross then was obviously not a doctrine of the early true church. It was not a part of the faith that was once delivered to the saints"

[Many authors] point out that the ancient cross was associated with the worship of the pagan savior Tammuz, whose death was lamented in the spring by many ancient nations — a practice that God condemns in His Word.

The so-called "Christian cross", then, is PAGAN TO THE CORE! As true worshippers of Jesus Christ, we should have nothing whatever to do with this vile symbol. We should repudiate it, abhor it, and put it far away from us!

Just because Jesus Christ, the Messiah, was hung and crucified on a stake, or stauros, in no means suggests that we should venerate or worship the implement of His torture and death! How obscene! How despicable a thought! How blasphemous and iniquitous! How cleverly Satan the devil is to get people to focus their attention on the pagan cross, calling it "Christian", instead of focusing their attention on Christ Jesus, the Savior Himself!

We must remember Jesus Christ, not remember the cross.

Nowhere in the New Testament do the apostles ever tell us, "Remember the cross!"

If you can find it, I would like to know where it is at. I have not seen it.

The Apostle Paul himself says rather we should be "Looking unto JESUS, the author and finisher of our faith;...

Well, finisher of faith.

...who for the joy that was set before him endured the cross, despising the shame, and is set down at the right hand of the throne of God. For CONSIDER HIM [not the "cross"!]...

Consider Him, not the cross.

...that endured such contradiction of sinners against himself, lest ye be wearied and faint in your minds".

That is Hebrews 12. We have looked at those verses many times.

To remember the cross, and to think on it, instead of Christ — is nothing less than the worship of the lifeless item itself — in other words, NOTHING LESS THAN MODERN IDOLATRY!

"Remember that Jesus Christ of the seed of David was raised from the dead, according to my gospel." That is Paul writing to Timothy in II Timothy 2:8. *"Remember that Jesus Christ of the seed of David..."* It does not ever say, remember the cross that Jesus Christ died on. It says, *"Remember that Jesus Christ of the seed of David was raised from the dead, according to my gospel."*

> *We should also, therefore, REMEMBER CHRIST, and what He accomplished for us, paying the penalty for our sins, and remember that He now sits at the right hand of God in heaven, as our eternal High Priest who ever lives to make intercession for us!.*
>
> *But the cross, on the other hand, has a distinctly pagan origin and history, and certainly is NOTHING that a true Christian and servant of the Living God would want to be associated with, love, adore, worship, remember, or keep in mind, as an object!*

I totally agree.

> *It is an IDOL! It is an object of SHAME...*

Especially if you know its history and where it came from. It was a mark and Satan craftily put together a plan using that mark that started all the way back in the time of Cain. I will get to that in a minute.

> *It is an IDOL! It is an object of SHAME, derision, and horror— not something we are to focus our attention on, or "remember" in times of crises, trial, or trouble! In the New Testament, the cross is nowhere regarded as an instrument or emblem of worship or adoration, nor does it have any power in itself to do good or evil. Theologically, the word stauros, "stake", or "cross", simply was used on occasion as a summary description of the Gospel of the Kingdom of God, and salvation, made possible by Jesus' death on the stake for us and for all mankind. We don't focus on human words of wisdom, "lest the cross [stauros] of Christ should be made of none effect".*

That is the instruction we are given in 1 Corinthians 1:17.

When Paul speaks of "the preaching of the cross" (verse 18), he is referring to the preaching of the entire Gospel, summarized by the "stake", as it is central to the theme of salvation, Christ's death being pivotal in the process. When Paul preached the "cross", he explained what he meant...

Salvation can only come to us through the death of Jesus Christ on the cross, or stake, in payment for our sins. There is no other way. There is no other means of entrance into the Kingdom of God for any of us! Certainly, therefore, in that sense, the "stake" or stauros, is a vital key to our salvation! However, it is the beginning point — not the ending point! As Paul wrote to the Romans, "Much more then, being now justified by his blood, we shall be saved from wrath through him. For if, when we were enemies, we were reconciled to God by the death of his Son, much more, being reconciled, we shall be saved by his life" (Romans 5:9-10).

Christ died for our sins; but now He lives at the right hand of God, to intercede for us, and He sends the Holy Spirit to dwell in us and to empower us...

Our emphasis, therefore, should be ON CHRIST HIMSELF, and what He DID and still DOES for us — and not on the physical sign of the "cross" itself! Let us not remember or focus on the cross itself, the object of shame and contempt, which Christ endured for us, but let us focus our minds and hearts on and remember CHRIST, who is "the author and finisher of [our] faith".

Let us have nothing whatsoever to do with PAGAN customs!

May God help us all to "earnestly contend for the faith which was ONCE delivered unto the saints".

So that was pretty much a summary of what was already taught in previous messages. I could not agree more. This cross has always been a symbol since God marked Cain to save his life from others that would want to do him physical harm. Satan took it and twisted it.

Now, God used a *Tav*. We already looked at that in the Old Testament, but it was an unseen mark, just as the Holy Spirit in the New Testament is an unseen mark. We do not go putting a *Tav* in our forehead or put tattoos of a *Tav* on our hands or body, so we can identify with Jesus Christ. The only way to be identified with Jesus Christ is if you recognize what He did for you and you are saved through His blood; and now being someone that can be reconciled back to God are now a candidate to have the Holy Spirit imputed in your life, which imputes righteousness into you. Then He goes to work in molding you. These are unseen things that happen. Jesus is not in the business of putting little crosses on your head or wherever you want them on your body.

And of course, Satan has confused the matter since Christ, especially a few hundred years after His departure when the apostles were no longer around to contest it. I believe Satan went to work, especially through the Roman Catholic Church, and especially shortly after Constantine claims he saw a sign from the heavens. He saw a sign all right. It was not the sign of Jesus Christ saying, "Hey, put this cross on your shield or wherever you want to put it". I believe it was the work of Satan and I have covered that before. But we saw that Cain was marked. God used a physical sign, so others could see it and know they should not touch him or do any physical harm to him because if they did they would get that plus sevenfold.

Now in the rabbinical and Jewish literature and viewpoints, especially the centric viewpoint, it teaches that the mark of Cain was the Hebrew letter *Tav*. Incidentally, it was just in one location written by one (let's just call him a) rabbi of the early period, even before Christ. He taught that the mark of Cain was the Hebrew letter *Tav*. Remember the *Tav*? The modern Hebrew *Tav* looks something like ת, remember? The ancient Hebrew *Tav* we covered before in the teachings looks like ✗. It is very similar to what the *chi* looks like. If you tilt the ancient *Tav* somewhat, you have this "+" mark.

Modern Hebrew
letter *tav*
(Hebrew square)

Hebrew letter
tav at the time
of Ezekiel
(Paleo-Hebrew)

The Hebrew letter *Tav* at the time of Ezekiel is the bottom image. The Modern Hebrew letter *Tav* is what has been used for over two millenniums, but it is not as ancient as you see there in Ezekiel. That even goes farther back than Ezekiel. So that is what I was referring to and that is what Jewish literature and rabbis are referring to, that lower letter or image you see there. That lower Hebrew letter *Tav* you see here was used during the Ezekiel passages that I already read before in previous teachings.

Now the *Tav* looks like the cross but it is also used in various ways as a plus sign shaped symbol. You can see in the beginning of middle and mostly Jewish-centric history how they would use this and explain this letter *Tav* as the mark that Cain wore. This is the sign which rabbis even today believe marked Cain, the mark for sin. So, that is why the rabbis still today believe that it was taught thousands of years ago that the mark of Cain was the Hebrew letter of *Tav*. This mark was the symbol of sin. Yes, Cain got marked but he got marked with the symbol of sin, so everyone would know what his deed was—and not only that but, even though his deed was murder, you were still not to touch him. He was God's problem in other words. Hands off. That is the covenant He made with Cain. And Satan went to work immediately to twist things, not only to copycat, but to twist things and meanings. So, this became a very popular mark shortly after the flood, even prior to Semiramis and Cush (the father of chaos, one of Ham's sons). Cush was the ringleader that taught and formed these false religions. And, of course, Satan found willing candidates in Nimrod and that evil queen Semiramis, and then of course after that Tammuz. So, this symbolism carried on and wherever you go; when you dig into the history around the Tower of Babel, or around the early periods of Babylonian mystery religions, you will find this cross symbol, this mark of sin, used not only on their buildings, in their steely work and other objects of worship, but also their pottery and so forth.

Now after the flood, man started to get together and they wanted to build a tower to reach to the heavens. Then God confused the languages. When God confused the languages, people started to spread out. People always ask me this question: How did people get across the oceans? You are assuming what you see today existed back then just like it does today. That is why I need to preach on Genesis especially the first four chapters because geology-wise it can be explained how this dispersion after this Tower of Babel experience was possible. The geographical changes had not quite progressed completely to the point we see in the geographical features of today, where we can see from above via satellite and looking down and say, Wow, most of it is water! That was not always the case. Why was that not always the case? There was more land mass than you think. I have taught somewhat on this before in the Spiritual Warfare Series and I even showed you how land masses disappeared, and more waters were on the earth after the flood. But I do not want to get into all that because it will take away from the topic at hand.

The plus (+) mark is the mark of sin, the mark of Cain. That is what was used and that is what you will find throughout whatever research you do… if you are into research and you don't want to take my word for it. Dig in and look at all the sources. This is one mark that was established worldwide and has worldwide acceptance. That is the one thing consistent about all the cultures, all the nations from Mexico to India to Japan to China, and obviously the Middle East. You find this mark everywhere, way before Christ. You find it used very often in Egypt, not only as a mark that is put on a tag with their false gods they were worshiping but also on their buildings, their literature, anything they could put this mark on including themselves! WHY? It was a mark that was used everywhere, and I mean everywhere. If you believe the flood story, and you believe the Tower of Babel story, and you believe there was a Cush, Semiramis, Nimrod and Tammuz, and you believe after that incident God confused the languages and man started to be dispersed, then that is the only explanation I can give you briefly as to why we can find this mark everywhere worldwide. They carried with them some of the pagan traditions they practiced in that area and it went worldwide.

John was told to write what he saw. I believe he did that. I believe, like Daniel, he did not have the answer, but I believe he wrote exactly what he saw. But what did John see? I believe he saw the *chi xi stigma* but not as we now see it. I believe he saw the Arabic. And why wouldn't it be in the Arabic? We know this letter ε in the Arabic. If we are dealing with Islam and when the Beast would be identified, then what John saw—even though he wrote it in the Greek, and that is part of the riddle—obviously would have been in the Arabic. What John saw and what it spells out now is bismallah or "in the name of Allah".

Now we know this word $X\xi\varsigma'$. The Greek letters *chi xi stigma* spells out a phrase in the Arabic. The *xi* part of the equation of the *chi xi stigma* means bismallah or "in the name of Allah". The *chi* part of the equation was a mark from the beginning, from the time of Cain - the mark, the cross, the *Tav*, any way that you can remember it. If you tilt X about 45 degrees off kilter, it resembles +. Just like Satan, by the way, to tilt things off kilter just as he does to the truth of God's Word. This mark X in the book of Revelation is like the mark of Cain. It is contained within the symbol that is in the name of the Beast itself. The mark of Cain, in a sense, is coded inside the *chi xi stigma* that spells "in the name of Allah". This can only be seen if you not only tie in the Arabic (which is a key component in translating this verse), but also choose the Option B (describing people) translation instead of Option A (a numbering system) to understand what this means… along with the correct definitions and describing what you must *determine* or *decide* about these people and who they are. Only then could you come to the ***chi xi stigma***, "in the name of Allah", and come to the point of recognizing that this is a CODE, a mark inside the ***chi xi stigma*** that spells out "in the name of Allah". This could only be seen after 1948, 1967, and the present age we are living in. We are that close to the end, folks.

The 8ᵗʰ Beast is Islam, the Beast's prophet is Muhammad, and the mark of the Beast is that infernal Arabic writing that you just saw. You can see "in the name of Allah" or bismallah across their arm, their armbands, and across their heads. I have shown that the cross symbol, this type of mark ✗ when tilted properly is the same kind of mark you see across the Islamic world, especially with the fanatical Jihadists, and not that fanatical in some cases.

Look at the image used as their symbolism. Isn't it kind of ironic?

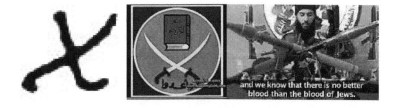

Of course, that is the Koran on top of those two swords in the center photo. How about that photo on the right? How often do you see that? Of course, the literal inscription on the bottom reads: "and we know there is no better blood than the blood of Jews." But so often with their swords, with their guns, with their bombs, their symbolism, their mark of Cain, their mark of sin, their mark period that identifies them for who they are and that they come "in the name of Allah" is the cross. Now the cross can have various meanings and Satan did a wonderful job for the Christians to idolize the cross for different purposes, but in Islam it serves a purpose of pronouncing sin; and what sin will produce is evil, and evil always produces death, not only temporary death but also eternal death. You see it everywhere in their symbolism.

In this photo, you can see "in the name of Allah" there. One starts to recognize all the different types of gibberish, as one of the HOFs called it. You can see the gibberish right there.

Then on the right (remember Arabic reads right to left), you can see especially towards the beginning and about one third of the way across, "in the name of Allah".

The Beast is Islam. The false prophet of the Beast is Muhammad. The mark of the beast is (along with everything else in the *chi xi stigma* translated correctly) the mark of Cain, $\mathcal{X}$. This $\mathcal{E}$ is "in the name of Allah", so what does this ς mean? I am going to give you a translation for the *chi xi stigma* — not a numbering system of 666; something totally different.

HERE IS A RIDDLE. LET HIM THAT HATH UNDERSTANDING DETERMINE OR DECIDE THE MULTITUDE OF THE BEAST: FOR IT IS A MULTITUDE OF MAN; AND THIS MULTITUDE IS SATAN'S MARK OF SIN IN THE NAME OF ALLAH TO SERVE.

Remember the badge of servitude? That is what this *ʕ* image means. Or better yet, because I have two ways that I have translated this: *Satan has marked you*. I like this translation better: *Satan has marked you in the name of Allah to serve*. Now let's read this verse again. *"Here is a riddle. Let him that hath understanding determine or decide the multitude of the beast: for it is a multitude of man, and this multitude is Satan has marked you in the name of Allah to serve."* This is probably a more literal translation and probably the translation you should stick with. *Satan has marked you in the name of Allah to serve*. Marked who? The multitude of men who are following the Beast, who we can now *determine* or *decide* or *reckon* who that Beast or multitude is, and that is Islam and its false prophet Muhammad. That is how it reads: The mark of Cain comes "in the name of Allah", so you can bow down to serve him. Period.

Yes, I do agree with the Jewish centric literature that rabbis out there present; the history that they believe the *Tav* is a mark of Cain used by God to be seen of men, that no one was to touch him. In other words, it was a mark that would preserve Cain's life. But in this case, how Satan twists it, it is a mark that will bring you eternal death if you are going to follow what Muhammad, the False Prophet, has lain out so you can bow down and serve "in the name of Allah," that false god.

Now I pretty much generalized everything because I wanted to just touch on it. I will be coming back to this in the future to add more details along the way. What I am seeking for you to understand is the translators, in a similar situation as Daniel, did not know how to translate this because while Islam did exist, it was not around at that time as a force to be reckoned with according to the perception of the early Greek translators. Islam came around 632 A.D. at the very earliest date. We know around 635/637 up to 642, Muhammad was putting all this together, and shortly after that it was developed into a more complete package following Muhammad's death. The earliest Greek translators did not have a clue. It really was a riddle to them. It took for time to pass to the point where we are at now to understand it. It could have been done probably a generation ago. We are at the point now where it is obvious who the 7th and 8th Beast is. I will be teaching on the Battle of Tours and Charles 'The Hammer' Martel. That historic time was the first death blow to the 7th Beast. We will also be delving into additional history that brought Islam to the point where it was revived and is now the 8th Beast. And more now than ever, it is alive and well and fighting against God's purposes.

I am sorry; we are to resist, we are to bring the truth out, we are to present it so people can be aware of it. I do not think we Christians in the here and now can defeat it, but Christ is going to when He returns in His second advent and guess what? I am going to be part of His army, so I will be part of that victory also. But you know what, folks? Most of the Christian world still do not have a clue about any of this that I have been presenting in this section of this series, The Mark of the Beast. They do not have any of this. They are still looking for people's names that add up to 666, like Ronald Reagan who has come and gone. They are still looking for people like Barack Obama. They are looking for anybody's name they can calculate using the Gematria, a numbering system that would result in the number 666, not to mention all the other silly Christian Science Fiction things that are going on. Bottom line: Most of the Christian world is in the dark and we need to change that.

There is no doubt about it; Satan has marked them *in the name of Allah to serve.* Well, we serve the Living God, we serve Jesus Christ. And, yes, we might be the laughingstock of the Christian world because they just do not see it this way, but as time marches on, I believe slowly but surely at least a portion of them will come to the knowledge of the truth. This will make an impact and they will see it for what it is. I will keep preaching it. We are unraveling the riddle and there is more to come. I just hope the Christian world wakes up before it is completely too late. The thing that bothers me more than anything else about the Christian Science Fiction theories is there are people so gullible in accepting it for what it is. We usually want proof of certain things before we make decisions. These false prophets use the phrase, "You have to take it in faith. You have to believe it in faith". Believe in what in faith? That this is the right interpretation? How do people have faith in something that you cannot really explain unless you bring some science fiction into it or all these possibilities? I am not bringing you possibilities. I was telling someone just a few days ago; I am not bringing you possibilities. I am bringing you history. I am laying out the facts through history.

Prove me wrong that this is not what it means in Arabic. Prove me wrong. If you believe Islam is the 8th Beast, then why not have an Arabic translation to decipher the riddle? That is my point. Prove me wrong. They can't. Their arguments always fall short. They argue in circles. They always divert to some other stupid argument that is not even related to what we started with. Well, I am going to change that. The mark of the beast is now exposed, not just a part of it as is done by the other few ministries that focus in on this, but a complete understanding. It is the mark of Cain which is Satan's mark because he has twisted what God's intentions were for Cain. He has twisted it and made a worldwide acceptance of it. God knows how many billions of people live in confusion about crosses and marks and everything else that goes along with it. The mark is exposed as Satan's mark to let someone know, YOU are now in the service of Allah. Well, I am not and hopefully there will be many more that understand what this mark is, including in the Islamic world - not to mention enlightening some Christians and really pulling them out of the dark ages of Christian Science Fiction theories. They are literally in the dark ages of Christian understanding of most of eschatology and what God has laid out for us to dig into. That is why it says, **Let him that hath understanding**, meaning that something is going to be happening to you as a person, to a preacher, or to a scholar, or to a professor that brings the information so you can have understanding - not just understanding of the Christian Science Fiction possibilities but understanding what God's Word says, TRUTH.

I have been in the business of showing off God's Word with **proof**. I have used Hebrews quite often, *faith is the substance...* No, faith there is the word *pistis; hearing and hearing to be persuaded by what you heard to be true.* That means the truth is being presented to you and you will either accept it or reject it. If you are persuaded it is the truth, it will be the foundation, the starting point where you will begin your journey to understanding. Why? *Of the things hoped for*, the things that you are expecting and desire, which is **the proof,** literally. What proof? This proof, The Holy Bible. We are living in an age where most things have already happened. That is why I like to tie in secular and biblical history to show you the proof, show off God's Word of things not seen. In Paul's day, yes, many things were not seen. In our day... very little, very little, folks. That is why we can say "by faith" in a lot of our personal problems, and not only that but also by faith as digging into God's Word and seeing what the truth is. You do not need that much faith any longer. You just need to be a serious researcher, a biblical detective with an open mind to say, "Wait a minute. There are so many things that have come to pass in God's Word. I have to take a second look" if you are not convinced. Yes, you have faith for your own personal life. You have faith for your trials, you have faith for your tribulations, you have faith during all those things, but when it comes to God's Word if you are a serious student of Jesus Christ, or not of Jesus Christ, the information is there. You can dig. There are more resources now than there ever were. The truth is not that hidden any longer. The foundations have been laid. You need to hear it to be persuaded and if you do not want to go through that route then dig in. I am convinced you are going to have a change of heart and a change of mind. You are going to be what Paul says, transformed, once you turn over your life to Jesus Christ and say, "You know what? This is it. He is the one. He is right, He is the way". He is the only way folks, and that is the way it has always been. Do not be misled into all this other stuff. See the truth for what it is.

The Last Days Study Guide
The Mark of The Beast Part 10

1. What does the Apostle Paul instruct disciples to do in II Timothy 2:8?

2. The pagan cross is a perversion of what Hebrew letter?

3. What does *tota* mean?

4. Give one example of how the saints are to identify with Christ?

5. What does centric rabbinical literature say the mark of Cain was?

6. How do the modern *tav* and the ancient *tav* differ?

7. The cross crept into Catholic and Protestant orthodoxy. What do some refer to this as?

8. Three things were necessary to obtain the correct understanding of *chi xi stigma*. What are the three things?

9. What is the most literal translation for Revelation 13:18?

10. How has this information helped you in recognizing the mark of the beast in everyday life?

The Mark of the Beast Part 11

In the last teaching segment, we looked at Revelation 13:17-18 and then translated 18 correctly. Revelation 13:18: *"Here is a riddle. Let him that hath understanding determine or decide the multitude of the beast: for it is the multitude of man; and the multitude is marked by Satan in the name of Allah or bismallah to serve."* That is the correct and rightly divided translation when you understand all of God's Word concerning the mark of the beast. Now I want to pick up from that point and go to Revelation 14:9 where it mentions the mark of the beast again.

"And the third angel followed them, saying with a loud voice, If any man worship the beast and his image, and receive his mark in his forehead, or in his hand, The same shall drink of the wine of the wrath of God, which is poured out without mixture into the cup of his indignation; and he shall be tormented with fire and brimstone in the presence of the holy angels, and in the presence of the Lamb:"

I am not going to go into if this "third angel" is an angel or not at this point. That is not the purpose of this message. *"And the third angel followed them, saying with a loud voice, If any man worship the beast and his image, and receive his mark"*—which we covered in chapter 13 and incidentally includes the false prophet also—*"in his forehead, or in his hand, The same..."*—the people that receive this mark and worship the Beast, the last evil empire in God's Word, the 8th Beast Islam; anyone that bows down to Islam either by worship or wearing that mark, period. No confusion there. — *"The same shall drink of the wine of the wrath of God, which is poured out without mixture into the cup of his indignation* [or again *wrath*] *; and he shall be tormented with fire and brimstone in the presence of the holy angels, and in the presence of the holy Lamb:"*

189

"And the smoke of their torment ascendeth up for ever and ever". Does that mean forever and ever? Now, that is another subject and I am not saying it does and I am not saying it does not, but does it? Oh! I know what Christian belief propaganda preaches, but they never really go into too much detail about that, whether it is this verse or other verses, do they? Is that forever and ever? "What are you saying! You are upsetting my world again." Good. I will come back to that.

"And the smoke of their torment ascendeth up for ever and ever: and they have no rest day nor night, who worship the beast and his image, and whosoever receiveth the mark of his name. " Hum. They are going to have the smoke of their torment sent up forever and ever (whatever that means) **and they have no rest day nor night who, worship the beast and his image, and whosoever receiveth the mark of his name.** Whether it means forever and ever is not the point right now, but we know they are going to have some torment because of who they follow now.

So what is this wrath of God? And what does it mean by *"they shall drink of the wine of the wrath of God, which is poured out without mixture into the cup of his wrath* [literally]*; and he shall be tormented with fire and brimstone in the presence of the holy angels, and in the presence of the Lamb... "*?

Go to Jeremiah 25:15. Here we have the cup of wrath for the nations. What nations? We are going to find out here in a minute. *"For thus saith the Lord GOD of Israel unto me; Take the wine cup of this fury at my hand, and cause all the nations, to whom I send thee, to drink it. "*

Cause all the nations… Does that mean everyone, every single nation on this earth? Read it again slowly: *"and cause all the nations, <u>to whom I send thee,</u> to drink it. "* So what God is saying is, Where I am sending you (and He is going to give instructions in the verses that follow), that is who is going to drink this cup referred to in Revelation 14, *"The same shall drink of the wine of the wrath of God, which is poured out without mixture into the cup of his wrath"*.

"Well, didn't this happen after Nebuchadnezzar and all those other evil kings and kingdoms?"

No, and the reason why is given to us in Jeremiah 25:27, *"Therefore thou shalt say unto them, Thus saith the LORD of hosts, the God of Israel; Drink ye, and be drunken, and spew, and fall, "*—and here are the key words and it checks out in the original— *"and rise no more"*. Circle those words: 'and rise no more'. That has not happened to any of these nations that I am going to show you in a few moments with a map that comes straight out of Jeremiah 25. That has not happened because these nations throughout the course of time, including at this present time, have risen and they are gaining strength. So, if this prophecy was already fulfilled and came to pass during Jeremiah's time or after, then God did not keep His Word because they did rise again. Verse 27 says *"and rise no more, because of the sword which I will send among you."* There is the conflict. Either God's Word is true, or it is not. Either it is believable, or it is not.

Some scholars interested in writing commentaries have misinterpreted these scriptures and bring so much confusion into the mindset of the Christian world. This has not happened yet, folks. We can tie in Jeremiah 25. Even prior to this, in this same chapter, he talks about the 70 years of desolation they would go through; so this would happen even after that period. In this case, many centuries after that 70 years of desolation took place. Understand?

Let's go back to verse 16, *"And they shall drink, and be moved, and be mad"*. Who? The ones that He causes to drink it according to verse 15. Then if you tie it in with Revelation 14, we know this has to pertain to Islam somehow. If this chapter and these scriptures in this chapter are related somehow to Revelation 14, which I am saying they are, do the areas that God says are going to drink the cup match up with present day Islam and the 8th Beast? Let's look and see if we can confirm that.

Verse 16: *"And they shall drink, and be moved"*. They are going to drink this cup of wrath *"and be moved, and be mad..."* Literally be driven to insanity, folks. If you think the Islamic world is not insane, then I do not know how to define what insanity is. Not just driven insane and be mad but *they shall drink, and be moved, and be* insane or come to a place of insanity to the point they are going to be boasting about what they are insane about. Literally in the Hebrew, they are going to be boasting about what they went insane over, Muhammad and his Koran which codified Islam.

"Yeah? I don't make that connection yet." Well, I figured you would be stubborn and cantankerous no matter how much I show off God's Word to be proven true. Sometimes I do not know what you need to be convinced, but in case you still need to be convinced let me keep convincing you with God's Word and how it verifies itself because we are speaking of the cup of wrath, both in Revelation 14 and now introduced here in Jeremiah 25.

"And they shall drink, and be moved, and be mad, because of the sword [really the *mouth of the sword*] *that I will send among them. Then took I the cup at the LORD'S hand, and made all the nations to drink, unto whom the LORD had sent me."* Like it or not, these nations are going to drink this cup of anger, this wrath that is coming! God will have the last word. The day of vengeance is coming, folks.

"But what about disobedient people, not followers of Jesus Christ, but are not part of Islam?" Their day is coming also but let's stay focused on what God is speaking of here.

"Then took I the cup at the LORD'S hand, and made all the nations to drink, unto whom the LORD had sent me: To wit, [scratch out *to wit*, that was added by the translator] *Jerusalem, and the cities of Judah, and the kings thereof, and the princes thereof, to make them a desolation, an astonishment, a hissing, and a curse; as it is this day."*

That is a loaded verse, but most read right through it. I believe this pertains to a certain section of Jerusalem and a certain area of Judah, what consists of Judah. Unless you break it down in the Hebrew and understand it is tied in with Revelation 14, you will miss the unbelievable riches in this verse that points to where we are now, folks. *"thereof, to make them a desolation, an astonishment, a hissing, and a curse; as it is* [scratch out *it is*] *this day."* This is how that latter part should be translated: *a place laid with desolation.* We are still speaking of Jerusalem here, folks. What is in Jerusalem? The Abomination of Desolation. Isn't it? The Abomination of Desolation. Remember, Jeremiah is writing before Daniel ever got the information from God about the Abomination of Desolation: *a place laid with desolation, mocking.* The Dome of the Rock sits there claiming that God had no Son and there is no such thing as the Holy Spirit. That Abomination of Desolation sits there and mocks TO THIS DAY. I will go into detail on that in future teaching. Of course, here before Daniel's time it is just called a desolation. *"A place laid with desolation, mocking, and a 'qelalah' at this time."* The Hebrew wording here can be translated *hour, time, day* or even *at a particular time*, but I translated it (if you fit it in with everything being communicated here in this verse) as *at this time.* So, the translation should read like this: *Jerusalem, and the cities of Judah, and the kings thereof, and the princes thereof, to make or a place that is laid with desolation, mocking, and a qelalah; at this time.*

Kind of a coincidence with *alah* being a part of the word *qelalah*, isn't it? *Qelalah* means *when God despises or curses.* That is how it is most often used in the King James and other translations. It means *when God despises or curses or holds something or someone in contempt.* We already covered the Abomination of Desolation that sits in Jerusalem. God despises, He does curse, and He holds it in contempt and what it represents. The way you find *qelalah* used, the way the Lord uses *qelalah*, is when someone or something is no longer sacred or holy according to Scriptures. In other words, it is a cursed person or thing; in this case, a thing.

Jeremiah did not know about the Abomination of Desolation. "You are just inputting that information without any verification." Well, what else sits in Jerusalem! And if these verses tie into Revelation 14 of what is still yet to come, what sits there now as a desolation, something that was laid that stands there mocking? WHAT ELSE? I am all ears. Let me know. You will see the contact information at the end of this teaching. Call or write me. What else is there in Jerusalem that is a desolation, which is an abomination that stands there mocking, **which God despises, curses and holds in contempt?**

So, He starts with Jerusalem, and of course that is where all the contention is. Iran wants to eliminate Israel and control Jerusalem; Egypt wants to eliminate Israel and control Jerusalem; Saudi Arabia, Syria, Lebanon, Turkey, Libya, anything that the 8th Beast controls as far as the nation's go. God starts with Jerusalem and He is talking about the cities of Jerusalem and the kings thereof and the princes. If you look at the structure now, especially the Palestinians and how they are structured, both in the Gaza Strip and in the Samaria area, where Bethlehem is located and north of that, there are different princes and rulers. God is going to deal with them. He is going to deal with that curse that is standing there on the mount, and then He is going to move onto *Pharaoh king of Egypt, and his servants.*

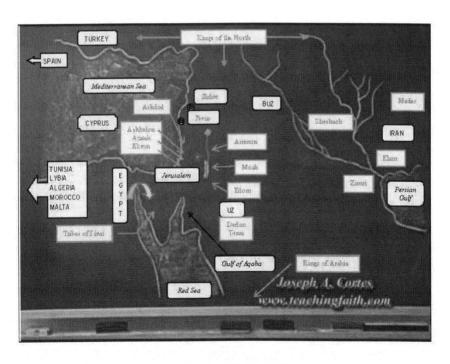

THE 8th BEAST NATIONS

Above is a map of the Middle East. Jerusalem is designated by the star. Of course, we see the Mediterranean Sea along with the Dead Sea and the Sea of Galilee which are just east of Jerusalem. We also have the Red Sea and the Gulf of Aqaba which Moses crossed. And then to the east we see the Persian Gulf along with the Tigris and Euphrates Rivers.

We already know Jerusalem and God is going to deal with that, but we also have Egypt and, of course, Egypt controls the Sinai Peninsula at this time so that is one of the locations. We know Egypt being the first location God is going to deal with when He comes back.

Now is it possible that Egypt and maybe even Syria might be dealt with by Israel in a war, which I have not gotten to yet, before God puts the last finishing touches on these nations that are part of the 8th Beast? That is possible. I will get to that but until I do, let's just go with who God says is going to receive His cup of wrath.

What is next on the list? *"Pharaoh king of Egypt, and his servants, and his princes, and all his people; And all the mingled people..."* Now mingled people means any foreigners and this could mean anywhere in the world that affiliates themselves and are on the side of the 8th Beast against Israel and Jerusalem. It could also mean tribes of Sinai because foreigners were also known as these tribes at the time when Jeremiah was writing this; but not The Lost Tribes, the Tribes of Sinai. Now, I think it has a multiple application. It could mean tribes that are in Sinai. I mean, Al-Qaeda is trying to get a stronghold in Sinai right now, the Sinai Peninsula, but it also means foreigners, or anyone that affiliates with the 8th Beast.

Let's move on: *"and all the kings of the land of Uz"*. Now where were the kings of the land of Uz? Remember, that is where Job was located in Scripture. You can see the location of Uz on the map. It would be located in the area of Southern Jordan today and the very northern part of Saudi Arabia at its border. That is Uz. "So, is Uz part of the Islamic 8th Beast today?" Absolutely. In fact, everything that I will point out on the map is part of the 8th Beast.

So what else do we have in scripture? *"And all the mingled people, and all the kings of the land of Uz, and all the kings of the land of the Philistines..."* This would be the general area designated by Ashkelon, Azzah, Ekron, and the remnant of Ashdod on our map. And actually, Ekron would cover even a bit more territory toward the east-south-east other than just the sea coast of Israel. Those are the areas here in Scripture. The question we must ask ourselves again is: Are those nations of this final beast, this 8th Beast? And, of course, the answer would be, absolutely. Ashdod, Ekron, Azzah, and Ashkelon (all these areas where the Philistines dwelt) are on the west side of Jerusalem.

Next on our list from Jeremiah 25 is Edom and Moab in verse 21, *"Edom, and Moab, and the children of Ammon."* They are located on the east side of the Dead Sea and the Sea of Galilee. So, all these three nations on the map would once again cover mostly all of Jordan. Some scholars that follow and map these out geographically believe that Edom could have touched the northern parts of Saudi Arabia also. I tend to believe that too. And Uz covers an additional area even a little further south from its simple designation on the map. Are they part of the 8th Beast? Yes. Jerusalem is covered on both sides. If you have a Bible map, I suggest you look at it also and write these things in if you do not have them in already. Some will include these different nations.

Verse 22, *"And all the kings of Tyrus, and all the kings of Zidon..."* Now where are Tyrus and Zidon? What is in the general area that comprises Zidon and Tyrus today? Well, this is Lebanon, folks.

Therefore, we have Lebanon, Jordan, Gaza, and we have so far just the northern tip of the Saudi Arabian nation in our Jeremiah 25 list. We have the Sinai Peninsula with the foreigners and we have Egypt (which also at this point controls the Sinai Peninsula.) So, we have all these areas so far in Scripture. And guess what? Do you think it is by coincidence that the Muslim Brotherhood is now in control of Egypt and are trying and get control of Syria also? They are getting control of Libya, Tunisia, Morocco, you name it. They are trying, at a very rapid pace, to overtake these areas and control the whole area because they want a caliphate to come on the scene that would control these 8th Beast areas of nations and then expand onto the rest of the world.

Now we have all the kings of Tyrus in verse 22, *"and all the kings of Zidon, and the kings of the isles which are beyond the sea. "*Now this is an interesting one; *the kings of the isles which are beyond the sea*. What does that mean? Literally it means coastland regions. Now I do not have time, but if you track the two areas that were coastland regions referred to in Scripture, over and over again it is Cyprus and Southern Spain. So, this is why you see Cyprus and Spain on the map. And, of course, it would be just the southern tip of Spain on the coastland and also, by the way, some southern islands that are just south of Italy today. So, you have Cyprus, southern islands of Italy, and the southern coastline of Spain. Interesting, isn't it?

In other words, the Muslims want to get back to areas they controlled before. The last time they controlled it, some of these areas were under the Ottoman Empire. But it was the last time where they had complete control and they were pretty much the dominant force. And, of course, if it wasn't for Charles 'The Hammer' Martel, they would have moved onto Northern France and most of northern Western Europe. Their goal was to get to the British Isles, what we call England today, which consists of Scotland and Ireland now, what we call the United Kingdom.

So, Cyprus is falling fast and is pretty much predominantly Islamic already. In Southern Spain, the influence of the Islamic Empire is becoming stronger and stronger. So is Southern France. Now, some people believe some southern coasts of France should also be included in this category of the *isles which are beyond the sea*. Now it can be, and if you look at France today, one of the biggest preoccupations outside of their financial crisis is dealing with the Islamics that are living there. And, of course, anyone that knows the Islamic overall plan, it is to so populate Europe with the Muslim people that by sheer numbers they would eventually control or put someone in political office or the offices that become available one after another so they can control the area with their political influence. Those things are happening. Can France or

Spain push back? If they want to. Will they be successful? I believe they could be, but I also believe that if it is Cyprus, then Cyprus has already lost the battle; but, if it is Spain also (because it could go either way or both ways) then only time will tell but the possibilities are there.

Now let's move on and look into another area. We have *"all the kings of Tyrus, and all the kings of Zidon, and the kings of the isles which are beyond the sea, Dedan, and Tema"*. Dedan and Tema are in Saudi Arabia country, the nation of Saudi Arabia. So back to the same question I asked at the beginning of this particular segment on the map: Are these 8th Beast nations? The answer is, yes, they are. Dedan and Tema are part of Saudi Arabia and part of the 8th Beast.

So everything that God is referring to, starting with Jerusalem and the Abomination of Desolation, is controlled by the 8th Beast. "Well I thought Israel controls Jerusalem?" Not yet, but listen, if Israel had their way that Dome of the Rock would be destroyed already but they don't. Do not think that they do because they do not. That is all I will say for now. So Dedan and Tema is Saudi Arabia.

"and Buz" - Buz is between the southeast section of Syria, the northeast section of Jordan, and the most westerly portions along the border of Iraq. That is where Buz is located.

Now Jeremiah is writing for his time by what he can identify with, so the question is once again, is this in the territory of the 8th Beast? Is this nation here described in Jeremiah part of that territory today? Once again, the answer is: Absolutely.

And then the next one (*the utmost corners*) is kind of interesting, so I want to come to that one last.

Verse 24: *"And all the kings of Arabia, and all the kings of the mingled people"*. All the kings of Arabia would go all the way down to what we call Oman and Yemen and all those areas along that Saudi Arabian Peninsula. Is that part of the geographical territory of the 8th Beast? The answer is yes.

Okay, moving on: *"and all the kings of the mingled people"*. "But what about the utmost corners?" I am going to come back to that last. *"and all the kings of the mingled people"*. What are *the kings of the mingled people that dwell in the desert?* That is everyone else in the Saudi Arabian Peninsula.

"And all the kings of Zimri". Now where is Zimri? Zimri would be the southwest section of Kuwait today and part of the northern eastern location of the border of Saudi Arabia. That is where Zimri would be located in biblical times, but it would be the southwestern part of Kuwait and also the northeastern part, but more the border location of where Saudi Arabia exists today. You got it. That is Zimri.

Who is next? *"And all the kings of Zimri, and all the kings of Elam..."* Now where is Elam? I have not preached that yet. That is the southern section of present day Iran.

"and all the kings of the Medes". That would be the northern section of Iran, and possibly even the most western northern location of Afghanistan.

So back to the question: Is Zimri part of the 8th Beast nations' geographical location? The answer is yes. Is Elam part of the 8th Beast? The answer is yes. Are the Medes (Northern Iran) part of that geographical location we find in Jeremiah 25 that God is still going to deal with in Revelation 14 when He makes them drink His cup of wrath, His cup of indignation? The answer is yes. Yes, yes, yes... to ALL of them. They are all in the area of the 8th Beast that God is dealing with and is going to be dealing with when He puts His closure on all this insanity that Jeremiah 25 refers to in verse 16, that they boast about and what is sitting there in Jerusalem as a desolation, mocking, a curse, a *qelalah* at this time. All this will be dealt with.

Verse 26: *"And all the kings of the north, far and near, one with another, and all the kingdoms of the world, which are upon the face of the earth: and the king of Sheshach shall drink after them."* Sheshach is the area of Babylon. Sheshach is Iraq. Okay, where are the other ones? Kings of The North: This includes Turkey, some areas of Eastern Europe, the Armenian areas, all the 'stans' and possibly even Russia! We will get to that. Those are considered The Kings of The North.

"Well what used to be the Soviet Union are not Islamic nations." Oh really! All those 'stans' no matter what they are or what they are called are predominantly Islamic and I will touch on that when I get to the Gog Magog war, but not yet.

So we have the Kings of The North. Are they influenced by the 8th Beast nations? Absolutely. Is Turkey? Well, I think you can see that for yourself. Absolutely. Nothing is left out in God's Word, folks.

"Okay, but you missed *the utmost corners* if you go back to verse 23. That has to mean everyone else." This is the error that a lot of scholars make. *"Dedan, and Tema, and Buz, and all that are in the utmost corners."* You know how that should be translated? Check the Hebrew. It should be translated *all having the corners of their hair pulled or polled.*

"What! What does that mean and who does that?" Well, you must dig in history to get the answer to that, folks. The Macians came along in history… and it is hard to find history, which is why you must become a biblical detective to find much history on the Macians. Let me read you something. This is a Pulpit Commentary, a very respected commentary. If you buy the hard cover editions, you could spend almost $400 for the set. *All that are in the utmost corners.* What does that mean?

> *Rather all that are corner clipped that have hair cut off about the ears and temples.*

Okay.

> *Herodotus tells us, speaking of the Arabs, their practice is to cut the hair in a ring away from the temples.*

That is pretty much it, folks. That does not really tell us much. Spend $400 for that?! Now I am not saying not to buy the Pulpit Commentary. What I am saying is they give just a little and you have to go dig for information if you want to find the truth of what these scriptures are really telling us. The information just leaps off the page if you know where to look. And, of course, you have to dig into history, and I do not have time to go into it right now, but the **utmost corners** refer to a people. In this case (and you have to take my word for it at this point), it was the people called the Macians. These are people that would cut their hair in a certain way and they could be identified as far back as 1500 BC. Now who were they? The Macians were people that were from the Phoenicians along the Lebanon area and some of the northern Gazan areas of today that first went to settle certain areas of Northern Africa as far back at 1500 BC. I believe it even goes further back than that.

Now everybody has heard of Carthage and the Punic Wars. If not, you could look up the history of that. Carthage was famous for it. Now where is Carthage? In Tunisia. Isn't that kind of ironic? The Arab Spring that we have been dealing with and watching on the news now for about a year and a half started in Tunisia, a stone's throw away from ancient Carthage. How ironic is that!

Now, the Macians were people that left the Phoenician areas and took a settlement group and went to Tunisia today, the Carthage area, and settled there. They were Baal worshippers. They were big on child sacrifices. There have been so many discoveries; archeological digs of babies after babies being buried that were sacrificed to these gods. Now the Macians also settled outside of Tunisia in areas such as Libya, which we find in Scripture that God is going to deal with them too. Are they part of those nations that will drink the cup of wrath? Absolutely. If you follow the coastline of Northern Africa there is Egypt, Libya, Tunisia, Algeria, Malta and the Morocco areas, from east to west and people that are defined here in Scripture as having the corners of their hair pulled. And of course, if you dig deep enough and you look for people who fit that description in history, the only ones that fit the bill are the Macians. Here is one of the traditions they had. Recalling Leviticus 19:27:

The tribes under Moses' direction, getting the instructions from God, were forbidden to shave or trim around the head or leaving a tuff of hair on top because that would be mimicking or emulating pagan deities.

So they were forbidden to do that because God did not want the children of Israel, when they went into these areas, to copy pagan traditions or practices which would lead to identifying them by association. Even if they did not practice, they were not to even by appearance seem connected with these pagan cults. God wanted Israel to have nothing to do with them.

Let's look at what the Macians' traditions were and if it fits the description in Jeremiah 25:23.

Among the ancients the hair was often used in divination. The worshippers of the stars and planets cut their hair evenly around, trimming the extremities. According to Herodotus, the Arabs were accustomed to shave the hair around their head and left the tuffs stand upon the crown in honor of Bacchus.

Bacchus came later in history, but he was a Roman god. What kind of god was he? He was a Roman god of wine. (How ironic.) He was a Roman god of intoxication. He was a Roman god of orgies. In fact, it became so bad the Romans around 120 BC (my date might be off a few decades) outlawed it. Now this false god was none other than the extension of Dionysus, which can be dated back as far as 1500 BC, the Macians' god that traveled with them when they went to these other areas. Now which false god they have is neither here nor there. What you do have to remember are the areas that Jeremiah 25 was referring to: Tunisia, Libya, Algeria, Morocco and Malta and all the areas along the northern part of Northern Africa all the way to the Atlantic Ocean.

When the 7th Beast was conquering, not only did it go east, it also went west. It crossed the Mediterranean at the Strait of Gibraltar and went into Spain, and then into Southern France where eventually it met up with Charles 'The Hammer' Martel. Retreating in defeat, they then settled in the areas of Buz and Sheshach spreading east and north. Then the Ottoman Empire developed and conquered Eastern Europe, which will be part of the Kings of the North, but that is for another subject for another time. So, Tunisia, Libya, Algeria, Morocco and Malta. The question again: Are these nations a part of the 8th Beast geographically? The answer is yes.

God is referring to the nations listed in Jeremiah 25 that we find existing on our map today. They are not in the 'no more' condition which we read in Jeremiah 25:27, *"Therefore thou shalt say unto them, thus saith the LORD of hosts, the God of Israel; Drink ye, and be drunken, and spew, and fall, and rise no more..."* That does not exist in today's world. They are there, every single one of these nations, including the Kings of the North which I will identify at a later time. They still exist today. Therefore, either God's Word is a lie or Jeremiah was not talking about this period shortly after Nebuchadnezzar but a time in the future, which we can now locate in Revelation 14.

Before we go there let's read Jeremiah 25:28, *"And it shall be, if they refuse to take the cup at thine hand to drink, then shalt thou say unto them, Thus saith the LORD of hosts; Ye shall certainly drink."* Ye shall certainly drink. They are not going to have a choice. They are going to drink that cup of wrath. See, God has already won this victory. They just refuse to believe it but they are going to be forced to drink it.

Back to Revelation 14:10, *"The same shall drink of the wine of the wrath of God"*. Who? The ones that worshipped the Beast. Do all these nations on the map worship the Beast? Yes. And receive his mark? Yes, because they do serve in the name of Allah and worship the Beast and his image. Yes, to all three. *"The same shall drink of the wine of the wrath of God, which is poured out without mixture into the cup of his wrath; and he shall be tormented with fire and brimstone in the presence of the holy angels, and in the presence of the [holy] Lamb: And the smoke of their torment ascendeth up for ever and ever: and they have no rest day nor night, who worship the beast and his image, and whosoever receiveth the mark of his name. Here is the patience of the saints: here are they that keep the commandments of God, and the faith of Jesus. And I heard a voice from heaven saying unto me, Write, Blessed are the dead which die in the Lord from henceforth: Yea, saith the Spirit, that they may rest from their labours; and their works".* The word there is *ergon.* It always involves the employment of something. In the secular sense, the work you do like a nine-to-five job. In the work of the Lord, the employment of the Word should be applied there. Let's read it that way: *"and the employment of the word do follow them."* Why? Because they are still yet to be rewarded.

My friends, God will have the last say. He will force every single one of these nations shown on the map, and the ones that I have not included yet because I have not gotten into the Kings of the North, to drink the cup of His wrath. All of them; those that associate and align themselves with the 8th Beast, which could mean anyone in the world, but more specifically those I've pointed out on the map. Jeremiah put the road map out their thousands of years in advance. These nations still exist today. They are still unified now under the 8th Beast with a purpose and that is to conquer Israel, eliminate God's people, the Jews. From the Muslim perspective, they are the Little Satan. Every one of these nations has a bigger plan that they hope they can achieve and that is to get rid of the Great Satan which is the United States of America, and any other country that might associate with it. That could mean Great Britain also and any other tribal location where the lost tribes went to, but let's just stick with Ephraim and Manasseh for now—Ephraim being the younger but stronger brother in this case.

This road map of nations that Jeremiah laid out thousands of years in advance, who still exists today, are not a Jeremiah verse 27 situation or else God's Word is a lie. They do exist. There is no such thing as '*no more*' with these nations. They still exist so Jeremiah was looking in the future not knowing exactly what we know today, knowing less than even Daniel knew, but he knew enough to lay it out in Scripture because God gave him the information.

Hebrews 11 says, *"faith is the substance of things hoped for";* more accurately stated, *Faith is the FOUNDATION of things hoped for:* the hearing and being persuaded that God's Word has already laid up a foundation for us. How can we not be convinced that God's Word is true? **The evidence is the proof!** We have it through Scripture. No matter how you look at it, Revelation 14 ties in with Jeremiah 25 and Jeremiah 25 ties in with Revelation 14. Jeremiah foresaw it. John also foreseeing the end does not really get into the 8th Beast, but all he knows is the followers of the 8th Beast that take his mark, that worship the image, and puts on the necessary garments that allows the world to see who they serve, and they are going to be dealt with. They are going to drink this cup of wrath.

So, the question is: Are these the only two locations that we have in God's Word or anything else that ties all this together? No! There is more.

The Last Days Study Guide
The Mark of The Beast Part 11

1. What clue do we have in Jeremiah 25:27 that tell us this prophecy was not fulfilled during the time of Nebuchadnezzar?

2. What is the definition of *qelalah*?

3. In Jeremiah 25:18, who is made an astonishment, a hissing and a curse?

4. Where is Sheshach located today?

5. Who is "**all in the utmost corners**" referring to?

6. Rome outlawed the worship of what pagan god?

7. What location is "**all the kings of the mingled people**" referring to?

8. Edom, Moab and Ammon comprise most of the area commonly known today as?

9. What is the desire of all these Muslim nations?

10. What is "*a place of desolation*" referencing?

The Mark of the Beast Part 12

Open your Bible to Revelation 14.

This Mark of the Beast segment of *The Last Days* series is not the commonly preached Christian science fiction teaching most have heard before. We looked at what the true mark of the beast is. We broke down the 666 theories. So, with that I want to pick up where I left off.

Revelation 14:9, *"And the third angel followed them, saying with a loud voice, If any man worship the beast and his image,* [we already covered what that is] *and receive his mark* [we also looked at that] *in his forehead, or in his hand,* [*or in his arm* literally] *The same shall drink of the wine of the wrath of God,* [that is what we looked at] *which is poured out without mixture into the cup of his indignation* [or *wrath*] *; and he shall be tormented with fire and brimstone in the presence of the holy angels, and in the presence of the Lamb. And the smoke of their torment ascendeth up for ever and ever: and they have no rest day nor night, who worship the beast and his image, and whosoever receiveth the mark of his name."*

At this point in Revelation 14 is where we went to Jeremiah 25 and looked at the cup of wrath for the nations and found how God is going to deal with those nations in the future. Then starting with Jeremiah 25:15, because Jeremiah is very precise and very specific to whom God is referring to, I mapped out the nations (pg. 140) one by one and where they are located geographically.

Let's just do a quick review of the cup of wrath nation starting at Jeremiah 25:15: We have Ammon, Moab, Edom, Uz, Dedan, Tema. And around the

Gaza area today, we looked at Ashdod, Ashkelon, and Ekron. Then we also looked at the Tribes of Sinai, which also includes Egypt because the Sinai Peninsula is part of Egypt today. We also listed who the individuals were in verse 23, *"Dedan, and Tema, and Buz, and all that are in the utmost corners."* I took at little bit of time and gave you the history on who these people *in the utmost corners* were. As I laid out the history, we found we could find these people in Libya, Algeria, Tunisia, Morocco and Malta; all the northern coast of Africa. Now, the nation of Islam is spreading into other areas of Africa today, moving south. Remember there are also a mingled people in this list in Jeremiah 25. The mingled people basically were foreigners which would include anybody that eventually would associate with the 8th Beast nations, any nation in this world that is going to associate and take up sides with the 8th Beast, Islam. These are the 8th Beast nations in Revelation 14. So one by one, we mapped these nations. We looked at Zimri. That would be in the northeastern section of Saudi Arabia and the southwestern section of Kuwait. We looked at Elam which is in Iran, and the Medes, Northern Iran, and even extending outward towards Afghanistan and possibly Pakistan. Then Sheshach would be the Iraq area, and then Tyrus and Zidon which are also listed in Jeremiah 25. The coastlands, which I said includes Cyprus, but it could also include as far west as the southern portions of the coastland of Spain and all the area around the Mediterranean coming back east all the way to Israel which means Southern Turkey, Greece, portions of Italy, portions of even Southern France.

Now the Kings of the North, which I did not get into, would also include Turkey and other Eastern European nations as far as Russia, meaning all the 'stans' that broke away from the Soviet Union but still, believe it or not, are under the control of the Soviet Union. It is called Russia today, but it is still the Soviet Union. Do not be fooled by just a name change. But anyway, I do not want to dwell on that because I said I would come back to the Kings of the North in the future, especially when I get into the Gog and Magog verses you find in Ezekiel and other places. So, that is the general area on the map listing all the nations God listed in Jeremiah 25 that would receive the cup of wrath.

Continuing with Jeremiah 25:30, it goes onto say, *"Therefore prophesy thou against them all;" everyone* on this list in Jeremiah 25 and all the nations on the map plus foreigners who will associate and take sides with the 8th Beast. *"Therefore prophesy thou against them all these words, and say unto them, The LORD shall roar..."* He is not going to be quiet. He is going to roar. The time is coming, folks. *"The LORD shall roar from on high, and utter his voice from his holy habitation; he shall mightily roar upon his habitation; he shall give a shout, as they that tread the grapes, against all the inhabitants of the earth* [or the land; either one is fine].*"* Which inhabitants? Everyone that is listed in chapter 25, all that geographical area on the map plus any foreigners, the mingled people. *"A noise shall come even to the ends of the earth* [or land]*; for the LORD hath a controversy with the nations: he will plead with all flesh; he will give them that are wicked to the sword".* You can find many references to that in the book of Revelation and other places. *"Thus saith the LORD of hosts, behold, evil shall go forth from nation to nation, and a great whirlwind shall be raised up from the coasts of the earth* [or land]. *And the slain of the LORD shall be at that day from one end of the earth* [or land] *even unto the other end of the earth* [or land]*: they shall not be lamented, neither gathered".* They shall not be lamented. Once God is finished, once Jesus Christ is done roaring from His holy habitation, these 8th Beast nations and anyone that associates with them shall not be lamented, *"neither gathered, nor buried; they shall be dung upon the ground."* I want to use street language and I cannot, but God says they shall be *dung* on the ground.

God's anger, God's wrath is not going away. It has been building up. The cup through the centuries and millenniums has become fuller and fuller to the brim, folks. It is full to the brim and it is about to spill over and God is going to deal with this 8th Beast nation and anyone that associates with it. He is going to deal with others outside of this. The book of Romans makes that very clear. All the ones not saved by the blood of Jesus Christ are going to be dealt with by God. That is coming. But in these verses in Revelation 14 & Jeremiah 25, He is dealing with the nations that will receive this particular cup of wrath because of their alignment with the 8th Beast, Islam and its false prophet Muhammad. They are not going to be on the right side. They will be against Israel, God's chosen people—and that is a little bit more than just that sliver of land, by the way. We will come back to that too in the future. So, do you understand? That is just a quick review. I just wanted to go a little further.

Now, God's wrath is not something we should be concerned with if we are in Christ Jesus. God took that wrath for us. Someone asked the question: "Could a Muslim become saved that is or isn't associated with this 8th Beast, because really they still worship a moon god, a false god?" Absolutely. "Well haven't they blasphemed against the Holy Spirit?" Well haven't all sinners! Those scriptures have been taken out of context to throw condemnation and guilt upon people; unfortunately, not to give them any hope in most cases but condemnation. Of course, they have the same opportunity. That is why we try to let people know in this particular area where the cup of wrath is about ready to be poured out, to know that there is hope in salvation. It is not in Allah, it is not in anything that Muhammad put together as a false religion. It is in Christ Jesus. That is why this ministry exists.

There are two cups: the **cup of redemption** offered by Christ that provides eternal life. It is available to those who trust and faithe in Him alone and what He did at the *stauros*. There is nothing that we can do to earn it. You can try to be a goodie-two-shoes all you want. See how far you get. Without Christ we are nothing. In Christ, there is eternal life and we are a precious gem in His eyes. Then there is the **cup of wrath** and that is what we have been generally looking at in this message and the last message. I want to continue that.

Before I go any further I want to look at Matthew 26. Why is the cup of wrath so important to understand? I had a message come in that said she has never heard anybody teach on it. I can tell you that you have never heard anybody preach on it the way I am going to present it because I have never heard it. It is something more should do. Hopefully this will encourage preachers to do it. Everyone knows the Matthew 26 story (Jesus praying in Gethsemane after the Lord's Supper). He takes a few disciples to go pray and prepare for what was lying ahead of Him still, and that was going to the *stauros*, the stake on which He was hung. Assuming you know the story let's just pick it up with verse 39.

"And he went a little farther, and fell on his face, and prayed, saying, O my Father, if it be possible..."

To tell you the truth, I do not think people really grasp completely what Christ went through on that stake. I do not think we can. Of course, everybody that teaches on this subject says that He suffered all kinds of pains and sorrows with both mental and physical anguish. The problem is that is where they stop, and they do not go any further. Believe me, that was enough; but if that is all that Christ suffered was on that *stauros*, that stake, it would not have been sufficient in God's eyes. Yes, you heard me right and you probably have never heard anybody say that before and that is the unfortunate part. It will become clearer to you as I progress in this message, so stay with me. Do not tune me out yet. I am not a nut. I base my messages on God's Word and I prove it out. Christ knew what was lying ahead for Him. He knew it was not just a mental anguish that He would suffer, not just all the physical beatings, the whippings, being punched, having thorns pierced in His skull, suffering abuse that would kill most men, then hung on a *stauros* (stake) to die, and pierced with a spear in His side. All the physical anguish and suffering is beyond anybody's comprehension. I am not taking anything away from that, God forbid, but that alone would not have fulfilled the requirement in God's eyes for our reconciliation back to the Father. Sorry, I know that is what you are taught, and I am not against those who teach that. They just have not gone far enough because Scripture tells us more than that. "Well, I have never seen it!" That is another problem.

That is why I present a different opinion about faith, *pistis*. Listen, I was taught that faith is 90% courage. Well, that is fine but not *pistis* faith. You have to be hearing something to become persuaded before you can even get to the level of having courage on what you heard to be true, to act upon it and to have the confidence that God's Word is real. That is why I broke down *pistis* as *the hearing and the persuading.* If you look at all the Greek classical writings, that is always what it meant for the most part. Translators and people that want to put their own definitions to how God would use the word if He was defining it have changed its meaning somewhat. But a *pistis* type of response means that you heard or are hearing something to become persuaded eventually, because faith comes by hearing and hearing. Most of the time it needs to be heard over and over, so you eventually become persuaded by what you hear, and you are convinced now it is true. Then you move onto a *pisteuo* level of faith, the so-be-it faith. Some people call it the amen faith. Look at Lockyer, he called it the "amen faith" 110 years ago. It is nothing new. I said it is the so-be-it faith: "God said it. I am not at that level, but I am so persuaded by what I heard to be true that you cannot convince me any different. My total confidence is in God's Word." That is the *pisteuo* level of faith. That is the level we need to maintain also, plus the *pistis*, hearing and becoming persuaded. There is an abundant amount of truth in God's Word, so much so that you cannot exhaust it. But I have gotten off track. I could go on another message with that, but I do not want to. I need to stay on course.

Christ knew what was ahead at that stake and it was not just the mental and physical anguish that He would go through and suffering. It goes way beyond that, folks, because like I said, if that is all He had to suffer and that was enough, it still would not satisfy God's requirement. Christ had to step in and take that **cup of wrath** for sinners. We will find as we move forward, and I get into all the vials and the plagues (when the cup of wrath is brought up again) some horrible, horrible things that have been happening and are going to happen that will cause a lot of suffering, but even that would not fulfill it if that is all Christ absorbed on that *stauros*, on that stake. Even that would not have been enough. He had to go somewhere that nobody ever went to and come back from it. That is why you find here (and I will get to that in a minute), *"O my Father, if it be possible..."* because He knew the consequences, *"let this cup pass from me"*. This is not the cup that we find earlier in this chapter when they are at the Last Supper meal. "Wasn't it the Passover meal?" I started to teach on that before, but I did not get a chance to finish that. I will come back to it. Let's just call it the Last Supper meal for now.

He had a chance and He said he would not drink of it, but He had to take the cup of wrath first for sinners which would involve something beyond just physical pain that He would suffer while He was still in the land of the living in the physical sense. *"O my Father, if it be possible, let this cup pass from me: nevertheless, not as I will..."* Remember that word *thelema*. *"but as thou wilt."* What Christ is saying is, "Not my desires, not my will, but Yours. The whole reason I am here in the first place is to eventually get to the point where that cup of wrath is something that I will absorb for the ones that will faithe in Me. Then they will never experience it because they are in Me. They became righteous because of Me. Now they are full of righteousness because they are imputed, because they trust and have faith in Me. So therefore God, you cannot reject them, and you cannot dish out the cup of wrath through Me on them, but eventually only to the ones that don't."

And, of course, His disciples fell asleep and then again in verse 42, *"He went away again the second time, and prayed, saying, O my Father, if this cup..."* knowing what cup it was, *"may not pass away from me, except I drink it, thy will be done."* Like I said before, everybody is looking for what the will of God is. The will of God, the way Christ uses, is always denying Himself first to put what His Father wanted first. You want to find the will of God? Start with denying yourself, take up the cross. If you never understood what I said before about taking up the cross, I am sure you are going to have a whole new understanding of it soon. Hopefully it will hit you to a point where you will have no doubts about it any longer "and follow Me. Follow Me" in His likeness. We are not going to be Jesus Christ, but in His likeness. Doing what? Bringing the message of how people can be delivered from receiving this cup of wrath. Like I said there are two cups: the earlier cup you see in the Last Supper that represents eternal life; or the cup of wrath, which is something we are going to get to here in a second.

213

Let's just cover a few more scriptures before I move on. Go to Luke 22:42. We see this same thing again. *"Saying, Father, if thou be willing, remove this cup from me..."* These are not just idle words here, folks. Christ knew what He was saying. *"nevertheless, not my will,* [*thelema* again] *but thine, be done."*

John 18:10-11. Here Peter drew his sword as Jesus is being taken away from the garden after the prayer. *"Then Simon Peter having a sword drew it, and smote the high priest's servant, and cut off his right ear. The servant's name was Malchus. Then said Jesus unto Peter, Put up thy sword into the sheath: the cup which my Father has given me, shall I not drink it?"* Christ is past the point of asking if it could possibly be something that He would not have to go through. He is beyond that. There was no sin by Him in asking the Father if there was something other He could do besides drink it. If it was a sin, it would have been the first time in the Gospel record we'd have found Him sinning against the Father, but He didn't because it wasn't a sin. He asked, and obviously He answered His own question if the Father didn't. But let's just assume the Father didn't and He answered His own question because He already knew the answer. "No, it is not my will, but thine. I will take the cup." For whose benefit? For ours. He is going to take the cup of wrath for our benefit.

That is why it is so important to really understand Isaiah 53. I want to look at it. I am going to read through most of it until I get to a certain point. Verse 1, *"Who hath believed our report?"* [or *who hath believed our hearing*] *and to whom is the arm of the LORD revealed? For he shall grow up before him as a tender plant, and as a root out of a dry ground: he hath no form nor comeliness; and when we shall see him, there is no beauty that we should desire him. He is despised and rejected of men; a man of sorrows, and acquainted with grief..."* This is where that physical and mental pain comes in. *"and we hid as it were our faces from him; he was despised, and we esteemed him not. Surely he hath borne our griefs, and carried our sorrows: yet we did esteem him stricken, smitten of God, and afflicted. But he was wounded* [or literally *tormented*] *for our transgressions..."* He was tormented for our transgressions. *"he was bruised for our iniquities: the chastisement of our peace was upon him; and with his stripes* [or *bruises* literally] *we are healed."*

Now everyone takes this verse and applies it to physical healing. Did that happen? Listen, I have seen people struggle over this verse. I have seen people say to themselves, "You have to heal me. Your Word says you cannot say no to my physical healing because of what Jesus suffered on His cross." If that is what it said, they would be right but that is not what it says. It has never said that. We developed a doctrine to make it sound like it says that, but it never said that. I saw a great man of God struggle with that at the end of his life who taught that. Then when God was not going to provide his healing, the last ailment that he was suffering from before he graduated to be with Christ, he was saying, "You have to heal me. Your word says it. You cannot go back on your word." If God's Word said that, he would have been right. That is why just a month before he went onto glory he decided to preach just faith messages until his dying day. "Do you believe in healing? Do you believe that Christ can heal?" Without a doubt. There is no argument from me that Christ can heal if He chooses to do so. Whether He does or not, it should not turn or change the way you trust and faith in Him. If anything, it is better to say, "Well, you healed these, why not heal me, O Lord" if you choose to go that route, than say, "Your word says it. You have to do it."

I know I am upsetting some people. Listen, truth first. All other emotions need to check in at the door and if some nugget of truth can jump out and say, "Hey you know what, now I see it," then you know that shows you are a work in progress just like me, forever getting knowledge in God's Word that sheds some light on some of the tough issues that you might be struggling with – something that maybe you have been taught in the past, or something that you never heard before and you wish you had more enlightenment on it.

Go to 1 Peter 2:23, *"Who, when he was reviled, reviled not again; when he suffered, he threatened not..."* speaking of Christ here, *"but committed himself to him that judgeth righteously: Who his own self bare our sins in his own body..."* He bore our sins in His own body *"on the tree, that we, being dead to sins..."* A lot of people like to tie together Isaiah 53 with 1 Peter and they should because it is tied in together, but this is not talking about a physical ailment here. *"Who his own self bare our sins in his own body on the tree, that we, being dead to sins..."* a spiritual problem, *"should live".* So, if we are dead in sins our spiritual problem is healed, is cured. Even though this flesh and body no longer might exist if the Lord does not come back sooner instead of later, then guess what? We will go meet the Lord. Instead of meeting Him in the clouds, we will meet Him in the third heaven. *"Who his own self bare our sins in his own body on the tree, that we, being dead to sins, should live* [or literally *be among the living with all fullness and vigor*] *unto righteousness: by whose stripes ye were healed."* What is it talking about? What is Peter referring to? He is not referring to a physical disease like cancer or Alzheimer's, or whatever. "Do you believe God can heal those?" Absolutely! Do not twist my words. I believe there is healing in Jesus Christ. I do not think there is any other option except trusting in Him for that healing. There is no Plan B outside of that. What if you get healed by using modern medicine? Fine. Let God direct the doctors and physicians or surgeons. I have no problem with that. I have a problem with people that try to pull verses out of context.

"Who his own self bare our sins in his own body on the tree, that we, being dead to sins, should live unto righteousness: by whose stripes ye were healed. For ye were as sheep going astray..." We are talking about a spiritual problem, *"but are now returned unto the Shepherd..."* So, when you tie this in with Isaiah 53:5, *"But he was wounded* [or *bruised*] *for our transgressions, he was bruised for our iniquities: the chastisement of our peace was upon him..."* It was going to be up to Him. *"and with his stripes* [or *bruises*] *we are healed.* [or *we are healed with His bruised wounds in order to be healed*] *All we like sheep have gone astray, we have turned every one to his own way; and the LORD hath laid on him the iniquity of us all."* The Lord took it all and put it on Himself. *"He was oppressed, and he was afflicted, yet he opened not his mouth: he is brought as a lamb to the slaughter, and as a sheep before her shearers is dumb, so he openeth not his mouth. He was taken from prison*

216

and from judgment: and who shall declare his generation? for he was cut off out of the land of the living... "He was cut off out of the land of the living, *"for the transgression of my people was he stricken."* Or *was the stroke upon Him.* That did happen on that stake.

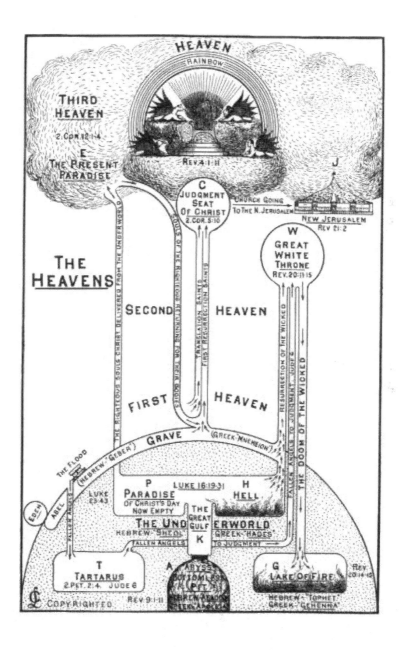

Therefore, I have redemption and why you have redemption but that is not the only reason why you have eternal life because if that is all that Christ accomplished on that stake, we would still have to bear the cup of wrath that someday at the end of all things is going to be poured, folks.

"What do you mean?"

Verse 9 (and this is where I wanted to get to), *"And he made his grave"*. The Hebrew word is very clear what type of grave; a pit or underworld. A pit or underworld with who? With the ones I have mentioned before that are in paradise—not paradise up in the air somewhere like the third heaven, no. Before Christ rose from the dead, there was no such thing. Well, it might have been there, but previous saints were not there waiting. They were somewhere else, and I already covered this in the Spiritual Warfare series. If you have never heard those messages, you need to hear them. Where was He? He was in the pit, the underworld, with the wicked. What a place to be! Remember, He had no sin, but He took all that upon Himself that we deserved. He took the cup of wrath. He took the iniquities, the transgressions, for the chastisement of our peace upon Him.

The photo above gives an illustration. The top left corner is the Third Heaven; then, of course, the Throne of God. Looking down you see the earth symbolized by that half circle. If you look straight down the center to the bottom of that picture you have the Abyss. Right above that you have the Gulf referenced to in Matthew 16, which I will go to in a minute. All that on the right and left side of the Gulf where you see Hell and Paradise is all considered Hades. See, saints that rose from the dead following the resurrection of Christ were not up in the Third Heaven. They were in Hades. Everyone thinks of Hades as just hell. I am sorry, it is not just hell. Scripture makes that very clear. Hades also included Paradise but there was a gulf between Hell and Paradise in the underworld. And on the bottom far left corner is Tartarus where the fallen angels before the flood reside until the very last Great White Throne Judgment where they will be judged and wind up in the Lake of Fire.

Go to Luke 16:19. This is just review of something I preached before in the Spiritual Warfare series. It kind of references what is shown in the photo. *"There was a certain rich man, which was clothed in purple and fine linen, and fared sumptuously every day: And there was a certain beggar named Lazarus* [basically a *helpless beggar*], *which was laid at his gate, full of sores, And desiring to be fed with the crumbs which fell from the rich man's table: moreover the dogs came and licked his sores. And it came to pass, that the beggar died, and was carried by the angels into Abraham's bosom: the rich man also died, and was buried;"* Now they are both dead *"and in hell,"* or literally Hades (Hades being that portion within the upper part of that half circle). *"And in Hades he lifted up his eyes, being in torments".* Who? That rich man. *"And in Hades he lifted up his eyes, being in torments, and seeth Abraham afar off, and Lazarus in his bosom* [or *in his arms*]. *"* If Abraham and all the saints prior to Christ's resurrection are in the third heaven, how in the world is this rich man seeing him? Scripture goes onto explain that. *"And he cried and said, Father Abraham, have mercy on me, and send Lazarus, that he may dip the tip of his finger in water, and cool my tongue; for I am tormented in this flame."* So, in that part of Hades, and let's just say the hell section, there were flames. *"But Abraham said, Son, remember that thou in thy lifetime receivedst thy good things, and likewise Lazarus evil things: but now he is comforted,* [or literally *strengthen and encouraged*] *and thou art tormented."* And here is something that you have to pay attention to in Scripture. *"And beside all this, between us and you there is a great gulf".* Literally *there is a gap, or a gulf or a chasm.* So, the bottom line is there is a section where you see hell on the right and paradise on the left and there is that great gulf in between. Lazarus the beggar was on the left in this case, according to this picture, in Abraham's arms being comforted and encouraged. *"there is a great gulf fixed: so that they which would pass from hence to you cannot".* So, this gulf is a gulf or gap that keeps them separated and is impassible. You cannot go from one side to another, in other words. *"so that they which would pass from hence to you cannot; neither can they pass to us, that would come from thence. Then he said, I pray thee therefore, father, that thou wouldest send him to my father's house: For I have five brethren, that he may testify* [or *earnestly repeatedly testify*] *unto them, lest they also come into this place of torment. Abraham saith unto him, They have Moses and the prophets; let them hear them. And he said, Nay, father Abraham: but if one went unto them from the dead, they will repent; And he said unto him, If they hear not Moses and the prophets, neither will they be persuaded, though one rose from the dead. "* Now obviously referring to something, that there will even be people in the future who will reject that Christ rose from the dead, so do not be so sure that they will listen.

So where did Christ go? Go back to Isaiah 53:9, *"And he made his grave".* He made his pit in the underworld. With that previous teaching, we just assumed that where Christ went was only in that underworld part where Paradise existed. Did He go there? Yes. Did He go there only? No. In fact, I believe He also went to Tartarus and I have already covered that in other teaching, but we see here in verse 9, *"And he made his grave* [in the pit or underworld] *with the wicked, and with the rich in his death".*

Every commentator that has ever written about these things wants to make the claim that because He was buried in Joseph of Arimathea's tomb, He was buried with the richer folk who could afford that type of tomb. If that is all you want to think on that verse that is fine. I cannot argue with that, but I think it goes into a deeper meaning which I am not going to go into at this time. It refers back also to the Lazarus story, but I want to move on from that point.

"And he made his grave in the pit or underworld *with the wicked".* Wicked there literally means *the godless and the unrighteous.* You are not going to find that where Abraham is dwelling, waiting for Christ to have victory over the grave. Because Christ rose and all the saints prior to Christ and after Christ rose from that paradise, they are now in the third heaven. That paradise section of Hades is empty now because if we die before the Lord comes back we would shoot straight to the third heaven waiting for all things to be fulfilled. *"And he made his grave".* He was placed in the pit or the underworld with the godless and the unrighteous. Why? *"and with the rich in his death".*

I do not know why the King James translated it just as death (singular) because it is plural — deaths. "Well what do you mean by that?" We know He died once. He died once on that cross. Remember when I said if that is all He did is to suffer the physical and mental anguish prior to the cross and on the cross that it still would not have satisfied the requirements His Father had for being reconciled back to Him? Christ knew that. That is why He could not say no and that is why He didn't. Even when He was sweating blood in that garden, He concluded that no matter what, this cup of wrath had to be endured by Him to save us from it. *"And he made his grave in the pit or underworld with the godless and unrighteous, and with the rich in his deaths"*. We know He was in the paradise section eventually, but I believe it was after experiencing this second death first.

What is this second death? The first death is when the physical body dies. The second death is something more horrible. Go back to Revelation 14 where the wrath of God is going to be poured out. The cup of His wrath is going to be poured into the cup *"and he shall be tormented with fire and brimstone in the presence of the holy angels, and in the presence of the Lamb. And the smoke of their torment ascendeth up for ever and ever: and they have no rest day nor night, who worship the beast and his image"*. I still have to get back to that forever and ever part, which I will do in the future. *"and they have no rest day nor night, who worship the beast and his image, and whosoever receiveth the mark of his name."* Not to mention what I already read in Jeremiah 25, plus other areas in Scripture that I do not have time to go into right now.

He had to suffer a second death just as the ones that are marked by the Islamic Beast and any of the ones that reject Jesus Christ will have the same experience. That is not just one death but two. Christ made His grave in the pit in the underworld with the wicked, the godless and the unrighteous, *"and with the rich in his deaths* [plural] *because he had done no violence, neither was any deceit in his mouth. Yet it pleased the LORD to bruise him; he hath put him to grief: when thou shalt make his soul an offering for sin,* [or literally *when his soul shall be made an offering for sin*] *he shall see his seed, he shall prolong his days, and the pleasure of the LORD shall prosper in his hand. He shall see of the travail of his soul, and shall be satisfied: by his knowledge shall my righteous servant justify many; for he shall bear their iniquities. Therefore will I divide him a portion with the great, and he shall divide the spoil with the strong; because he hath poured out his soul unto death: and he was numbered with the transgressors; and he bare the sin of many, and made intercession for the transgressors."*

He not only suffered the first death, but also the second death. The second death, the full cup of God's wrath, has experiences in the first death and what comes right before that, and the second death. God is not through once this physical body experiences the first death if we are not in Christ, but His cup of wrath also extends into the second death.

Like I said earlier, I am in awe. People around me say, "What are you thinking now?" Usually because they know I am thinking about something. Usually when I am dealing with secular things, I do not find myself in this state of mind and people around me that are very close know this. They know when I am in awe of something now because they know my habits, my personality and my characteristics. They know that I am in awe about something that Christ has done for us. I live in a state of awe, I live in a state of amazement because, like I said, no man could ever describe to you, including me, what Christ not only went through on that cross but what He had to experience in Hades in that second death. He had to experience both to fulfill God's requirement, what the cup of wrath for all mankind would be like and what they would experience if they did not faithe and trust in His Son. But those who do, those who do, will <u>never</u> have to experience that. "Well what if we are still here and the cup of wrath is being poured and sometime before the end of time we experience some of the physical ailments of that?" It is not directed towards you. You are in the world but not of the world. You are still going to experience some of the experiences of the world, but you are not of the world and the grave surely does not have any victory or sting as scripture declares. Christ has already given us that victory.

That is why I am in awe daily. I cannot go to the table of the Lord and not be in awe. What Christ went through… which no man can tell of because no man has ever done this and come back to tell the story in the first place; even the ones that died the first death because Father Time came calling for them—even if they are in Christ, they cannot come back and tell the story that Christ can tell because they never experienced the second death. They out their faith in God so they would not experience that second death. All they were waiting for before Christ is for God to deliver them from that part of the underworld paradise into the third heaven, a little closer to the throne of God. You get it?

I am in awe; I am speechless most of the time. That is why it has been hard for me to preach the resurrection message and I have heard some great ones, but even the greatest resurrection message I have heard or read leaves out this element that Christ had to suffer not just one death, and a horrible one, but a second one also to fulfill God's requirement that someone had to take the cup of wrath, so we could be reconciled back to Him. Christ did that. That is why I am dumbfounded when people are presented the truth and do not respond to it for whatever reasons they want to give or make excuses for.

Now we know that Christ went to the Paradise part because He made that statement and a promise to the thief on the cross, 'This day you shall be with me in paradise'. So Christ did go there too and I believe He went to Tartarus. I believe when He rose from the dead, prior to that physical resurrection into a new body that He had, or He was going to get, He had to spend time in Hades. I would not even doubt, and I cannot say this with any certainty, but it would not be a stretch of anyone's imagination that He had to spend time in the Lake of Fire also, not because of any sin that He did because He was sinless. He was the perfect unblemished Lamb. He was Jesus Christ, Son of God. The only way that He could finally bruise the head of the serpent which was promised in the beginning chapters of Genesis is He would have to experience everything that was delegated to us because of Adam's sin, and He did it. Once He fulfilled those requirements, He marched on through Paradise and He said, "Follow me saints! We are headed toward the heavenlies as I present my blood to my Father and say payment fulfilled. I have fulfilled all the requirements. I went into the pit, the underworld, where the godless and unrighteous are. I experienced that second death also." That curse was upon all of us but God and His Son, Jesus Christ, provided the way that we would no longer be cursed but rescued.

That is why this ministry exists. That is why we understand how important it is to not just think about ourselves. I said to you throughout this ministry, it starts with your connection with the Vine; be severed from it and see how long you last. But once that is connected and you keep that strong daily, **we are here for a purpose**. We have been rescued. So, let's start rescuing others. Deny yourself. It is not all about you. Thank God you have been saved by the blood of Jesus Christ and everything that He had to go through to fulfill God's requirement. Deny yourself. Take up the stake that Christ had to endure. That is why it says, "Remember Me, what I went through on that stake and beyond in the pit of the underworld and follow Me in my likeness. In other words, remember Me and tell others what I did for them and what I did for you."

Let's not rest until we are called home, or He comes back for us. I won't. That is why I get on your case on occasion. Did you forget the state of awe you should be in? Unfortunately, you do not hear that in too many churches these days because they are always trying to cater to your carnal flesh – How to make a better you and get what you want out of this world when you should be more concerned about the eternal rewards that are still yet to come, that go throughout eternity, presented to you, distributed because of what you did here. "Well, are you saying it is works for salvation?" No! What I referred to in that last statement has nothing to do with salvation. There is nothing you can do to be saved, that all depends upon Jesus Christ and whether you trust and faithe in Him. If you do not, guess what? You are probably following some false religion, some false god or just no god at all. But if you do, there is redemption.

That is why I want to go to the table of the Lord in this message. Christ suffered the first and second deaths, so you would not have to experience the torment of eternal damnation, for however long that is.

Go to Luke 22. Hopefully you have the elements to go to the table of the Lord. Verse 19, *"And he took bread, and gave thanks, and brake it, and gave unto them, saying, This is my body which is given for you: this do in remembrance of me."* Do this and remember the greatness of the sacrifice. *"Likewise also the cup after supper, saying, This cup is the new testament in my blood, which is shed for you."* That too you should do in remembrance according to Paul's letter to the Corinthians. His body, His blood, His life, taken from the land of the living, a man without any sin, the Son of God without any sin, the Son of man without any sin, the unblemished Lamb.

When I say the greatness of the sacrifice, in my opinion it goes beyond any understanding of the human mind because like I said earlier, there is no way we could understand both deaths if you never experienced it and lived to tell about it. That is why the rich man was pleading, "Go tell people in my family what it is like here; the torment that we are suffering, including myself. You do not want to come here." That is someone that was only concerned about himself throughout his life. Cared less about God, cared less about Jesus Christ. His only concern was for himself. "Go tell my family members. Tell them there is a rescue plan. Listen. Act upon it. Be saved by the blood of Jesus Christ. Do not come here." Well, guess what? Christ went there. Isaiah makes it very clear that He did. He went there so we would not have to absorb that part of the cup of wrath. Why wouldn't anybody want to be covered by the blood of Jesus Christ, and recognize the greatness of the sacrifice?

Most people go to the table of the Lord these days, so they can get something out of it. Do you not realize what you already got out of it? I am in awe of what Christ has done for me, what He had done for all of us. Do this in remembrance of Him. Do this and do not forget to tell others what Christ has done for all of us — ALL OF US. No exceptions.

Christians, especially in this country, and more developed countries around the world, have been fed a bunch of hogwash about how to make a better person out of yourself. First, any time you start doing that on your own, you probably form some self-righteous list to follow that would just put you right back where you started, not covered by the blood of Jesus Christ because you developed your own righteousness and are not imputed with God's righteousness which can only be provided through His son, Jesus Christ. Don't find yourself in that camp, folks.

Remember what He has done for us. Remember the greatness of His sacrifice. Remember the whole trip He took and not just what most people preach, only the first half of it. He took the WHOLE cup of wrath. He took the torment of Hades and even possibly the Lake of Fire for our benefit. Because of Adam's sin, we are all destined to wind up in that Lake of Fire and we have been rescued from that. The only way you can thank God is through His Son Jesus Christ who provided the opportunity for you to avoid that cup of wrath that someday will be poured out and poured out completely. God's anger is going to be poured. My message is, do not be caught receiving it. The mark of the beast and its followers will. The godless and unrighteous will.

Be in Jesus Christ and remember by taking the bread and taking the wine (or whatever you have) and when you do, say, "Thank you Jesus! Even though I may not comprehend all of it, because I will never experience it because you did it for me, I will not forget. Not only will I not forget, I understand what you are asking me to do to be a facilitator of letting others know." A facilitator, no matter how God called you to do it, whether to participate with people that are doing it or going out there and doing it yourself. Your mission, your commission, is to be in a place where you want to bring people into the land of the living not into the land of the dead.

Thank you, Jesus… as we take these elements. First the bread and then the wine and say, "Lord I do remember, and I want to continually remember the price You paid for me. What I deserved you took upon yourself and all the facets and elements of what that means". And like I said earlier, no one can really understand what He did take on completely, but we know enough to know what we deserve. He said, "I take it for them and when I come out of this grave and I rise and sail into the blue and come back for them, the only option you have Father, if your word is true, is to say through My Son you are right with Me again." That is a great place to be, right with God through His Son.

That is what we remember. So, take the bread and take the cup now and say thank you Jesus for your rescue plan and saving me. Thank you.

The Last Days Study Guide
The Mark of The Beast Part 12

1. God gives a specific word about the outcome for those who are Muslim and those who support them. What does He specifically say will become of their persons?

2. While the beast and those who associate with the beast will drink the cup of God's wrath, what cup is He still offering all sinners, including Muslims, at this time?

3. Isaiah 53 and 1 Peter are both speaking of what type of healing?

4. What is the Greek word so-be-it faith?

5. Before Christ rose from the dead, where did the dead in Christ rest awaiting His resurrection?

6. Where did Christ make his grave?

7. What specifically was made as an offering for our sin?

8. Christ suffered two deaths. What were they?

9. Now that we have received the cup of redemption, what does the Lord Jesus call us to do?

The Mark of the Beast Part 13

Open your Bibles to Revelation chapter 14. I have been preaching about the cup of wrath in a general sense and I want to continue with that.

We have been looking at verses 9 and 10 in Revelation 14 among other verses in Scripture, but let's just read these two verses again as our starting point. *"And the third angel followed them, saying with a loud voice, If any man worship the beast and his image, and receive his mark in his forehead, or in his hand."* Now, I already covered all of this on Revelation 13:17-18. I already preached on the mark of the beast, the image of the beast, and the number. In verse 10 it says, *"The same shall drink of the wine of the wrath of God..."* Wine of the wrath of God! *"which is poured out without mixture into the cup of his indignation*[or *wrath*]*; and he shall be tormented with fire and brimstone in the presence of the holy angels, and in the presence of the Lamb."*

The last time I preached on the cup of wrath, I mentioned there are two cups in scripture: the cup of redemption and the cup of wrath. Those who are saved by the blood of Jesus Christ who trust in Him will not experience the cup of wrath because they already drank from the cup that provided redemption. We looked at a few of the verses but I want to look at a few more that gives us that promise.

If you go to Paul's letter to the Romans starting with chapter 5 verse 8 we see, *"But God commendeth his love toward us, in that, while we were yet sinners, Christ died for us."* I do not have time to break this whole verse down, but I want to look at 'God commendeth'. Once you dig down deeper to get to the heart of the definition and go beyond some simple Greek definition of what they say it is it means *God committed to His care*. It is usually committed to someone's care or committing your care for someone else's sake. *"But God committed* [his care]*, his love"*. Scripture says God committed His care because He cared for us. *"But God committed* [his care] *and his love toward us, in that, while we were yet sinners, Christ died for us. Much more then, being now justified* [or *being made right with God again*, God the Father through Christ] *by his blood, we shall be saved..."* From what? What does it say there in that verse? *"from wrath..."* The wrath that is still yet to come.

I do not want you to confuse this. There is a difference between God's wrath and the tribulation, or the Great Tribulation. A lot of the Christian science fiction world wants to combine those two, preaching that they are one and the same. No, they are not! They are not.

"But God commendeth [or *God committed his care*] *his love toward us, in that, while we were yet sinners, Christ died for us. Much more then, being now once again right with God through the blood of Jesus Christ, we shall be saved..."* From what? *"from that wrath"*, which is what I have been describing in the last few messages on this subject. Refresh your memory as we move forward. It is only going to happen through Jesus Christ, my friend.

Verse 10, *"For if, when we were enemies..."* Enemies! *"we were reconciled to God by the death of his Son; much more, being reconciled we shall be saved by his life. And not only so, but we also joy in God through our Lord Jesus Christ, by whom we have now received the atonement."* A better translation for atonement would be *reconciliation*. Those of us who are in Christ Jesus, those of us who have been made right with God again by the blood of Christ Jesus have been saved from this wrath. We were once enemies but now we are not. We are no longer enemies. We have been saved by His life and now we are, as Jesus would say in John 15, His friends.

Let's go to a couple more places just to drive that point home. Go to 1 Thessalonians 1:9. *"For they themselves show of us what manner of entering in we had unto you, and how ye turned to God from idols to serve the living and true God;"* And, by the way, idols there can even mean serving yourself. Let's say you do not believe in any other religion, any other belief system, and you believe your way is the right way. That just became your own idol — worshipping of self. So, no one is excused here. Paul was saying, *"...how ye turned to God from idols to serve the living and true God"*. There are only two options folks: serving an idol, whatever that is, and serving the true God. *"And to wait..."* This word is only used once in the New Testament. It means *to wait with the notion to trust or to endure.* So that notion that you are going to have to trust something and trust something that will create you to endure whatever you are going to endure through. *"And to wait..."* To *trust and to endure* whatever is going to happen until then, for what? *"for his Son from heaven, whom he raised from the dead, [even] Jesus, which delivered..."* I like the translation *rescued. "us from the..."* What? *"wrath..."* Not tribulation or Great Tribulation. *"wrath to come."* True disciples of Jesus Christ will not experience the wrath of God. I want you to remember that. What a promise!

1 Thessalonians 5:9, *"For God hath not appointed us to wrath..."* The hot anger of God's wrath, He has not appointed us to that. *"...but to obtain salvation by our Lord Jesus Christ."* There again is our promise. Sorry, no wrath on the horizon. Tribulation, yes. No wrath, folks. That is a promise. *"Who died for us, that, whether we wake or sleep, we should live together with him. Wherefore comfort* [or *exhort*] *yourselves together, and edify one another, even as also ye do."* That is what I am doing right now here with you. I am letting you know, yes, there are going to be hard times. Yes, there is even going to be tribulation, but we will be spared from the wrath of God. When you understand what that wrath of God is, as much as we can understand it as given in Scripture, there is no comparison my friend.

When God's Word repeats itself and verifies itself over and over through different books, epistles, letters, or verses, whatever you want to call it, pay close attention to the fact my friend. Romans 1:18 declares, *"For the wrath..."* This entails *hot surging anger that is slow in rising* if you want a complete definition. When it hits, it is going to be like one of those volcanoes where all the pressure builds up over the years, decades, even centuries. It might be silent, but it seems like overnight it reaches its boiling point. Remember Mount St. Helens in Washington State back in the early 80's? When it blew, it blew my friend. There was no question whether we had a volcano explode or not. It was slow in getting to that point but when it got to that point, brimstone and fire came out of that volcano my friend. God's anger is the same. That is what that word 'wrath' means when it is defined completely. It is hot surging anger, slow in rising, but when it blows it is going to blow. We have some outline in Scripture what it is going to look like. You cannot compare anything with that wrath of God when it does explode to any tribulation that you might experience.

"For the wrath of God is revealed from heaven..." Here it says, *"For the wrath of God is revealed from heaven..."*. How? Most people just say it was because Jesus Christ came down from heaven. *"...against all ungodliness and unrighteousness of men, who hold the truth in unrighteousness"*. Ungodliness is neglect or violation of worship towards the true God. Unrighteousness means those who are wrong with God, who hold the truth and who suppress or restrain the truth in unrighteousness. But how was it revealed from heaven? When Christ came down here, He revealed it Himself to a certain extent but not completely because remember the book of Revelation was not written yet, it was not given yet. To completely understand the wrath of God, you must include, no question about it, the book of Revelation to have a complete understanding as much as God wants us to know about His wrath. He made a point to make sure that we would have some idea what that is going to be like. He revealed that through Christ through John. But how was it revealed in heaven?

Remember I told you there is a gospel of the stars. There is a gospel written in the heavens. There is a history of this world and how Jesus, and not only Jesus, but how Satan would play a part in history revealed in the stars. The world would have no excuse *"Because that which may be known of God is manifest in them; for God hath shown it unto them. For the invisible things of him from the creation of the world are clearly seen, being understood by the things that are made..."* Aha! So 'the things that are made' is referring to something else and not what Christ said but 'the things that were made'. ***"his eternal power and Godhead..."*** For what reason? ***"so that they are without excuse."*** If you don't want to believe ***thus saith the word of the Lord*** (up to recent history, compared to how many thousands of years have gone by), then there was a language in the heavens that people knew. Then Satan got hold of it and twisted it, and now his perversion is much more popular.

In today's world, all we can do is look back at what it was like. Most people live in heavily populated areas, so we cannot even see the stars any longer to learn about what the heavens have declared. Thank God for His Word. The world never had an excuse about His first advent, about what He would do when He was here, providing a rescue plan, dying, rising from the dead, coming back and then also bringing everything to a conclusion. That conclusion for the ones that are not in Christ, for those in the world, is going to be horrific my friend, no matter if it is written or expressed through the heavenlies, through the written gospel of the stars. There is a book which is a good introduction to the gospel in the stars entitled *The Glory of the Stars*. I want you to know the information. I just do not want you to take my word for it.

Let me read you something:

> *In the Bible, we are told Adam named the large animals and birds, but God named the stars. When we look at the ancient names some interesting things emerge. However, because of the perversion of astrology today, many Christians are afraid to take a look at these names and see if God had a purpose in what He named them.*
>
> *It is wise to remember, however, that names in the past always meant something. Today we choose names for our children because they sound pretty or we are perhaps honoring a relative or a friend, but the ancients used names that meant something. For instance, David means 'hero, commander, prince.' This list is, for all intents and purposes, endless. So it should not surprise us when we find*

that the original names of the stars had meanings. Finding the original meanings is not always easy, and can take a lot of time and research going back into different languages, root words, etc. But for enough of the stars it is possible, and when this is done, something quite remarkable emerges. Today, astrology says a man can tell something about himself in the stars. That is nonsense.

Oh, I agree!

In fact, it may go beyond nonsense and into demonic.

Now that did not just start today. That started over 4,000 years ago.

The original purpose, as we will see (and which is also stated in the Bible) was to tell us something about God and His plan for the world. Please recall, "In the past God spoke to our forefathers through the prophets many times and in various ways, but in these last days He has spoken to us by His Son whom He appointed heir of all things and through whom He made the universe." So let's take a look at what we find when we look into this.

The constellations themselves have been known from antiquity. Their identities have remained basically unchanged although a few of the ancient large constellations have been divided up by modern astronomers into smaller constellations, but for many the identities remain.

For instance, the constellation of Taurus, the bull, and Orion appear in cave art dating back to 3000 and 2900 BC.

In cave art! This is not some modern invention.

The book of Job is the earliest completed book of the Old Testament. In Job 38: 31 and 32, the Pleiades and Orion are both mentioned by name.

Let's verify that. Let's not just take someone's word for it without looking at it. Go to Job 38. What does it say in verses 31 and 32? I have been here before. *"Canst thou bind the sweet influences of Pleiades..."* or the seven stars, sometimes called the Seven Sisters. *"Canst thou bind the sweet influences of Pleiades, or loose the bands of Orion? Canst thou bring forth Mazzaroth",* which means literally the 12 signs. The 12 signs of what? The 12 signs of the zodiac. This is in the book of Job. Just because man and his evil ways have twisted it by representing the stars for something that they are not, does not mean that you throw it away. Satan is the greatest mimicker of anything that God ever put in place for our understanding of His salvation plan, and our understanding on how history is going to play out. Nothing new there. *"Canst thou bring forth the zodiac in his season? Or canst thou guide Arcturus with his sons?"*

So far, this author is on track. We have verified that yes, Job being probably the oldest book in the Old Testament mentions Pleiades, Orion, and we find even the 12 signs of the zodiac are mentioned by him. Where did he get that information from?

> *Around 2700 to 2500 BC the Samarians recorded the existence of the tablet of the stars in the heavens.*

Archeologists know that. That is nothing new.

> *Mesopotamian tablets dating around 1800 BC recorded both star names and observations of planetary movements.*

Once again, that is 1800 BC.

> *Dating about 1400 BC are Chinese oracle bones which list the Chinese star names.*

> *Babylonian and Chaldean tablets dating from 800 to 600 BC recorded zodiac signs by name.*

In Genesis 1:14 we read that the sun, moon and stars are for signs, seasons, days and years. Most of that is not hard to understand: a day is determined by the earth's rotation in relation to the sun in the year by its orbit around the sun. The word translated 'season' in that passage does not mean spring, summer, autumn and winter. It is a word meaning a specifically designed time, such as for a feast. Israelite feasts and memorials were based on new moons and times relative to new moons. What about signs? Signs carry a message. If you see a sign that reads 'San Francisco, 300 miles' that sign is giving you information you understand.

Signs give information.

So how can the stars actually give information. We read in Psalms 147:4 and Isaiah 40:26 that God himself named the stars. "He determined the number of the stars and called them each by name." "Lift up your eyes and look to the heavens: who created all these? He who brings out the starry host one by one, and calls them each by name. Because of His great power and mighty strength, not one of them is missing."

Not one of them is missing! We find that in Psalms 147:4. I have been there before. ***"He telleth..."*** or *he counts.* In other words, counting is like recounting ***"the number of the stars"*** or, *the appointment of the stars.* ***"he calleth..."*** I told you to circle that word before. It means *proclaim, or call out, or preach.* Proclaim ***"them all by [their] names. Great is our Lord, and of great power: his understanding is infinite."*** Or *of his understanding there is no number.* (I do not have time to go to Isaiah 40:26.) Because of His great power and mighty strength not one of them is missing because He placed them there by design to recount the story. Just like Abraham, as I already preached, had to recount the message of the stars about the Promised One that would come from his lineage.

Interestingly, we trace star and constellation names back in time, we find that the names meant the same thing for various stars, although the actual words in the various languages may have been different. A good example is the constellation Virgo which means 'virgin'. This constellation is Bethulah in Hebrew, Parthenos in Greek, Kanya in Indian and they all mean 'virgin'. This would point, linguistically, to a common origin before the separation of the tribes and peoples. Biblically, this would mean the name meanings were known before Babel. It is quite probable they were known by Adam and passed down through the generations, to Noah, and to our present age. Today, because the astronomical names are now fixed by Convention, it is very difficult...

By the way, that convention started about 1603 and I do not agree with all the convention rules that were applied to the astronomical sign posts, (let's just call it that) which they presented and literally changed some of the meanings of what the message there in the heavens was all about. That is another story and I do not have time to get into all that history; maybe some other time, because there are plenty of messages that I could introduce the stars into, in the future.

Today, because the astronomical names are now fixed by Convention, it is very difficult to find some original names and meanings. Some appear to be lost for good. Star and constellation names were fixed in process...

Now it has kind of lost its meaning.

...so to find the meanings if they are to be found we must search back into the 16th century.

Before things were changed by the Conventions of the scientific world of that day and before. I do not have time to read everything, so let me jump ahead.

Aside from cold and warm, new flowers and harvest, the time of the year is also seen by which constellations are where in the sky as seen from the earth in its orbits around the sun. Because of the earth's orbits around the sun, the background of the stars and constellations in which the sun appears changes. This is called the zodiac. The word itself comes from 'zoad,' the Greek word for a way, a path, a step, or circuit. In Sanskrit, the word is 'sodi.' The specific twelve constellations we recognize today as the zodiac is referred to as the Mazzaroth in Hebrew. We find this word used in Job 38:32 which means the word was in use extraordinarily early, as Job is probably the earliest completed book of the Bible. In Job 26:13, Job says God formed the constellation figures. The fleeing serpent mentioned there is Hydra, a constellation that would take seven hours to pass overhead because of its length.

"What does this have to do with the cup of wrath?" Hang on!

Let's go to Job 26:11. What does that say? ***"The pillars of heaven tremble, and are astonished at his reproof. He divideth the sea with his power, and by his understanding he smiteth through the proud*** [or *through pride*]. ***By his Spirit he hath garnished*** [or *cleared*] ***the heavens; his hand hath formed..."*** [a better translation is *twist*] ***"his hand hath twist the crooked serpent."*** Of course, some translate it *fleeing serpent*. A better translation would be *fleeing serpent*. So, he became known as the *crooked fleeing serpent* or the *twisted fleeing serpent*. So in Job 26:13, Job said God formed the constellation figures. The fleeing serpent mentioned there is Hydra. Now Hydra is in the Leo constellation and it takes seven hours for Hydra to pass overhead because of its length.

This is really a hard picture to look at and try to distinguish anything. So, a red arrow points out Hydra's location just outside of the circle on the left side. The crooked or twisted fleeing serpent's head is at the bottom and its tail towards the top of the picture. Now Leo, which represents Christ, had his foot stamped on the head of the serpent in the zodiac declaration that God placed in the stars.

In the picture above we see on the bottom the twisted fleeing serpent or the crooked serpent. You see the constellation Leo on the right side and Virgo on the left side. And, of course, to the right of Leo is Cancer. You do not see the serpent's head there because it is cut off on the right, but Leo is treading on the head of Satan, in this case the serpent, as Scripture declares would happen.

Now you also see a cup there. You see Corvus, but you also see Crater, a cup. The heavens already knew way before the written Word we have because God already penned it in the heavens through His mighty power and His ability to create things for our benefit. That cup there represents the cup of wrath my friends. Where is that cup of wrath located in the heavens? On that twisted fleeing serpent which is none other than Satan and anyone that aligns and joins up with him.

Is there any indication the star and constellation names have any significance, biblically or otherwise? Certainly, they appear to biblically. Read what Paul says in the passage from Romans 10.

Let's go to Romans 10:14.

"How then can they call on the one that they have not believed in? How can they believe in the one of whom they have not heard, and how can they hear without someone preaching to them? And how can they preach unless they are sent? As it is written, how beautiful are the feet of those who bring good news, for not all Israelites accepted the good news. For Isaiah says, Lord, who has believed our message. Consequently, faith comes from hearing the message and the message is heard through the word of Christ, but I ask, did they not hear? Of course, they did."

In the King James, verse 18, *"But I say, Have they not heard? Yes, verily, Their sound went into all the earth, and their words unto the ends of the world."* Well, that sure did not happen through the written Word at this point, so what Paul was saying was, How else could that have happened?

Let me continue with this translation:

> *"Consequently, faith comes from hearing the message and the message is heard through the word of Christ, but I ask, did they not hear? Of course, they did. Their voice has gone out into all the earth, their words to the ends of the world."*

> *So, what is Paul talking about? What quote is he using at the end here which he thinks proves his point? He is quoting from Psalms 19.*

Let's look at the Psalm. I am going read it from the same translation.

> *"The heavens declare the glory of God; the sky proclaims the work of his hands. Day after day they put forth speech; night after night they display knowledge. There is no speech or language, where their voice is not heard. Their voice goes out into all the earth, their words to the end of the world."*

Before we had any gospel, Psalms 19 was already declaring what? What the heavens declared!

> *In the ancient Alexandrian Septuagint...*

This is the only one that I recommend you read in the first place if you are going to use the Septuagint. By the way, I came to that conclusion for many reasons that I do not have time to get to. Maybe some other time.

> *...the heavens declare the glory of God; and the firmament proclaims the work of his hands. Day unto day utters speech; and night unto night proclaims knowledge. There are no speeches or words of which their voices are not heard. Their voice has gone out into all the earth, and their words to the ends of the world.*

> *Therefore if we allow Bible to explain Bible, there is something about the heavens which declares Christ. Look at the fourth line of Psalms 19: night after night they display knowledge.*

Night after night they display knowledge. Was the author of Psalms 19 just trying to be poetic? I do not think so, folks. *"Their line is gone out through all the earth, and their words to the end of the world. In them hath he set a tabernacle for the sun, Which is as a bridegroom coming out of his chamber, and rejoiceth as a strong man to run a race. His going forth is from the end of the heaven, and his circuit unto the ends of it: and there is nothing hid from the heat thereof."*

Verse 2, *"Day unto day uttereth speech, and night unto night showeth knowledge."*

> *Night after night they displayed the knowledge. What knowledge? Whatever it was, Paul seems to indicate it has something to do with everyone hearing the Word of Christ.*

Everything that can be clearly seen through the written Word has already been declared, night after night, day after day in the heavens.

Now I am going to skip along because I do not have time to go through the rest of what I wanted to go through, but I think you get the point about what is declared in the heavens. See, when Paul is referring to the cup, the wrath of God in Romans 1, he is referring to that cup of wrath that John is referring to in verse 14, and all the Old Testament scriptures we already looked at. It is the same cup seen in the last picture, Crater.

The heavens declared it is the cup reserved for Satan and his followers. It is the cup reserved for the Beast and his followers; those who bow down and worship the image and take what the Beast has declared and declared that as the truth and say *thus saith the word of the Lord.* You see that over and over.

I could go to the Gospel of the Stars and I could read about the crater of the cup of wrath.

> *The Psalmist in 75:8, For in the hand of the LORD there is a cup, and the wine is red; and is full of mixture...*

That is the one you just saw on the fleeing serpent.

> *...and he poureth out of the same: but the dregs thereof, all the wicked of the earth shall wring them out, and drink them.*

> *Upon the wicked he shall rain burning coals of fire and brimstone.*

That is what the crater on that cup of wrath signifies in the picture you just saw that the heavens declare, which verifies scripture and scripture verifies the heavens.

> *Upon the wicked shall remain burning coals with fire and brimstone and the fiery tempest. This shall be the portion of their cup concerning every worship of the beast. John heard the angel proclaim, The same shall drink of the wine of the wrath of God, which is poured out without mixture into the cup of his indignation; and he shall be tormented with fire and brimstone in the presence of the holy angels, and in the presence of the Lamb: And the smoke of their torment ascendeth up for ever and ever: and they have no rest day nor night.*

That is Revelation 14 which we have been looking at.

> *The portion of the worshippers of the son of perdition is the lake of fire and the same is likewise dealt out to the beast and the false prophet. And ultimately to the devil himself, for John saw him cast into the lake of fire and brimstone where the beast and the false prophet are, and where he shall be tormented day and night for ever and ever.*

> *In other words, he and all his are to drink of the wine of the wrath of God which is poured out with adulteration or delusion to the cup of divine indignation. And lo, here is the second decan of Leo...*

I showed you in that picture. (pg. 171)

> *...of that cup, broad, deep, full to the brim and placed directly in the body of this serpent. The same as is something to his very substance...*

Something to his very substance.

> *...for the same stars which mark the bottom of the cup are part of the body of the cursed monster, so that curse is fastened down on him and in him as an element of all his after being. Dreadful beyond all thought is the picture John gives of this cup of unmingled and eternal wrath, but not a wit more dreadful than the picture in which the prophets have thus inscribed upon the stars.*

Of course, it goes into Corvus, which I will get to at a later time. The heavens declared it.

> *So the story ends with the victorious line of Judah, the mighty God and the coming judge who will tread under the foot the enemy.*

You do not see it in the picture, but it is Satan's head.

> *Leo is treading under foot the fleeing serpent, Hydra, the old serpent whose brightest star is Alphard, the cursed one. When that happens, Corvus the crow and the other stars are called to the battle of the great day of God, Armageddon.*

Which, I will get to in the future.

> *...where they shall feed on the flesh of the armies. This is a day when the cup of God's wrath is outpoured, which is the significance of the constellation Crater, the cup.*

I will get to that and see if that is true or not because the timing is a little bit different than the way I present it, but I will give it to you in the future.

Paul knew it. All the prophets of the Old Testament knew it. The heavens knew it. Jesus declared it through John. So, what do you need to be convinced?

Romans 1:18, *"For the wrath of God is revealed from heaven against all ungodliness and unrighteousness and men, who hold the truth* [who suppress or restrain the truth] *in unrighteousness.* Verse 20, *"For the invisible things of him from the creation of the world are clearly seen, being understood by the things that are made, [even] his eternal power and Godhead; so that they are without excuse:* [or you could also translate it *that they may be without excuse*] *Because that, when they knew God, and glorified him not as God, neither were thankful; but became vain in their imaginations, and their foolish heart was darkened. Professing themselves to be wise, they became fools, And changed the glory of the uncorruptible God into an image made like to corruptible man, and to birds, and four-footed beasts, and creeping things. Wherefore God also gave them up to uncleanness, through the lusts* [*through the desires* really] *of their own hearts, to dishonour their own bodies between themselves: Who changed the truth of God into a lie, and worshipped and served the creature more than* [*rather than* really] *the Creator, who is blessed for ever. Amen."*

Then he gives you a list. It is a partial list of not only what we find in Revelation 14 by the way, but a partial list of who is going to experience this wrath of God. Most preachers avoid this list. It is not PC these days, it is not PC. I do not have time to go into this list. If you are interested I might do that in a future teaching. Maybe next time.

I am telling you right now, folks, I have good news for those of you who are in Christ. All this, whether it is declared in the heavens, whether it is declared in His Word, we are not subject to that cup of wrath that is going to be poured out to the Father of Lies, and anyone that worships the Beast, or anyone that worships themselves and desire not to worship the true God, or desire to change the truth into a lie and worship themselves more than the One that created them. For those of you who will not see the truth for what it is, your future is not promising. It is horrific. But the ones that are in Christ Jesus, saved by the blood of our precious Lord, we will be rescued from this. We are not destined for this kind of wrath. We will be plucked away before it is poured out.

Hallelujah, hallelujah! That is something to shout about. **RUWA!** Thank you, Jesus.

The Last Days Study Guide
Mark of the Beast Part 13

1. What is ungodliness?
2. What was the purpose of Jesus' resurrection?
3. What is unrighteousness?
4. What is the mazzaroth?
5. What is the oldest book of the Bible?
6. When were we reconciled to God?
7. How is the wrath of God revealed from heaven?
8. What is the significance of the constellation Crater?
9. What is the original purpose of the constellations?
10. Who will be subject to the wrath of God?

The Mark of the Beast Part 14

Open your Bibles to Revelation 14:9. I have a lot of messages that are coming in to me from those who have been following this series, especially the last few messages, and are confused about what the difference is between the great tribulation and God's wrath.

Like I said, I am just giving you a general outline now concerning God's wrath. I cannot even conclude the topic in a dozen messages on God's wrath when it does come down. It takes up so much of Scripture, especially in the book of Revelation, that it will take some time to go through. I have been trying to generalize the messages to give you quick footnotes, so to speak, so you have an idea, a timeline, some type of understanding of what God's wrath is. If we are disciples of Jesus Christ, just like the Thessalonian letters I went to, we are not destined for God's wrath. Thank God we have been saved by grace for those disciples who keep trusting in Jesus to the very end, that have been saved by His blood. I think I have made that clear.

GREAT TRIBULATION
vs.
GOD'S WRATH

It is 'Great Tribulation' because I have already said before there is no such thing as '*The* Great Tribulation'. That is why you see "*Great Tribulation vs. God's Wrath*". I have many messages trying to combine these two into a future event, or a set of events, that are going to take place sometime in the future. You must separate them, folks. They are not one and the same. Let's just read the verses first as our starting point.

Revelation 14:9, *"And the third angel followed them, saying with a loud voice, If any man worship the beast and his image, and receive his mark in his forehead, or in his hand, The same shall drink of the wine of the wrath of God"*.

Now, they are not the only ones, but we know for sure God has called out probably about a third of the population that will fall for the Beast's trickery, his *methodeia,* the 8ᵗʰ Beast, Islam, convincing people to take his mark and worship Islam. We have already covered that. *"If any man worship the beast"*. And, of course, I also looked in Romans 1. The wrath of God is also destined for a whole list of other categories of rebellion that you do not necessarily see here in verses 9 and 10. I did not get into all those categories, but they are listed in Romans 1.

"And the third angel followed them, saying with a loud voice, If any man worship the beast and his image, and receive his mark in his forehead, or in his hand, The same shall drink of the wine of the wrath of God…"

I have spent now I think about three or four messages talking about the wrath of God, showing you in Scripture that Christian disciples of Jesus Christ are not going to be destined for this wrath *"…which is poured out without mixture into the cup of his indignation* [or *wrath*]*; and he shall be tormented with fire and brimstone in the presence of the holy angels, and in the presence of the Lamb."*

The wrath of God is something that is going to take place. It is a judgment that is coming but it is not great tribulation. And, there is no such thing as 'The Great Tribulation'. Find it anywhere in scripture. Find it in the Greek; let's just go to the Greek. Find it anywhere, I challenge you. There is no such thing as 'The Great Tribulation'. If there is, then prove me wrong. I challenge you. People mix these two up thinking all of these are going to happen somewhere in the seven-year period depending on, like I said, your doctrinal view. No, separate them! Great tribulation described by Jesus, when He described it in the Gospel record of Matthew, did not even start on the timeline of events. Was there tribulation in the world? Absolutely. There has been tribulation ever since Adam sinned. But a certain *type* of tribulation did not start even in Jesus' time. He was talking about a future event. Now this obviously is a future event reserved for the end. So, never mix these two up.

Great tribulation is demonic in origin. It includes persecution, killing, etc. by Satan's human controlled instruments.

Wrath of God is a godly judgment against evil. The purpose of the wrath of God is to punish the Beast and his followers, etcetera. Etcetera being Romans 1 for one example.

These are two different events from two different sources for two different purposes. Do not combine them. The wrath of God is a judgment which will be poured out. His purpose is to punish the Beast and those who have taken the mark, during a set period—which fits in the timeline of 'Great Tribulation' but that is the only thing that they have in common. You got it? God's wrath is not the Christian Science Fiction. 'The Great Tribulation' does not exist. So, strike that out. It is not great tribulation either. There is no separate event or the kind of tribulation that Christian Science Fiction theories people try to convince you of when we look at Matthew 25.

Now with that, go to Matthew 24. The reason why I am preaching this message is because there has been a lot of confusion about what people think 'The Great Tribulation' is – which it's not. Let's just call it *"Great Tribulation vs. God's Wrath"*. So, that is the purpose of this message.

Now I have to assume that you have already studied the previous teachings in this series that gave you a lot of history about when this abomination of desolation began. [But if not, you will find that information in the following volumes of this series.] Remember the Dome of the Rock began to be built in 688 AD to 691 AD. So, they have starting points. Remember those messages on "the middle of the week"?

Let's start with Matthew 24:15, *"When ye therefore shall see the abomination of desolation, spoken of"*. That is the Dome of the Rock, which has inscribed on it that God basically did not have any children in modern language. He did not have any son. *"When ye therefore shall see the abomination of desolation, spoken of by Daniel the prophet, stand in the holy place, (whoso readeth, let him understand,) Then let them which be in Judea flee into the mountains:"* So we have a starting point. *"Let him which is on the housetop not come down to take any thing out of his house: Neither let him which is in the field return back to take his clothes. And woe unto them that are with child, and to them that give suck in those days! But pray ye that your flight be not in the winter, neither on the sabbath day."*

Now this is the verse I really wanted you to look at closely. *"For then shall be great tribulation"*. This is the closest you will ever get to 'The Great Tribulation'. Jesus did not say this is going to be '*The* Great Tribulation'. He never said that, even if some other blasphemous versions of the Bible say He did. They also have been brainwashed to believe in this Christian Science Fiction theory, so they added their own point of view and are just trying to be creatively cute in modern-day language but that is not what the original says. *"For then shall be great tribulation, such as was not since the beginning of the world to this time, no, nor ever shall be."*

And, of course, the Christian Science Fiction theory people say, "Wow! This is so awful, so horrific that the world is going to experience something that has never happened before." Of course, they see all the plagues, all the vials being poured, the trumpets being blown, and all the things that are supposedly going to happen, which will happen, taking place in the book of Revelation and say, "Ah, this is what Matthew 24 is *probably* referring to". Really! Prove it with 100% certainty. But then again, they cannot because they would still have to figure out what the abomination of desolation is. Since they say it has not happen yet, and it is going to happen in that seven-year period, they do not know what the heck it is. So, their assumption is the Temple is going to be re-built and somebody is going to walk into it, sit in the Holy of Holies, and say they are lord.

Ah, heck! How many people brainwash you continuously, whether religious or not; that try to convince you that you do not need Jesus Christ daily, whether it is the media or whether it is even false doctrines. Aren't you the temple of the Holy Ghost? What do you think would be worse: Something affecting you, who belong to Christ and Christ came and died for; or, somebody sitting in a building somewhere that the Jews rebuilt? It is stupid, folks. I just turned off a whole bunch more people in the Christian Science Fiction world because I called their theory stupid. God would call it something far worse than that.

So let's look at verse 21. *"For then"* — scratch that out. Write in your notes *"For at that time"*. It is a better translation. *"For at that time shall be"* - circle that word 'be'. The word tense there when Jesus spoke it was still a future time if you apply the rules of Greek grammar. I do not get into all that stuff too much. Some people claim to be experts on it. That is fine. There is enough information out there about languages, both Hebrew and Greek, and other languages, but you can decipher what is real and what is not real by the last and the most important way to decipher anything, God's verifiable word. *"For at that time shall be..."* is referring to a future time still to come. And we already have a timeline that already began in 688 AD. [See following volumes of the series.] So, what Jesus is referring to is something that comes after 688 AD. It begins, and if the abomination of desolation is the Dome of the Rock, the al-Aqsa right next to it, even the stupid Dome of the Tablets which sits where the Holy of Holies used to sit (not the Dome of the Rock but the Dome of the Tablets), if that is the timeline that Jesus is referring to as the starting point, GREAT! We then have a marker.

"For at that time shall be" – future event – *"great tribulation"*. Not *'The Great Tribulation'*, there is no such thing. You cannot find it in the original language, so why make it up? They did because it fits an agenda to try to prove 'our Christian Science Fiction theories are correct'. Well, unfortunately too many people have fallen for it.

"For at that time shall be great tribulation". The word there for 'great' is *megas*. What does *megas* mean? This word comes with many definitions

attached to it. "Well why didn't you preach this the first time around?" I told you I would keep adding things on. The problem with most listeners/students is you want everything all at once. It has to be laid down in layers. So, as we keep going back to the verses I have already covered, you will now see how it even fits in more to what has already been preached and more clarification comes by it. Many definitions come attached to this word *megas*. Some of you will immediately look at *mega* as *great*; usually saying great, or mega, or mega awesome, or mega this and mega that. I will just give you several examples of what *megas* can translate to in the Greek: Great mass or in weight. Great amount of weight. Great in mass or size of something. Great in measure or height. Great in quantity. Great in number. Great in age. For instance, comparing someone who is 10 years old to someone 90 years old, and the 90-year-old would be called great in age because they have been around for a while. Great in affections and emotions that affects the mind, for instance. Great in rank. For instance, a private or sergeant. Obviously, a sergeant has a higher or greater rank than a private in the military. Great in external appearance. But the one the Christian Science Fiction theories do not use is *Great in space and time or dimensions.*

I think the best translation is great in space and time. Great in space and time from what? From 688 AD, the starting point and what Jesus referred to as the abomination of desolation, the Dome of the Rock, to what time? Well, we know 1,400 years (to round it off) have come and gone. We know all the worldly empires (e.g. Egyptian, Babylonian, Assyrian, e Medo-Persian, etc.). We covered the lion, bear and leopard or the LBL Beast. (Rev. 13:2) There have been other beasts but as far as great in space, occupying a certain space in time, there has been nothing that has taken the place of Islam as far as accomplishing *megas*, folks. "What about the Egyptians?" What about the Egyptians! Prior to the LBL Beast even the Egyptians had an upper kingdom and a lower kingdom. Then there were the outside kingdoms such as the Hyskos that came in. So, even though you want to consider everything that is in Egypt Egyptian, you must break up the differences between what is upper rule and what is lower rule, when they ruled, and how they ruled in the period of space and time, which means the rule was broken up. Nothing has lasted this 1,400 years.

Did the Roman Empire last that long? That is another beast. No, it did not. Did the Hyskos in Egypt last that long? No, they did not. Did the Medo-Persian Empire last that long? No, it did not. Find anyone that is considered a beast in biblical history that coincides with secular history that has lasted and taken up that much space and time. I am sure some of you are historian buffs. Find it. But not only has it taken up great space and time, consider how much it affects the mind and body. Which beast ever had such influence over a population of the world, the world it exists in, which it conquered, which it controlled, then Islam?

So, we could break this down into many kinds of 'greats' but the one I want to look at is *great in space and time*. For instance, let's just call 688 AD, Point A. Fourteen hundred years later (which we still have not had a conclusion to, and is just a very conservative estimate) is Point B. Remember this is called great tribulation. Why? Because of the persecutions, killings, torture... how it affects a person's mind and body. Very conservative numbers by experts in the field that try to put this information together have calculated for this period between Point A and Point B that there have been about 270 million killed by the 7th and 8th Beast. I believe it is way more, much more. That figure doesn't even include people that have been tortured or enslaved throughout Islam's 1400-year history. These numbers are conservative numbers: 270 million starting with the 7th beast, now the 8th Beast, over a 1400-year period. The conservative estimates are about 60 million Christians, which I think is low, or people professing they are Christians by title, and 80 million Hindus. So, it is not just Christians.

Back to the scriptures. Verse 21, *"For at that time shall be"*—a future tense; what Jesus was referring to with the beginning point of the abomination of desolation— *"great tribulation"*. From Point A to Point B, in that great amount of space and time, and how it affects the mind and body. No beast prior to the 7th and 8th Beast, which is really one beast with different time periods, has ever accomplished (if it is called an accomplishment; it kind of sickens me to say that but for lack of better words) what Islam has. That is why you will see tribulation used a lot in scriptures. The word there is *thlipsis*. Remember I preached on *thlipsis*, "Enduring Faith". Remember that? The word here is *megas thlipsis*. In the Greek it is in the reverse, *thlipsis megas*.

Nowhere in history…. Jesus was correct, once again. Not since the beginning of the world have we seen anything like it. We haven't, if you know your history. I am just giving you very brief information here for this message, that has been accumulated and that for some reason the world does not really want to understand or learn. That is why they keep making the same mistake over and over with Islam. *"such as was not since the beginning of the world to this time…"* And Jesus goes onto say, *"no, nor ever shall be."* That 'be' again is used in a future tense.

This is it. This last Beast, the 8th Beast, which started with the 7th Beast, back in Jesus' timeline with the abomination of desolation, has been going on now for about 1,400 years give or take a few years, and the Beast is called Islam. *"And there shall be megas thlipsis".*

Now, what did I tell you about *thlipsis*? I am going to use my own words. I pulled this from my book, "Faith Pleases God". What does *thlipsis* mean? Not the cute little quick translation of it; I am talking about a deep understanding of what *thlipsis* means. It means *a pressing together — a pressing together*. In this space of time from Point A and Point B, people are going to experience a pressing together. Now a Christian could be experiencing that in their own personal lives, but let's stay in the context with what Jesus is describing here. It means *a pressing together*. These are my own words in the book:

> *"Just imagine being in a vice, and that vice is just pressing in on both sides."*

In other words, squeezing you tight. It means pressing together.

> *"In other words, you are in a tight squeeze and it is only going to get tighter."*

And as the world concludes, believe me, that pressing is going to really squeeze tight. Just imagine yourself in a vice and it is becoming tighter and tighter.

"Put your circumstance in that position."

Of course, I was personalizing about your own *thlipsis* in your own personal life in my book but put those circumstances on the timeline of history.

"Your circumstance is in that vice with you…"

You are in there with it.

"It is not getting easier, and it is starting to create pain in your life."

Like one message said, in the West we have not experienced much of that. But where Islamic practices are encouraged and exercised, and I read you a few articles before, they want to pretty much murder you, eliminate your life for criticizing Muhammad. Talk about being pressed together. Talk about creating pain in your life. And why? Because it is closing in on you. It is squeezing the life out of you. That is what Islam is. It squeezes the life out of existence. That is what Satan's purpose always has been, to squeeze life out of you. And, until he can squeeze every ounce of life and any hope of eternal life out of you, he will not stop, whether on a personal level or on the timeline of history and how he will try to dictate how things go down. It does not matter to him.

"It is squeezing the life out of you. That is an illustration of what the word means in the Greek. These circumstances press together for one purpose and one purpose only, to see how you can handle the pressures though your situations and circumstances."

Of course, I was preaching that on the personal level and focusing on your situations and circumstances.

This is a Greek word that I think you need to remember. I added two other words with it. Remember Romans 5:3 and 4. If you have not read the message, I recommend you get "Faith Pleases God" and read "Enduring Faith". I think it is chapter three in the book.

"Remember this word when you are going through thlipsis, or tribulation."

There is no such thing, my friend, called 'The Great *Thlipsis*' or 'The *Megas Thlipsis*'.

There is great tribulation, and that great tribulation as Jesus described would begin and warn us about what would be Islam, otherwise there is just tribulation, folks. You can have tribulation over many different things, but in reference to what Jesus was referring to in verse 21, it was Islam. Verse 21, nothing else.

Go to Acts 14:22. You see over and over the apostles used this word, but it never came with any connection that there is something in the future that is 'The Great Tribulation'. They were experiencing tribulation on a personal level in their time. Early New Testament Christians experienced it throughout history. *"Confirming the souls of the disciples, and exhorting* [or *calling to one's side*] *them to continue* [literally *to persevere*] *in the faith, and that we must through much tribulation"*. The word there is *thlipsis* again. That is just one example. You will see it over and over being used.

Let's go to Romans 5:3. You see the word *thlipsis* used here again as I have just described that you can find in the book "Faith Pleases God". *"And not only so, but we glory in…"* Paul did not say 'The Great Tribulation' did he? He said tribulations, *thlipsis*. Jesus said from a starting point there would be great tribulations. He was referring to **who** would bring on those tribulations that would be *megas* in the Greek.

No matter where you go throughout scripture, where you see this word *thlipsis*, the disciples are describing the pressing together, what life circumstances in your everyday activities will try to do to you to squeeze the life out of you. Satan will send his agents to do that, but that is not what Jesus was referring to. That is something different in type. You get it?

There are many more verses I can go to describing tribulations as the apostles use it and never, NOT ONCE, was it directed back to what Jesus said about great tribulation, not 'The Great Tribulation', great tribulation. There is no future 'The Great Tribulation'.

And, of course, there is John, and I will probably finish here. Go to John 16:31, *"Jesus answered them, Do ye now believe?"* The word there is *pisteuo* — *Do you now have trust and confidence in me? "Behold, the hour cometh, yea, is now come, that ye shall be scattered, every man to his own, and shall leave me alone: and yet I am not alone, because the Father is with me."*

What a great way of understanding when you go through tribulation that you are never left alone. You might think you are alone but if you are trusting, and that is what *pisteuo* is, you are having trust —you have gone beyond the *pistis* level. *Pistis* is the hearing and hearing and becoming persuaded by what you heard to be true. *Pisteuo* now says you are going to act on that truth and you are going to start trusting and having confidence without any doubt, the so-be-it faith, in Christ. Then when you go through any of your own personal *thlipsis* — forget about Islam right now — guess what? Just as Jesus was not left alone because the Father was with Him, Christ is with us. We are not alone. It might seem that way sometimes, and believe me, I have been there plenty of times, BUT WE ARE NOT!

Jesus goes onto say, *"These things I have spoken unto you, that in me ye might have peace."* The Greek word is *eirene. "In the world ye shall have tribulation"*. Now this is Jesus speaking about tribulation. He did not say in the world you are going to have great tribulation because the only time He used that was in Matthew, with the exception by the way, once when John is writing to the seven churches in Revelation 2:22, *"Behold, I will cast her into a bed, and them that commit adultery with her into great* [*megas*] *tribulation, except they repent of their deeds."* I will have to get to what that refers to in the book of Revelation. That is the closest thing you can get to that. Well, no, you can also get it in Revelation 7:14 where it says, *"These are they which came out of great tribulation"* but they are talking about those who will be washed by the blood of the Lamb that came out of the period of when most of them were murdered by Islam during that Point A to Point B period starting from 688 AD.

Over and over, even the churches, Revelation 2:9, *"I know thy works, and tribulation"*. Revelation 1:9, *"I John, who also am your brother, and companion in tribulation"*. John did not write 'in the great tribulation'. Of course, you are going to say he could not write that because it did not happen yet. Well none of the apostles wrote about that. Only Jesus did, and like I said, if you believe what I have preached, what you can listen to or read about the abomination of desolation, Jesus was referring to that starting timeline from that point on when great tribulation would come into human history, and it is so great because it takes up space and time, and how it affects the mind and body. Great in those elements, especially the space and time, because it is still going strong and it is getting stronger even in 2012 AD, about 1,400 years. You get it, folks?

What about the corresponding gospel records that refers to Matthew 24? Mark says, *"For in those days shall be affliction"*. He did not call it great tribulation. He just called it tribulation. If it was not for the Matthew record, we would not even know it would be *megas*. *"In those days shall be affliction,* [or *tribulation* is the correct translation] *such as was not since the beginning of creation which God created unto this time, and neither shall be."* Referring to what I just read and we translated in Matthew 24. Then again in Mark 13:24 it says, *"But in those days, after that tribulation, the sun shall be darkened, and the moon shall not give her light."* Why is the sun darkened and why would the moon not give her light? Why? What happens? What happens for that to take effect? Do you know? Do you want to know? You will have to stick around.

Back to John and I will finish here, *"These things I have spoken unto you, that in me ye might have peace."* You are not alone. If that does not give you peace, nothing will. Christ is there with you. *"In the world ye shall have thlipsis:* [once again *tribulation*] *but be of good cheer"*. "Have courage. You know why? I am with you! And guess what! I have victory over the grave. I have overcome the world." If He could overcome the world, and if you are caught in the middle of great tribulation, that period that still exists today, that no other beast had that much power and influence over a great space and time, guess what? The Beast has lost. Islam has lost. Christ is with us. Have good courage. Christ conquered this world including the Beast that is still left and He will deal with it when He comes back. His wrath will be poured.

God's wrath is not to be confused with great tribulation. They are two different subjects. One, God is going to pour out, and Satan has been trying to pull out his own type of great tribulation, the kind of tribulation which Jesus started the time clock on by giving us information in Matthew 24:15. Don't ever confuse it and I don't think you will.

It is very clear when the clock started ticking in Matthew 24:15 and it is still ticking. It is a ticking time bomb, and the bomb that is going to be delivered by Christ himself is still yet to come. The Beast will be dealt with, but Christ overcame the world. Whatever great tribulation you might experience because of the Islam influence, I have news for you. Hang in there! He has overcome the world and our enemies. He has won the victory, and all the other tribulation that you experience in life on a personal level, He is there also. We are not left alone, folks. Praise Jesus, PRAISE JESUS. **RUWA!** Now some of you might wonder what *ruwa* means. Well, you will have to listen to that message to find out, won't you?

RUWA! That is something to shout about.

The Last Days Study Guide
Mark of the Beast Part 14

---

1. How does great tribulation differ from God's Wrath?

2. How has the common definition of *megas* limited the understanding God has desired to convey through His word?

3. Why is there no such thing as "The" Great Tribulation?

4. In Matthew 24:21 it says "***For then shall be great tribulation…***" Why is "*For at that time shall be…*" a better and more accurate translation for this verse?

5. What does "great" in Matthew 24:21 refer to?

6. Describe what enduring *thelipsis* is like.

7. Did Jesus ever promise that His saints would be snatched away from great tribulation?

8. Why is the Christian warned about tribulation?

9. When you are suffering, where is Jesus?

Lucifer and Allah

Turn in your Bible to Isaiah 14:1.

Here Isaiah is giving a prophecy, which starts in chapter 13. In our day, some of it has already been fulfilled but most of these prophecies have not. We see this demonstrated in chapters 14-21 when he is dealing with Babylon, the Assyrians, the Philistines, Moab, Damascus (Ch. 17), Ethiopia, Egypt, and then Babylon again (Ch. 21), followed by Edom, Arabia, Phoenicia and others. Then eventually the whole world. We are starting at verse one, but the focus is going to be on verses 12-14.

Isaiah 14:1-2, *"For the LORD will have mercy on Jacob, and will yet choose Israel, and set them in their own land: and the strangers shall be joined with them, and they shall cleave to the house of Jacob. And the people shall take them, and bring them to their place: and the house of Israel shall possess them in the land of the LORD for servants and handmaids: and they shall take them captives, whose captives they were; and they shall rule over their oppressors."*

"For the LORD will have mercy on Jacob". That was clear from the day He promised that, and it is still true today. *"For the LORD will have mercy on Jacob, and will yet choose Israel"*. Israel from this point would still be in bondage and they will come out of that. So, part of this chapter did get fulfilled but most of it did not and that is the point. *"...and set them in their own land: and the strangers shall be joined with them, and they shall cleave to the house of Jacob."* That partially happened and is happening even today. *"And the people shall take them, and bring them to their place: and the house of Israel shall possess them in the land of the LORD for servants and*

handmaids: and they shall take them captives, whose captives they were; and they shall rule over their oppressors." Now if that was true and that was fulfilled completely 2500 years ago then we would have to question what God's Word is saying here because Israel, for most of its history, has been the oppressed and it is not over yet. Yes, they are in their own land. Yes, God has been faithful and had mercy on the house of Jacob, but you cannot say that they have ruled over their oppressors completely. That has never been fulfilled anywhere. If you can, show me.

Verse 3, *"And it shall come to pass in the day that the LORD shall give thee, rest from thy sorrow, and from thy fear, and from the hard bondage wherein thou wast made to serve..."*

Yes, they served in Babylon and the LORD delivered them from that, but it did not end their sorrow. Trace the history of Israel. Eventually, the Roman Empire came on the scene and before the Roman Empire, the Grecian Empire, Alexander the Great. They were controlled by gentile forces. It was not until 1948 that they were even an independent country, called Israel once again. They did not have Jerusalem back until 1967. But even after all that is said and done, that does not mean they do not have any more sorrow, that they do not live in fear. Listen, you do not hear about it but if you were connected to the sources which report how many missiles come across every month, how would you not be living in fear? Maybe someday I will share story after story (really miracle after miracle) about those just leaving their homes minutes before a missile landed either near or in their home, sometimes exploding and other times just a dud. They are still living in fear. There is still sorrow in the land. Yes, there is independence and freedom, but all of this has not been fulfilled. You cannot find that anywhere including after they came out of exile. All we have to do is look at the Zachariah record and the other Minor Prophets to see the trouble they had just rebuilding Jerusalem again. They had enemies as soon as they got back in town from exile.

Verse 4, *"That thou shalt take up this proverb* [or literally, taunting speech] *against the king of Babylon, and say..."* Who is the king of Babylon? Do you think it is just referring to Nebuchadnezzar or some other king? It could but there is a bigger picture here, folks. *"How hath the oppressor ceased! the golden city ceased! The LORD hath broken the staff of the wicked, and the scepter of the rulers. He who smote the people in wrath with a continual stroke, he that ruled the nations in anger, is persecuted, and none hindereth. The whole earth is at rest..."*

I am sorry but when has that ever happened? Scholars may debate this but even if the whole earth was referring only to the general area of the Middle East and surrounding areas, find in history anywhere where the whole earth has been "at rest and quiet".

Who were the original kings of Babylon, by the way? We know Satan's influence immediately went to work and shortly thereafter Cush, a son of Ham (his grandfather was Noah) began creating a new false idol worship system, developing false gods. Where? In the Mesopotamian Valley, in the Babylonian area: present day Iraq, some parts of Saudi Arabia, some parts of Syria as we know it today, Transjordan, Kuwait, and so forth, even some parts of south eastern Turkey – to mention a few. Those were the physical kings of Babylon.

Now everyone thinks that Cush just went down to Sudan or Ethiopia or southern parts of Egypt. He had sons that did go down to those areas and populate those areas but there are enough records to see that he went back and forth. He was the family father figure and an evil family father figure. Of course, the most notorious son that came from his lineage was Nimrod through Semiramis. There they developed the moon-god worship, which started as a moon-goddess. Baal's mother, according to their evil tradition, produced Baal. That can be traced all the way back to Semiramis. There is plenty of history on this, folks. Most Christians do not know about it because most Christians just about like anybody else today, at least here in the United States, think history is boring. So, they tune that part out or they were never taught it in the first place—and especially when it comes to ancient history. They cannot relate to it. These are the original physical kings, controlled by

Satan, who then went to work almost immediately after the flood to establish another false worship system. And in this case, at the beginning Satan would stick with that system. Each would take its turn and shape it a little bit differently as the centuries and millenniums went by but eventually Mohammed would shape it in such a way that Satan in the last days would use that false worship system to create the last and final 8th Beast Empire, which Satan does have control over, with a system in place which I have declared over and over is none other than Islam.

Verse 6, *"He who smote the people in wrath with a continual stroke, he that ruled the nations in anger, is persecuted, and none hindereth. The whole earth is at rest..."* Like I said, that has not happened; so this has not been fulfilled yet. *"...and is quiet: they break forth into singing. Yea, the fir trees rejoice at thee, and the cedars of Lebannon, saying, since thou art laid down, no feller is come up against us."* Well, that still has not happened. *"Hell* [or the grave] *from beneath is moved for thee to meet thee at thy coming: it stirreth up the dead for thee, even all the chief ones of the earth; it hath raised up from their thrones all the kings of the nations. All they shall speak and say unto thee, Art thou also become weak as we?"* Who? What? *"...art thou become like unto us? Thy pomp is brought down to the grave, and the noise of thy viols: the worm is spread under thee, and the worms cover thee."*

Then in verse 12, *"How art thou fallen from heaven, O Lucifer, son of the morning!"*

O Lucifer, son of the morning—what does the Hebrew actually say? *Heylel ben shachar*; How art thou fallen from heaven, *heylel ben shachar*. That is the Hebrew.

"... how art thou cut down to the ground, which didst weaken the nations! For thou hast said in thine heart, I will ascend into heaven, I will exalt my throne above the stars of God: I will sit also upon the mount of the congregation, in the sides of the north: I will ascend above the heights of the clouds; I will be like the most High. Yet thou shalt be brought down to hell, to the sides of the pit."

Well, if we are speaking of just Lucifer alone, we know that has not been fulfilled completely, right? Most of this chapter has not been fulfilled.

"How art thou fallen from heaven, O Lucifer, son of the morning!"

HEYLEL Hebrew	HILAL Arabic
Morning Star or Day Star	Crescent Moon

Above are the Hebrew and Arabic words for Lucifer. Do you see the difference? There is not much difference. So what is the meaning of these two words?

The name Lucifer in Hebrew, as I said, is *heylel*. Most of you have a Strong's Concordance and that is okay. It is not complete. In my opinion, it is not descriptive enough of what the words originally meant in most cases, but that is okay. It is a good starter. Most of you will find in the concordance that *heylel* just means brightness. Now *heylel* in the Hebrew meaning has the same meaning in the Arabic. In the Arabic, what do you think the term, or the meaning is associated with? It is associated with the crescent moon, which was first developed before the Islamic period.

Hilal is associated with the crescent moon. *Heylel* in some of your margins even has a correction which says, "O day star," which means shining or brightness or born of the morning dawn. It could be the rays of the sun, but it could also be the day star or what is known in most corrections as the morning star. You will see in the New Testament that Satan is transformed into an angel of light. How was he transformed? That is a subject for another time.

Heylel in the Hebrew; *Hilal* in the Arabic: one means morning star or day star; one means crescent moon.

In this part of Scripture in verse 12, we are given the name that has been around a long time. It has come down through the centuries, the millenniums, to signify Satan. It is the name Lucifer. You will see it in the King James version and most other versions as Lucifer, O Lucifer, son of the morning or Day Star. And most of us have heard Satan referred to as Lucifer.

Now the truth of the matter is this passage, this verse, may not so much have been given to us here in the Scriptures as a proper name but as giving us the description of who Satan really is. He is described here as the son of the dawn or the son of the morning. And as I said, the words in the Hebrew are translated *heylel ben shachar*. What is even more fascinating about this word *heylel* is how it is translated in the King James as Lucifer and how it is similar to the Arabic word *hilal*, which is defined as the crescent moon. Between Day Star and Crescent Moon, it almost has an identical meaning or definition.

"Well, it is not written in Arabic."

That is right; but considering when this was written, are these given to us as clues for what was still yet to come? Remember Isaiah in context is describing future events. Only a very few of those events have been fulfilled. We can find those partial fulfillments after this was written but most of it is not—and not just for Babylon, but all the nations listed in 15, 16…21, all the surrounding nations, which is the focus in prophecy. Sorry, South America is not included. The North Pole is not included. Australia is not included. Do the rest of these countries have some involvement in end-time events? Absolutely. But prophecy is focused on one general area and how those countries relate to those areas that they are associated with—for instance, the tribes and where they went come into play more than others. That does not mean the other have an excuse. That does mean that they are not going to be involved and that does not mean that they are not going to be accountable.

When you put the whole phrase together in the Arabic, "*O Lucifer, son of the morning*", it simply means Crescent Moon, son of the morning star (or dawn). So, what is Scripture telling us here? Is it a clue? Is it an identification that only when the time was right someone could, for instance, in our day and age when this would be understood see the significance of the two, compare it, and see if it does fit in with Scripture and who the Satan-controlled end players would be? Are there more clues?

Now we know Islam has a crescent moon and it has a star lingering over it. It has become the symbol of Islam, the flag in many Islamic countries. The *hilal* is the Arabic word for the lunar crescent of the new moon. The crescent moon in Islam is the most important symbol in the Muslim tradition. The Muslim calendar is a lunar one and it is used to determine such days as when the Muslims celebrate their festivals and their holy days, the beginning and end of Ramadan, the month of their fast; the beginning of the annual month of their pilgrimage to Mecca, etc.

The symbolism of the crescent moon behind the *hilal* is intended to convey that the moon is in the act of devouring the star within the horns of the crescent moon, having been consumed by the moon. The horns of the moon are the tips and that is why they would make a lot of their idols with the horns facing upward as a crescent-shaped crown, whether it was an animalistic type of idol or a person or whatever. The horns are the jaws of the mouth and are still considered so today. The crescent is a mouth and the *hilal* regardless of whether the star or sun (in an eclipse, by the way) is entering or within the shaded part of the moon's face. What does this mean? It shows that the moon is in the act of eating. In other words, let me just say it the way Peter did in the New Testament, Satan is roaming to see whom he can devour with his jaws. Islam is just the tool. It is just the agent. It is just the 7th and now the 8th Beast, the last in history, in which Satan will carry out his false religion, his false worship system which he started with Cush, Nimrod and Semiramis. As it migrated to other areas of the Middle East and beyond, it took on other names but it all falls under the category of the moon-god or goddess, an association with Baal and other gods, Molech being one of them.

Incidentally, why do you think the Amalekites had to be eliminated? It was not just because they attacked from the rear, they picked off the weak and the elderly, what we would call the have-nots of society that could not defend themselves—which is why Israel had to stop and deal with them and that is where we get to Moses, Aaron, Hur and Joshua down in the valley fighting the Amalekites—there were other reasons. I know some scholars believe the Chronicle letter is the last event we will see of the Amalekites. Well, do not be so sure. We find them in the book of Esther (and I know that is prior to that story) but where else can we find the Amalekites? I am going to present to you something very interesting that will take it all the way back to the last century. It will take you back about 70 or 80 years. "Do you mean that you can find Amalekites?" It is possible. You just have to know how to look for them.

The Amalekites had to be destroyed.

Most people think that Molech was just some false idol that people would worship or sacrifice their children to. Some of those idols were created into human being like shapes. In fact, they would heat some of these idols to such a point that unwanted children or children that were dedicated for the sacrifice would be placed on the out-stretched arms of Molech. Because it was so searing hot, it would just burn to death the child. It was a torturing situation. It was sick and that was just one of the ways.

The original beginning of Molech was not just a statue or a false system. It was a king that wanted allegiance and everybody bowing down to him. That is why I am not a fan of quick-hit dictionaries that just give you minute information, common information that is out there, the short-cut, what I call the Cliff Notes of religion and do not dig deep into these subject matters to find out the truth. Maybe I will come back to this again when I deal with the Amalekites to give us further insight of their practices and why God wanted them destroyed, men, women, children and animals. Anything belonging to the Amalekites had to be destroyed. Why do you think the greatest sin Saul committed was his disobedience in destroying EVERYTHING concerning the Amalekites? He spared the king, spared the people, and saved the best of the animals to sacrifice to God. God wanted obedience right from the beginning. And I have not really touched on this before but, in that first battle with the Amalekites in Scripture, the way it is written in the Hebrew, the Amalekites cooled them off from trusting God. Remember, Israel is coming through. Yes, they lacked faith, but they were full of faith at one point. Scripture makes it very clear once you can read the language and understand what it is saying. The Amalekite situation cooled them off; literally cooled them off from trusting God. No matter where you turn, the Amalekites angered God.

So again, we have the jaws of the crescent moon devouring, the mouth of Satan's representation of a false religious empire with the real intention of devouring God's saints. Now, as I said, every Islamic flag carries this symbol and not just their flags, but mosques have these placed on their pinnacles, domes, or their minarets. The very symbol that the Lord is describing here is the symbol that Satan will eventually use to apply to Islam. Think about it.

Now I am going to share with you some Koranic literature.

> *Not surprisingly, one particular Koranic narrative contains several of the very same elements that we find in the biblical account of the fall of Lucifer or Satan here in Isaiah. In the Koranic surah entitled Qadr, (power or fate), we find a passage that speaks directly of the dawn (son of the morning)—when the angelic host came down from heaven. It is described as a night vision in Koranic literature, quote:*

> *"We have sent it to thee in the Night of Vision, what do you know of this Night of Vision. The Night of Vision is better than a thousand months. The angelic hosts descend [to earth] in it with the spirit by command of their lord. Peace shall it be until the rising of the Dawn (Morning star)." —Surah 97:1-5*

You still have some that say that Islam is the religion of peace. In fact, they try to brainwash us and convince us that they are the religion of peace and that Christianity is the religion of war. Look it up. You can find hundreds of articles and write-ups mostly by Muslims and Imams declaring that they are the religion of peace and that Christians and Jews are the ones that want war and not to live in peace. But we know by the way we have been studying these last days and the subject matters that we have been covering that is not the case. In fact, that is a very big falsehood.

Paralleling the biblical narrative, we have: angels descending; the rising of the morning star or the Dawn, or Satan… or something else. This is how we see Scripture confirming itself and what I believe it means here in these verses. And it probably was not until very recently that this could be clearly understood. And, a so-called peace is established from that point onwards.

> Now, according to Islam, this rising of the son of the morning star or dawn, (their hilal in the Arabic; or heylel in the Hebrew, the morning star or day star, or what has come to be known as Lucifer and by the way, is the only place you will find it), happened on the 27th day of the month of Ramadan.
>
> It was at that point, centuries ago, Mohammed declared his encounter with the "angel" who revealed this important information and other information that eventually established the Koran. Ramadan is the same month during which Muslims fast from dawn to dusk, basing the fasting season on the appearance of the moon, including the crescent moon. These two words, in fact, parallel each other in Scripture regarding Satan (the morning star or day star or the son of the morning star or dawn).

So they are paralleling each other. With just this information alone, even though it may sound convincing to you already, I was not convinced. Is there something else in these scriptures that makes the connection that ties this all together and what this is referring to—since most of this was not yet fulfilled in Isaiah's time, and still for at least 1500 years was not fulfilled in the time after this was written? Then in which time can we start seeing at least a partial fulfillment, though now we can see the full fulfillment of it? Do we have any clues in these particular scriptures that can point to that understanding?

I hope you have the clear understanding of how closely related these two words are. In fact, they mean the same thing. In the Hebrew, it means morning star or day star but that does not mean that is all it says. That is why in most of Christianity it refers to Lucifer and Lucifer is referred to Satan. Due to this understanding, we will think by reading these passages that these passages refer to Satan falling from heaven. Well, it is a heck of a lot more than that, my friend. It is pointing to a time period and not just when Satan fell from heaven. This talks about his falling and what it produced, which eventually did weaken the nations. The nations? What nations? Stay in context; the nations in 15, 16, 17, 18, and 19 and so on. I hope you understand that. As we continue to read, then, let us look for the clues.

In verse 13, *"For thou has said in thine heart, I* [here come the five I's] *will ascend into heaven, I will exalt my throne above the stars of God: I will sit also upon the mount of the congregation, in the sides of the north: I will ascend above the heights of the clouds: I will be like the most High."*

Now, everyone thinks this is the reason why Satan was kicked out of heaven. Well, he still had access in Job's day. In fact, I declared and preached this before using the book of Revelation, to show you exactly when he got kicked out and that was when Christ presented His blood and said, Nope. You will no longer be an accuser here in the heavenlies. The heavenlies were cleansed of Satan also and he was cast down for a short time to do his last and final damage to destroy mankind's relationship with Christ and the Father. Remember, a short time is not just a few years; a short time, a period of time, or an age of time.

"For thou has said in thine heart, I will ascend into heaven, I will exalt my throne above the stars of God: I will sit also upon the mount of the congregation, in the sides of the north: I will ascend above the heights of the clouds: I will be like the most High. Yet thou shalt be brought down to hell, to the sides of the pit."

How come you want to believe verses 13 and 14 are describing Satan's fall and the reasons for his fall? If that is true, then put a line between verses 14 and 15 because there is one heck of a gap since that has not been fulfilled yet. **OR, this whole series of verses here in this chapter are describing something else.** If you only used a basic understanding of what the scriptures are saying because you did not have the insight to see how these last days would play out, because you had not been given the privilege; or you just refuse to see it because you are stuck in the Christian science fiction mode and you cannot snap yourself out of it because you are afraid to be the laughing stock, then Yes! you are going to perceive these scriptures saying exactly how "they" (the rest of the Christian world) want you to perceive it because they all are like robots merely following a message and a doctrine that has been preached for several hundred years, the same way defined today as it was hundreds of years ago.

I have been asking you: Do you want to be a robot Christian? Or do you want to dig into the truth of God's Word layer by layer and piece by piece? In that journey, you are going to have to destroy some of your pre-conceived concepts just like I had to. I am still doing that today as I see the Bible really concerns the First Advent and the Second Advent, and, how we are participants in the process; that God has elected and chosen us in the capacity that we were called to be participants. And thank God He did choose us because if He did not choose us we would not have the benefit of being saved and all the benefits that come with it, to be reconciled back to the Father through the Son.

"So, what are you saying?"

I should just dangle you right here... but I will not.

> *"For thou has said in thine heart, I will ascend..."*

He also says,

> *"I will exalt my throne"*

And in verse 14,

"I will be like the most High"

The Hebrew word for ascend is *alah*. "I will *alah*". WHO will *alah*? *"I will be like the most High"*; and like I said, the Hebrew word is *alah*. Of course, this is the same name used by Muslims for their god. Who is going to ascend? *Alah*. Today they add an additional letter to it, but that was not always so. What does this mean? We have *alah* in the Hebrew, which incidentally, there are three different ways you can say it in the Hebrew; or there are three different definitions for *alah*, but only one way in which it means ascend. Now I want to share with you something about the word:

> *"From a primitive ancient semitic root alah developed in Arabic to Allah. It is thought to be the equivalent of the Hebrew God Elohim. "* I am telling you right now, it is not. That is what they made their followers to believe. *"Translated by some as El-yah (the god who ascends, the god who is mighty). The name Allah was never used in the Old Testament as a name for God. "* The Hebrews never used Allah, whether Alah or Allah. *"The god Allah was worshiped among the pantheon of pagan deities in Arabia. His name appears in the name of Mohammed's father 'Abdullah', with 'lah' being an abbreviation of Allah, the last three letters. "*

> *"According to Jewish sources, the word 'alah' in the Hebrew language means 'to ascend'".* And I told you this already, there are actually three words that can be used. Alah is always used as "to ascend". *"Alah is found in the Hebrew Bible 688 times and translated a number of ways: "went up" [Gen 2:6] or "arose" [Gen 19:15]. "*

But here in Isaiah 14:13 it is translated *alah* and the way it was used in the Hebrew language, one of three possibilities, was "ascend". So, "I will *alah*". So, what is Satan declaring? And since, in context again, most of this chapter has not been fulfilled, is this a statement being made that Isaiah through the gift of seeing what God wanted him to see and putting it down in words for us to know when it does happen who the final players will be, along with the other nations that he talks about that would be under the control of Allah, the god of the 8th Beast, the Islamic Empire?

"There is only one text of Scripture in which 'alah' is used that comes near describing a god and that is Isaiah 14:13. In this text Lucifer, the great Satan, claims he will 'alah' [ascend] into heaven and replace God."

If you have been a Christian for some time, that is what we are always under the assumption of, that Satan will ascend. And yes, it is Satan in the unseen world that will ascend, but by what instrument is the question I am trying to point out. What instrument will he finally develop—which he started shortly after the flood to destroy mankind, to put them off track, to break that relationship, which he was successful in doing—for man to go down the wrong road again? That is why God had to separate Abram from Ur, from all that false worship and deities, including the moon-god. Could this be a glimpse of the system that Satan would use, who controls the unseen spiritual things that he creates to his advantage, to come against God? I am sure Isaiah probably did not even have a clue of what was still yet to come. It is here now though and has been for quite a while, but never as strong as they are today. They have not had the ability for destruction as they are putting together today, and they have never been so large. Listen; there are about 1.4 billion people under the control of Allah, the 8th Beast of Scripture.

"In this text, Lucifer, the great Satan, claims he is Allah." **In what I just explained to you, I am declaring that there is more to it than just that.** *"This boast by the great Satan is believed by many Christians to be the origin of the use of the name Allah for a god."*

"Prior to Mohammed's conversion to the Jewish religion from which he fashioned his new religion of Islam, the god "Allah" among the pagan Arabs of Arabia was the highest or the mighty

god. Since this god was the family god of Mohammed's father, it is no mystery then why Allah became the mighty god of Islam.

If indeed the great Satan made his boast to be "Alah" in Isaiah 14:13, and if indeed, he has impregnated over a billion people upon the earth to shout his name, then Lucifer has indeed become a mighty god for a billion people upon the earth. The Koran would by implication be the Bible of Lucifer as written or dictated by Mohammed."

Oh, it is going to be more than that! I will show you all the implications of that in the future.

"Nowhere in the Jewish Bible or the Christian Bible is the name Alah or Allah used for the name of the true God. The Jews would never mention or pronounce the name of a pagan god (Ex. 23:13). That 'Alah, Allah' was deemed to be the name of a pagan god would be indicated by the absence of this name from the Bible. Jews today do not accept 'Alah or Allah' to be the name of God or to be the same God as Elohim. Most Christians today do not accept 'Alah or Allah' to be the name of God or to be the same God as Elohim.

The meaning of the word Alah or Allah from the more ancient Hebrew language <u>always means</u> 'to ascend' in one manner or another. Only in the Koran and within Islam does Alah or Allah represent the name of a god. The question for Christians is whether or not they will ever accept 'Alah or Allah' as the name of the true God of the Old and New Testaments?"

A TRUE Christian will not; that much I can tell you.

I will ascend. I will be like the most High. The word in the Hebrew is *alah*. Do you think that is just a coincidence? Or, is it a description since we are talking about where these false pagan religions originated from, from the area of Babylon, and it is giving us a clue of what to expect and the nations that would become subject to it in the following and preceding chapters? Or, is it just one big accident again? The word for *alah* in Hebrew is to ascend, in the same way that Allah has laid claim to the title of the almighty God of the universe—even though he is just simply a moon-god, an Arabian moon-god.

So we see a desire through the *alah,* Satan accomplish ascending to where? Into heaven. To do what? To exalt his throne above the stars of God, to sit at the mount of the congregation. *"I will ascend above the heights of the clouds."* Isn't it ironic that Mohammed supposedly did that? And *"I will be like the most High."* The Most High: Satan's desire is always to be exalted as an equal to God no matter what form or fashion it takes. There is a hint found in this word *heylel* and it means both morning star and crescent moon. Now, that could just be a coincidence but when you also tie it in with the word *alah* in the very same passage, this is more than just a prophetic hint, folks. This is unveiling the identity of an ancient evil behind the title of Satan and what he is trying to accomplish. And we have it; there is no doubt about it! —the *alah,* the crescent moon or the morning star (or dawn), as a representative of things on this earth in the physical sense, being Islam. It is not a coincidence. *I will ascend.* That is the whole purpose and understanding of the Islamic religion; that Mohammed ascended, and he will come back again, and he will set things in order, and the whole world will have to bow down to the crescent moon, the son of the morning (the star or dawn). Satan, the *heylel/hilal,* whether Hebrew or Arabic, is the morning star, crescent moon. His intention was to weaken the nations as Scripture says because in his heart, if not at the beginning, then very close to the beginning, he wanted to be equal, as God. He knew he could not do it in His realm, in the spiritual existence he was created in and what was still available to him. So, being against God, he would come down to this planet and form a false religion. He tried to do it before the flood and he tried to create a different kind of human population. That failed! They were wiped out. But immediately after that, he went right to work, and it was shortly after wherein Cush and Nimrod (settled in the Mesopotamian Valley, the Babylonian-ish area, the Fertile Crescent, no matter what you want to call it) started creating the false moon-god worship, Baal and everything else that came from that evil part of the world where these people dwelt and expanded out.

It is kind of ironic; the expansions of these evil pagan deities that were developed and created all came through the family, in this case through the Hamitic line. And you still see that today if you understand where the Hamitic line, Ham's son and sons, migrated to. Satan wants to ascend to the heavens again and the only way, in a sense, that Satan could try to get back at God was by creating a system that has God's creation believing that the way to be equal with God is through the moon-god worship.

Eventually it was called Hubal before Mohammed changed the meaning, but Hubal is from the moon-god worship of the pre-mohammedin time, which Mohammed then remolded. He supposedly got messages from "angels" which we know is a falsehood. Satan created a system through the Koran and other literature and leadership that started the 7th and the 8th Beast. These scriptures here give us a clue of not only how Satan through his Islamic Empire was going to do it, but who is going to be involved, the players, the creation of Satan/Allah. The only way Satan could get man to follow this is to eventually send a false prophet (which I have already said is Mohammed and which God already prophesied through His prophets) to lay down this system through the 7th & 8th Beast. It would be formulated and would go through the end of time to deceive not only that part of the world but many around the world – and God does deal with that in the latter chapters. It is Satan through the system that has mankind believe that they can ascend into the heavens to sit and exalt at the throne of God, to be equal, to be like the most High. But I have news for him; in verse 15 it says, *"Yet thou shalt be brought down to hell, to the sides of the pit."* That has not happened yet. It is coming.

We will continue more on this, but I just wanted to lay out a brief outline— and not what the same *'ol same 'ol* declared about these verses because they just did not know. I do not think it is a coincidence or an accident. We have the prophetic hints here in Scripture of who the final players will be of things that were not yet fulfilled. And now, we are living in a time when these chapters will be fulfilled. And if they are going to be fulfilled, we have been given the prophetic events of who these players, institutions, religious or whatever organizations will be under the guidance of their supreme leader, Allah, their false god and their prophet.

The Last Days Study Guide
Lucifer and Allah

1. Give two reasons why most of Isaiah 14 is not yet fulfilled?
2. What is the crescent moon symbolism meant to represent?
3. What was King Saul's greatest sin?
4. What is the meaning of *heylel*?
5. What was Molech originally?
6. What is the meaning of *hilal*?
7. Most understand Isaiah 14:12-14 to be merely describing Satan's fall. Why is it more than just that?
8. List the *Five I's* claims.
9. What is the Hebrew word which means "ascend"?
10. What is Isaiah 14:12-14 actually describing?
11. By what instrument does 'alah' ascend?
12. How did Lucifer try to get back at God?

Who is Allah

Open your Bible to the book of Deuteronomy.

We are now at a point in *The Last Days* series where I want to move from the Old Testament period to a point in the New Testament age after the Church had been established and Mohammed comes on the scene. Mohammed was born in 570 AD. He started promoting his new religion in 610 AD. I am going to give you an introduction to who Allah is. I hope you have a grasp of these two characters, Lucifer and Allah, and how it has always been Satan's plan "A" to use a false system that was based on false gods (no matter what name was used at any given time). God warned about it even coming out of Egypt in the wilderness at Mount Sinai, giving the warning to not worship anything in the heavens including the sun, the moon, and the stars. Of course, it did not take man very long to do the opposite of what God instructed.

Islam is just an extension of the moon-god religion, which not only can be traced all the way back to after the flood but even before the flood in Enoch and Lamech's day. I will return to that in the near future because I do have more to say on that particular subject but, I want to make some strides forward to bring us more into the present time of Islam and how we can deal with it today, and what to expect that still needs to be fulfilled in God's Word.

What religion were they practicing in the pagan rites of the moon-god? It is not called Ashtoreth anymore. It is not called Baal any longer. It is not called any other god whether Egyptian or Greek—which many of those gods were extensions of the moon-god religion as well. What is it called? It is called Islam. Islam is what was prophesied, the 7th and the 8th Beast. According to God's Word for our time, it is the 8th Beast's moment to be front and center once again and for Satan's plan "A" to take the headlines. But God someday will send His only begotten son, Jesus Christ, to wipe the 8th Beast off this planet once and for all.

From an article:

> *"Islam is the fastest growing religion in the world today. Many times it has been a violent religion in which one has two choices: either convert or die."*

It always has been a violent religion, not just "many times".

> *"The religion of Islam has as its focus of worship a deity by the name of Allah. Allah was a pagan moon-god in Arabia during pre-Islamic times. Moon worship has been practiced in Arabia and the Middle East since about 2000 BC."*

Actually, it goes further back than that. It is pre-flood.

> *"The crescent moon is the most common symbol of this pagan moon worship. The moon-god was also referred to as "al-ilah".*

You need to remember these names because I will refer to them often. Al-ilah eventually became just Allah. (ref. *Lucifer and Allah*, Isaiah 14:12-15)

Then there was Al-Lat, Al-Uzza, and Manat; the three different names of the daughters of Al-ilah.

> *"Originally this was not a proper name of a single specific god, but a generic name meaning "the god". Each local Arab tribe would refer to their own local tribal pagan god as "al-ilah".*

So, it was a generic name depending on who would use it. It was a generic name so any tribe could use it.

> *"Al-ilah" was later shortened to Allah before Mohammed began promoting his new religion in 610 AD."*

This is not something Mohammed came up with. This was already in existence.

> *"Mohammed retained almost all the pagan rituals of the Arabs at the temple, Kabah, and redefined them in monotheistic terms. Today Islam is a false monotheistic religion with its roots in polytheistic paganism.*
>
> *The Old Testament regularly forbade the worship of the moon-god and other false gods. When the children of Israel came out of Egyptian bondage they were warned..."*

They were warned not to follow these other gods. Where does it say that?

Deuteronomy 16:18, *"Judges and officers shalt thou make thee in all thy gates, which the LORD thy God giveth thee, throughout thy tribes: and they shall judge the people with just judgment."* These are instructions given to the children of Israel. [17] *"Thou shalt not wrest judgment; thou shalt not respect persons, neither take a gift: for a gift doth blind the eyes of the wise, and pervert the words, of the righteous."*

Ha, how true that has become. God foresaw, and he warned against problems in the judicial system: You are going to take some money from the people, and they will expect a decision in their favor and it will cloud your judgment. In other words, they will finance your campaign. They will finance your causes, things you will want to associate yourself with. They will give you the support you necessarily need to get it done. Things like this will cloud your vision and judgment. Why? Because you are going to lean toward those peoples' desires and what they want to see done, or what decisions they want to see come to pass.

"Thou shalt not wrest judgment; thou shalt not respect persons, neither take a gift: for a gift doth blind the eyes of the wise, and pervert the words, of the righteous." If only our politicians and our judicial system would heed to that, no matter what governmental system, how much better off we would be, but that has not happened. *"and pervert the words of the righteous"*. That is right; pervert.

Deuteronomy 16:20, *"That which is altogether just shalt thou follow, that thou mayest live, and inherit the land which the LORD thy God giveth thee. Thou shalt not plant thee a grove* [asherah] *..."*

Here is the *asherah* again in the Hebrew. And where were asherahs planted? Near the altars, usually the altars of Baal. And then they would make false images of these asherah groves into moon-god or moon-goddess representations. *"Thou shalt not plant thee a grove* [asherah] *of any trees near unto the altar..."* Remember, they were just coming out of Egypt, but this stuff was already being practiced in the land of Canaan by the pagans, by the Canaanites and other cultures.

Deuteronomy 16:21-22, *"Thou shalt not plant thee a grove of any trees near unto the altar of the LORD thy God, which thou shalt make thee. Neither shalt thou set thee up any image; which the LORD thy God hateth."* In the Hebrew, it is very clear what that word hateth means. It means to hate with intensity. God hates with intensity any false images. Then Scripture continues on with verse one in chapter 17:

"Thou shalt not sacrifice unto the LORD thy God any bullock, or sheep, wherein is blemish..." Here, in this set of instructions, God is not only dealing with the possibility of the children of Israel eventually following false gods, creating false images, practicing a false religion, but in one verse He also throws in giving and how it should be done in their day and age under the Mosaic Law.

"Thou shalt not sacrifice unto the LORD thy God any bullock, or sheep, wherein is blemish..." Circle the word blemish. The definition comes with a certain understanding. You would not give as an offering anything, in this case an animal (sheep or goat), that was second best or third best. It had to be the best! Most New Testament Christians in our day and age have forgotten that concept—which in God's Word has never been changed as a manner of practice including the here and now. He still wants your best. He will be your provider. He will still make sure you have whatever is the best for you to give.

"Thou shalt not sacrifice unto the LORD thy God any bullock, or sheep, wherein is blemish, or any evilfavouredness: for that is an abomination unto the LORD thy God."

Circle evilfavouredness. Hmm... He hates with intensity images, asherah groves (everything that is related to the moon-god or other gods, by the way); and He does not want your second or third best. He wants the best and not only your best, He also doesn't want you thinking or talking evil about the act. That is what *evilfavouredness* designates in the Hebrew: it means a speech of evil or evil speech. In other words, through thought, you are going to express in words and convince yourself to give a second or third best. You are going to talk yourself out of giving your best, by whatever silly excuse and usually because you want to keep your best and not be obedient to the Lord's requirements. He considered that an abomination, an abomination unto Him.

So here He hates false images and false gods with intensity and He does not like your second or third best. "Well, my second or third best is still a sacrifice to me." Big deal! You are still disobedient. He wants the best.

Thou shalt not sacrifice unto the LORD thy God any bullock, or sheep, wherein is blemish, or... if you even speak or create an excuse why the Lord just has to accept the second or third best for now, those thoughts are evil in His mind and it is an abomination unto Him.

"If there be found among you, within any of thy gates which the LORD thy God giveth thee, man or woman, that hath wrought wickedness [usually associated with something that is bad or in this case, inferior in quality] *in the sight of the LORD thy God, in transgressing his covenant..."*

Do you get it? The Lord just does not want your second or third best. <u>He wants your best</u>. And the promise throughout God's Word is He will keep providing you the resources that give you the ability to give Him the best. If that is prosperity, that is the true prosperity doctrine; that God will be the provider so that you will be able to give Him your best, not the second or third best.

Too many people reading this are just giving their second or third best or nothing at all. You think you are right in God's eyes because you profess a few things and say a few words. Sorry; you are coming up short. God has never changed. Man has changed, and they have redefined how worshipping God or being His disciple is—which is mostly by reducing the situation down to their level, which falls short from God's level.

And here in verse 3 again: *"...and hath gone and served other gods, and worshipped them..."* Remember what I was reading to you and how this started, *"When the children of Israel came out of Egyptian bondage they were warned..."* They were warned over and over. Here in Deuteronomy 17 you see it once again, *"...and hath gone and served other gods, and worshipped them, either the sun, or moon, or any of the host of heaven* [God is even telling them what they are going to fall into again], *which I have not commanded; and it be told thee, and thou hast heard of it, and enquired diligently, and, behold, it be true, and the thing is certain, that such abomination is wrought in Israel".*

286

Now we have two things to be concerned with here in these verses, TWO DIFFERENT TYPES OF ABOMINATION: the way you give to God; and if you put another god before Him. That takes us back to Exodus 20, if you really think about it long enough. God hates you worshipping other gods. He is a jealous God—because He knows they are not real. They are Satan's creation!

In the Ten Commandments section, what does it say in Exodus 20:1? *"And God spake all these words, saying, I am the LORD thy God, which have brought thee out of the land of Egypt, out of the house of bondage. Thou shalt have no other gods before me."* That is our first commandment. God does not waste any time with the children of Israel once they were out of Egypt, does He? They got their fill of the false religions and the false moon-god worship in Egypt. Now God sets them straight and He gives them the Ten Commandments to follow and THE FIRST COMMANDMENT is? Think about it folks.

Go to Romans 3 because I can already hear some saying, "Well, I am not under the Law anymore." And you are not...but, there is a reason why you are not. Everything in these Ten Commandments including *thou shalt have no other gods before Me* is fulfilled in you by Christ, through Christ. We will get to that. But let us look at Romans 3:21.

"But now the righteousness of God without the law is manifested, being witnessed by the law and the prophets; [vs. 22] *Even the righteousness of God which is by faith of Jesus Christ unto all and upon all them that believe* [*pisteuo*: them that have trust and confidence in the Lord Jesus Christ]: *for there is no difference: For all have sinned, and come short of the glory of God* [no exceptions to the rule]; *Being justified freely by his grace through the redemption that is in Christ Jesus: Whom God hath set forth to be a propitiation through faith in his blood, to declare his righteousness for the remission of sins that are past, through the forbearance of God; To declare, I say, at this time his righteousness: that he might be the just, and the justifier of him which believeth in Jesus. Where is boasting then? It is excluded. By what law? Of works? Nay; but by the law of faith."*

We cannot boast in the Mosaic Law any longer. No one ever really could. Why? Because no one could ever fulfill it. No one could keep it. It was there to show us how morally wrong, and like Scripture says, how *"short of the glory of God"* we are. No matter how hard we try, we would fall short of meeting His standard of the Law. But now since Christ did, do we fall short any longer? That is the question. That is one of the questions Paul raises and not just in this chapter.

Romans 3:28, *"Therefore we conclude that a man is justified by faith without the deeds of the law"*—without the employment of the Law in their lives any longer. They tried to employ it but were unsuccessful. They always fell short. Verse 29, *"Is he the God of the Jews only? Is he not also of the Gentiles? Yes, of the Gentiles also; Seeing it is one God, which shall justify the circumcision by faith, and uncircumcision through faith. Do we then make void the law through faith?"*

Now most of you will see the answer right after that. But you have to ask the question: Do we then make void the Law through faith? Is the Law void? Paul answers it, *"God forbid."* If the Law is void, Christ came for nothing. That is what it is saying here. He had to come to fulfill the Law, which He did. And He was not a second or third best. He was not blemished. He was unblemished. He is God's best. He is His only begotten Son.

"Do we then make void the Word of God through faith? God forbid: yea, we establish the law."

How do we establish the Law? Well literally, we bring the Law into existence once again or into our being through Christ. There is nothing we can do. Do not twist my words into some package that we have to follow the Law. We do not because the Law is fulfilled in us by Jesus Christ who is in us with His righteousness.

So, why have I brought this up? Because the first commandment is *thou shalt have no other gods before Me* and I know a lot of you will say we do not have to follow the Ten Commandments. You are right, but do you know why? You are living it. You are not under the bondage of the Law because Christ fulfilled it and He is in you. So, it comes into existence again, into your being because Christ fulfilled it – not as incomplete, but as complete now. That is the theme that Paul uses throughout the rest of the book of Romans and not just Romans. A fulfillment took place. We did not fulfill it. Christ did. His blood accomplished it. That is why Paul goes on to say, *"Do we then make void the law through faith?"* He answered, *"God forbid"* because he knew *"yea, we establish the law."* The only way we can establish the Law is if we faithe in Christ who has fulfilled the Law and now He is in us. He completes us. The Law is not our standard any longer, Christ is. That is why Paul in a different portion of Romans says, "Do we keep on sinning?" He also answers, God forbid. We do not keep on sinning, so we can have more grace. Enough grace has already been provided. That is the confusion. And I am not with the Christians who say we need to live the Ten Commandments or else we fall short. I want to say to all of you who believe that, you have already fallen short—but the Law is not extinguished; the Law is fulfilled. The Law is fulfilled through Christ. And because He is in us and we are in Him, we establish it. By establishing it, we do not deny it existed, and we do not think we are not morally under the Law anymore or else we could follow false gods. Think about it; the only way you become under the bondage of the Law again is if you are not in Christ. If you are in Christ, you are not going to go against the Law because it would be going against Christ. I really want you to stop and think about that because there is a lot of confusion about Law and Grace, *a lot* of confusion.

Now there are several different sects and there are hardheaded individuals in all of them. Their argument in this case is if we are not under the Law any longer, then why does worshipping other gods even matter? What would it matter? I could believe in Jesus Christ, but also believe in this god and that god and this god as long as I also believe in Jesus Christ. Sorry; it does not work that way. You cannot have your cake and eat it too because the Law is fulfilled and established in you by Christ. You cannot establish it on your own unless that "own" is trusting in Christ who did – which now He is in you and you are in Him and it is complete.

Exodus 20:2, *"Thou shalt have no other gods before me."* If this did not upset God throughout history, if you did not think it did, then why even make this the first (really) of several commandments at the beginning of the Ten Commandments? Now there are a lot of commandments of the Law, over 600 of them. But of the first few, it says thou shalt have no other gods before me.

Exodus 20:4-5, *"Thou shalt not make unto thee any graven image, or any likeness of anything that is in heaven above, or that is in earth beneath, or that is in the water under the earth: Thou shalt not bow down thyself to them, nor serve them: for I the LORD thy God am a jealous God."*

Do you think God the Father is not jealous any longer when you bow down to anything other than Jesus Christ? That would be a slap in the face of His son if that were true.

Verses 5-7, *"Thou shalt not bow down thyself to them, nor serve them: for I the LORD thy God am a jealous God, visiting the iniquity of the fathers upon the children unto the third and fourth generation of them that hate me... Thou shalt not take the name of the LORD in thy God in vain; for the LORD will not hold him guiltless that taketh his name in vain."*

Going back to Deuteronomy 17:3-4, *"And hath gone and served other gods, and worshipped them, either the sun, or moon, or any of the host of heaven, which I have not commanded. And it be told thee, and thou hast heard of it, and enquired diligently, and, behold, it be true, and the thing be certain, that such abomination is wrought in Israel"*. It has always been an abomination.

By the way, there is an abomination there in the Dome of the Rock that was built in 688-691 AD. If Christians are not under the Law any longer, that would not be a problem to God, would it? But by the same token, we are not under the Law because it is not our moral compass anymore; Christ is, amongst other things. And the only way we could fulfill any of the Law is through Christ who has done it for us. So in that case, He has released the bondage of our actions and the pressure of trying to do it in the flesh because He has already done it and He has imputed His Holy Spirit in us because of our faith in Him, which releases that righteousness from God to bring it to a completed state.

"Well, what if I sin?"

Well, that is where the blood comes in. I want you to understand that. Maybe in the future I will break this down even further. If the Law does not exist any longer as a compass point, then why should it matter what sits there (the Dome of the Rock) on The Mount? And why should it matter if any other god was ever created if we are not under any type of Law which includes *"thou shalt have no other gods before me"*? *"Thou shalt not make any graven image"* of any sort in heaven, earth or what is below the earth. Why would it matter? I really want you to think this through. Why would it matter?

In fact, it was so important to God that people were not to be falsely accused of worshipping anything but Him. The requirement was to bring forth any man or woman (in verse 5) which *"committed that wicked thing, unto thy gates, even that man and that woman, and shalt stone them with stones..."* Now, we do not do that any longer, but this was in Old Testament days. And, *"At the mouth of the two witnesses, or three witnesses, shall he that is worthy of death be put to death"*. Someone could not just come up to someone else and accuse them on a hunch. There had to be witnesses: *"of two witnesses or three witnesses, shall he that is worthy of death be put to death; but at the mouth of one witness he shall not be put to death."* No hearsay allowed. And they would put that evil thing away from the people or from among the people.

This has always concerned God. Why? Scripture makes it very clear. He is a jealous God. He will not have any gods before Him. That was the Law;

actually, it was even before the Law. But He is emphatic during the time of the Law. If the Law does not mean anything any longer, then this really should not be a problem—but it is. It is quite clear in Scripture. In fact, Christ Himself will come and wipe out the last great false religion of the last age of time, the religion of the 8th Beast, Islam. He will finish it Himself. Oh, there will be things up to that point that need to happen still—including wars, which I will get to in this series. But when the final second of the end-time clock has ticked, He will take care of the 8th Beast. He will place Satan and the Beast in the locations that He has already declared in the book of Revelation, where they will eventually be spending an eternity, including the false prophet which came up with this new religion—which is nothing more than an extension of a religion which God hated from the beginning. God has come against Satan's plan "A" as I have said so many times. If I were to rewrite the first commandment, *thou shalt have no other gods before me*, it would mean thou shalt not have Satan's plan "A" before me, which has always been the extension of false religions, false gods, false images predominantly controlled by a moon-god type of worship throughout history, especially and not long after the flood.

I wanted to point out two things God intensely hated: the asherah groves, the worshipping of false gods; and how you presented and cared for the offerings that were presented, even the thoughts that would lead to your words and how it was presented through your heart and mine. You even had to be careful about what you said. "Oh, I cannot give Him my best animal this time, but I will give this other one. It is pretty good." You could not even say it in that manner without it being an abomination unto the Lord! The way you give demonstrates what you think of Him. Does He deserve your best; or just second or third best? And then once again, He brings it back to the false gods, other gods: Do not fall back again into the worship of the sun, moon or any other host of heaven—which they did over and over, and eventually, the moon-god became the predominate worship as time ticked away in the B.C. centuries leading up to Christ. The Arab world was still practicing a moon-god type religion in their geographical area and you can also find at the same time traces of it in India, China and other areas. Just because we do not readily see Islam in biblical history does not mean it just went away. It was there behind the scenes waiting for the moment that was predicted and prophesied when the false prophet would come and establish, eventually, the 7th and 8th Beast, the two last beasts that God would deal with, with a two-horned lamb in-between, all heading toward the last days where all things will be fulfilled.

You need to be ready. You need to be prepared. You need to know what God's Word says and what it has promised. I will pick up in Deuteronomy 17:3-4 later and I will finish the introduction. Then we will move forward from that point and take a look at Mohammed, his daughters, and the name changes, plus all the different aspects of Islam, the Kabbah, the black stone, maybe even take a look at some habit patterns that the children of Israel in Israel today and outside of Israel still practice that reminds Satan that he still has a certain control over how people will respond to the moon-god worship… and they do not even realize they are doing it. That will be interesting also.

The Last Days Study Guide
Who is Allah?

1. When did moon-god worship begin?
2. Where were asherahs usually planted?
3. What does evilfavoredness mean?
4. What two abominations listed in Deuteronomy 17: 1-3 does God intensely hate?
5. Who is Al-ilah?
6. How is the Law established in us?
7. What does God want from us?

Notes

1. Unless otherwise noted, Scripture quotations are from The King James Version. All Scripture references are italicized.
2. Clarence Larkin (Mark of the Beast Part 12)
3. Walid Shoebat (Mark of the Beast Part 3 and 9)
4. Yoel Natan
5. Jewish Virtual Library

Made in the USA
Las Vegas, NV
23 August 2021